SURVIVING
STRATEGY &
ARCHITECTURE

Getting out of your own way to survive and thrive in strategy and architecture

MICHAEL D. STARK

In loving memory of my mum who passed away shortly before publishing.

SURVIVING
STRATEGY &
ARCHITECTURE

Getting out of your own way to survive and thrive in strategy and architecture

MICHAEL D. STARK

F FACTORY

Factory Books
(Self-Published)
2024

Book Cover Design by Michael D. Stark
Cover Photo by Jordy Meow, CC0
(check out his portfolio at www.jordymeow.com)
First printing edition 2024

ISBN: 978-0-473-73349-0

Michael D. Stark
www.michaeldstark.com
www.thinkingea.com
www.linkedin.com/in/michael-stark-thinkingea

DEDICATION

Alan Watts

Decades after his physical body returned to the earth in 1973, Alan Watts still reaches out with his voice, wisdom, wit, and warm humor, to entertain and inspire us. Alan Watts continues to open our eyes to a whole new way of seeing and understanding existence and provides us with many tempting pathways to explore. Thank you for illuminating our universe.

"The meaning of life is just to be alive. It is so plain and so obvious and so simple. And yet, everybody rushes around in a great panic as if it were necessary to achieve something beyond themselves."

Alan Watts 1915 - 1973

TABLE OF CONTENTS

INTRODUCTION

If you do not know about strategy and architecture before reading this book, then I'm sorry but you will not know about strategy and architecture after reading it either. There are other good books about business and technology strategy, and about technology architecture; these are both big tents and there is much to explore. What you will read here, in contrast, is not a book about strategy or architecture, it is a book about you, the technology strategist, enterprise architect, or solution architect. This book is about you, the perfectly imperfect human being.

This book is about how to survive and thrive in the highly rewarding, but emotionally taxing, world of technology strategy and architecture.

In our profession, we can feel like we are expected to be beyond human. We are supposed to be like Spock on Star Trek. As architects or strategists, we must at all times, be logical and rational. We must follow the deterministic tramlines that lead to the irrefutable ideal target state for our company or organisation. Yet here we are, being human. Getting disillusioned. Getting frustrated. Getting disappointed.

We often find we love our work life, but it is also rather unsatisfactory, and there are many fantastic people, but they seem to be frustratingly illogical. It doesn't have to be this way. The world won't just change for us. It is up to us to change our viewpoint, to empower us to do the most good we can, and that is the point of this book.

What is in the tin?

This book is divided into three parts, each centred around a way of thinking about ourselves and our profession. These parts align to a core theme. That theme is the subtitle for this book:

**Getting out of your own way to survive
and thrive in strategy and
architecture.**

Here is a brief overview of the three parts of the book.

Part 1: Getting Out of Your Own Way

We need to tackle this issue head on to try to jolt our way of thinking and open ourselves up to other concepts. It took me about 10 years to explore many of these ideas and adapt my way of being. Trying to achieve this in one part of a book is rather ambitious, but if you can glimpse that something is there, then that is all I can ask. If you just cannot connect with this part of the book, you might need to skip it, but do give it a good try as it is the key. You could perhaps even come back to it at the end, or even at some future time when you are ready. This content only works when you are ready.

Part 2: Understanding the Game

To really survive and thrive we need to dig deeper into the various games that we play as companies, organisations, divisions, teams, and as humans. This part of the book ideally builds on Part 1 to help you understand what is, and is not, within your control. By understanding the game better, you can be more successful and more accepting of your situation. We all need to consider how we will play the game and how we will stay true to our beliefs and values.

Part 3: The Other Strategy and Architecture Skills

The many books, videos, podcasts, articles, and courses about strategy and architecture cover the central concepts we need in our careers. Part 3 takes a different lens and explores other useful skills that we can leverage from the worlds of business, engineering, sports, psychology, philosophy, technology, and even nature.

Where are the citations?

Ok, so I will be honest. In this book I want to have a conversation with you. Strategy and architecture roles have treated me very well over the years and I have had many great leaders who have cared enough to take the time to mentor and coach me. At this point in my career, I want to give something back. I find this very rewarding.

This book takes some of what I picked up from those leaders, along with many of the great Eastern and Western thought leaders of history and contemporary thinkers. I try to blend all this with my own observations and thoughts and then take from this mix the things that make it through my own inevitable biases and filters.

This book is not an academic work. I will often touch lightly on my viewpoint of these topics. I will not be citing references like you would expect in an academic work or a book stating facts about the world; I claim no facts. I take a minimalist approach aimed at providing just enough information to be useful and point you towards various paths you might wish to explore. You only gain the benefit if you explore the paths yourself, all I can do is point to them.

Everything in this book is my understanding and interpretation of what I have seen, heard, and read. I will refer to and credit all the original sources that my porous memory can recall within the main text. One thing I have learnt is that nothing is independently original in the endless chain of causation. As nicely stated by Carl Sagan: "If you wish to make an apple pie from scratch, you must first invent the universe". We all stand on the shoulders of giants, to paraphrase Isaac Newton.

If I cover a concept that you know in depth, you might like to skip over it, so you don't get frustrated by the relatively light treatment needed here; we have much of the planet and about 3000 years to cover. However, if I cover a topic that you find interesting and useful, then consider doing your research as there will likely be more to it than I can cover here. I know you can research your topics as that is a core skill you use every day. YouTube is a great source – as are podcasts, books, and audiobooks. I have learnt the information in this book by an even balance of each of these sources and you can find recommendations at thinkingea.com or michael.d.stark.com, along with any new thinking on these topics.

Why Strategy and Architecture?

Let's clear up the 'and' between Strategy and Architecture. I tend to be in the camp that enterprise architecture includes technology strategy and overlaps with, or is a subset of, business strategy and it would be hard to do one without the other. However, I have experienced operating models where strategy and architecture were closely related but separate and I can see the merit in this approach. In this situation, some strategists had strong management consulting experience which is rare for pure enterprise architects, and some other strategists had strong merger and acquisition experience, which also proved very helpful. People are unique and have many different experiences and skills, so popping people in any one box is often unhelpful.

Another reason for the arguably contrasting focus is to get the right key words in the name of the book so it would have appropriate hits on the distribution platforms. As an enterprise architect I naturally explored the business model for self-publishing platforms and determined how they work. Having both strategy and architecture in the name keeps the audience segment tight enough to not get lost in the crowd, but broad enough to have the desired audience included.

What will you get?

What I am giving you in this book are some stand-alone useful concepts, a broadening of perspective, and above all, breadcrumbs that you can (if you choose) follow down the very rich and rewarding paths that are open to anyone who is curious. My own trail of breadcrumbs started with Alan Watts and expanded out in many directions.

I am writing this book with the audiobook in mind as a first-class product along with the physical book. This means that I largely stick to straight text paragraphs with few lists, tables, diagrams, or bullet points, and without reference citations outside the main text. This makes it much more audio friendly while not detracting from the physical experience of the book.

My hope is that by listening to or reading this book you will be a more successful Strategist and Architect; however, my deepest motivation is that you might become a happier one with more satisfaction, understanding, and contentment in your journey, wherever it might take you. Thank you for trusting me with your valuable attention.

Kindest regards,

Michael D. Stark

PART 1

GETTING OUT OF YOUR OWN WAY

———————————————

"What is a bad day? There is never a bad day in the universe,
only some idiots are having a bad time … hello … so it's a
beautiful day already, even if you and me did not exist it's still a
beautiful day, isn't it?
But it is our fortune we are here"

Sadhguru (Jaggi Vasudev)
Know Thyself podcast with André Duqum

CHAPTER 1

GETTING OUT OF YOUR OWN WAY

"An empty stomach is one problem: hunger. But a full
stomach? A hundred problems!"

Sadhguru

When Dante described his journey through Hell, in what is known as
Dante's Inferno, he may well have been describing a year in the life of a
Technology Strategist or Architect. The first part of Dante's 14th century
poem *Divine Comedy* describes nine concentric circles of torment; most of
us know that experience.

If we are expecting our torment will end once we find the *correctly* behaving
company that finally *gets it*, then we are setting ourselves up for a long
painful career. The corporate world we operate in exists in one way, but
we perceive that it exists in another. This is unhelpful. This is an illusion
we don't need.

How do we find out how our corporate world really exists? How do we get it to behave as it ought to behave? It is not our corporate environment that we need to change, it is *ourselves*. We need to get out of our own way.

People in both the East and the West have been thinking about this problem, getting out of our own way, for thousands of years. It is achievable. I cannot give you all the answers here, even if I could explain Buddhism, trying to would take 10,000 pages or more, and Hinduism would take 100,000 pages or more. On the other hand, Zen would take one page, and that would be blank. The Tao would take maybe five pages, but not even I would comprehend what I had said.

I aim to give you some nuggets of gold that you can use directly. I also hope to make you curious and point you in the right direction to find the *start* of the path, or more accurately paths. You can choose to explore these paths if, and when, you wish to.

We need to talk about a few key Eastern philosophy concepts

In these remaining chapters of Part 1, getting out of our own way, we will talk mostly about a few key Eastern philosophy concepts.

Why do we start with Eastern concepts? Many Eastern traditions focus on our thinking, and they use our own consciousness as a laboratory to experiment and learn how the world works. They have been doing this for thousands of years.

The *Upanishads*, which originated in India between 700BCE and 300BCE, has a great analogy that explains this. If you know about one thing made of gold, then you know about all things made of gold; the only difference is the shape and the form of the item. Consciousness is like this.

If you know consciousness then you know all, as everything we know is made of consciousness. We will talk about how consciousness, in one sense, *creates* our universe in Chapter 5.

CHAPTER 2

LETTING GO OF ATTACHMENTS!

"[DT] Suzuki was once asked how it feels to have attained
satori, the Zen experience of awakening, he answered,
'just like ordinary, everyday experience, except about two
inches off the ground!'"

From The Way of Zen, Alan Watts

There is nothing more important to your success and wellbeing, as a strategist or architect, than letting go of *attachments*. This is not something people in Western cultures are familiar with hearing and at first it is hard to even understand what an attachment is. Western cultures are built on attachments.

Let's use a very simple example - perhaps you wear Nike when you are training in the gym and elsewhere; that is your thing. Your partner buys you a nice Adidas top for your birthday. You smile and say you like it. Next time you go to the gym your partner asks you to wear it and you reluctantly put it on. You don't want to be ungrateful, or precious, but you are a Nike person. That is part of who you are and perhaps even part of how you build and keep your identity. You keep telling yourself it doesn't matter, it is just a top, but you can't quite shake that discomfort. That feeling is clinging, and that clinging is to an attachment. This is a simple example, but we can all think of things we are attached to. Pay very close attention to the source of that feeling. Pay attention to how deep it is and how hard it is to let go. Humans are highly prone to developing attachments and marketers are very good at reinforcing and exploiting them. There is a concept closely related to clinging called grasping; we cling to things we are attached to, and we grasp at things we think we need to be attached to, or that will complete our attachment – like those Nike Air Jordan IV Retro Eminem 'ENCORE' trainers. If I had those, I really would be much better at banging out my reps on the bench-press.

There are also many things in Strategy and Architecture that we find ourselves getting *attached* to and these things tends to lead to *clinging* onto the object of that attachment. It could be a particular technology, vendor, pattern, or even principle. It could be a favourite storyline, diagram, or presentation slide. Something we have invested in that we don't want to let go of. We attach ourselves very quickly and it takes a lot of effort, or several well-defined processes to avoid these attachments. At least, that is the standard approach.

Importantly we also cling to our image of ourselves. Our *identity* and beliefs about who we are. There is more on our identity and our clinging soon.

Perhaps the most useful methodology in the West for avoiding the pitfalls of attachment is the scientific method. If we think about it, the methodology pits us against ourselves and each other to try to prove ourselves and each other wrong. The scientific method recognises how attached we are to proving ourselves right about ideas we have invested in and identified with, and then seeks to turn this attachment around in a very ingenious way. Assuming you know the basics of falsifiability and replication, we can see the approach is basically that we don't declare anything right, only that it is not proven wrong yet; so paradoxically we are right by proving ourselves or others wrong. The scientific method uses a very clever countermeasure to turn a weakness into a strength. I talk a lot about the wisdom from the East, but to give the West its due credit, the scientific method really is one of humanity's greatest accomplishments.

I knew a Head of Data Engineering who would often wear a Kafka t-shirt in meetings. I know what you're thinking, what's wrong with that, Kafka is a fantastic author! No, not the guy that wrote *The Metamorphosis*, I am talking about Kafka the distributed event streaming platform from Apache (but *Metamorphosis*, makes sense right). It is a great technology, but I always did wonder if the Head of Data Engineering was *attached* to it as a technology platform. It made me think of the saying: '*to a little boy with a hammer all the world is a nail*'. However, as I got to know the Head of Data Engineering better, he was not particularly attached to Kafka, he just knew it was a good platform to add to our toolbox of options, and besides, the t-shirt was kind of cool. Incidentally, if you want a great parody of the modern corporation, read *The Trial* by Franz Kafka (intended as a parody of the USSR, but it still works).

If we pay careful attention, we find that we not only cling to the *object* of attachment, but we also cling to the *attachment* itself. We cling to the idea of being attached to something, anything. We desire to have stable beliefs about the world; this could be a methodology, pattern, or anything that seems stable. Think of this like the passengers from the Titanic in the icy North Atlantic water at the end of the movie. They *cling* onto anything that floats, and don't care, or perhaps even realise, what it is they are clinging to. They try to climb up on unstable objects that can't support them. That is what we are like in the icy corporate waters we are trying to survive in. That might be us in our life overall. If we are brave enough to let go, we might just find we can float without holding on to anything. We might find that the thing we were holding onto is actually dragging us down.

Not a new concept

Identifying and reducing attachment was one of the core teachings of the historical Buddha who lived 2,600 years ago in India. Having spent many hours over the years looking at Buddhism I would have to describe it as a blend of psychology, philosophy, and self-help. Yes, there is a lot of other cultural traditions and rituals *attached* to it, but essentially it can be understood as being like an early version of psychotherapy, yet arguably it is still more extensive.

This isn't a book about Buddhism, however, the teachings have had a significant impact on how I understand myself, so I need to be open about that. Buddhism is a big topic, so we'll leave it there, but to call on one key pieces of advice from the historical Buddha that will apply to all the Eastern and Western concepts in this book: If you hear an idea and it makes sense, why wouldn't you try it? If you try it and it doesn't work, then why would you *keep* doing it? If you try it and it helps you then why wouldn't you *keep* doing it? You decide. It is your life and your wellbeing. You need to make the best decisions for yourself, as nobody else can, or will.

Where to start

So how do you let go of attachment? Well, there is no magic answer, it is subtle and takes a lot of practice. Very few people really master it, but the good news is that people get great benefits from making even modest gains.

Starting is simple: pay attention.

Slow down and really pay attention. Noticing when you feel you don't want to let go of something and working out if you are *attached* and if you can the *causation* of that attachment. Importantly you are not trying to separate yourself completely from the *object* of attachment; it is not about that. It is about creating a *little space*. A gap. It is not about becoming cold and detached. It is not about becoming Spock. It is about not being *identified* by the object of attachment, remember Nike does not define who you are. Attachment is about building you identity with the objects of attachment, either physical or conceptual objects. Wear Nike if you want, just don't get attached to Nike. If you persist with this, you will experience the loosening of attachment, there will be a little gap. And it starts with paying attention.

This clinging also applies to our thoughts and feelings. There is a useful analogy used in Buddhist teachings around sitting on a riverbank watching boats go past. We can run over, wade through the river, and hold on to the boats or climb onto them. However, we don't have to. We can relax a little, notice the boats, perhaps even reflect on where they came from and how they move, and we can wait for them to pass, as they will. Our thoughts are like this; we can notice them, without judgement, and we can wait for them to pass as they must, because all created things are impermanent. We don't have to cling to our thoughts. We don't have to follow them around all day. We can still observe them and where they come from, just don't try to push them away, as that is more clinging. To push thoughts away you still hold them or at least connect with them. Notice the thoughts and let them go. It takes practice, but this is very powerful for us. Once you get used to it you will find it so liberating. Give it a try. Let go.

What are you attached to as a strategist or architect? Microservice architecture, decoupled digital layers (CQRS perhaps), relentless focus on turning off legacy, multi-cloud, loose coupling? None of these are bad things, but are you *attached* to them? When these concepts are dismissed do you feel a little disruption to your identity? These concepts manifest as thoughts, from memories, and we don't have to be attached to them. This doesn't mean we throw them away; we just don't cling to them. We create just a little gap, so it is a very small change; hence the quote from D.T. Suzuki at the top of this chapter about being *two inches off the ground*.

CHAPTER 3

LETTING GO OF YOURSELF!

"Other people teach us who we are. Their attitudes to us
are the mirror in which we learn to see ourselves, but the
mirror is distorted. We are, perhaps, rather dimly aware of
the immense power of our social environment."

Alan Watts

Now that we have considered our attachments, we move to identifying
their causes and in turn the root cause of many of the frustrations that we
have as Strategists, as Architects, and as people. This root cause is our *ego*,
which is largely constructed by our *identity*.

The cause of attachments is our identification with ourselves. Put plainly,
it is about our *identity*, how we construct that identity, and importantly, our
attachment to that constructed identity. It also is related to what we will
do to protect that constructed identity. There are complex interactions
between collections of autonomous beings, people, protecting their own
constructed identities within our organisational environment. This is a

complex topic, and I'd encourage you to explore it further outside this book. But let's start a brief overview of it with a famous, perhaps the most famous, Western Philosophical statement: "Cogito, ergo sum".

I think, therefore I am not!

"Cogito, ergo sum", is typically translated to "I think, therefore I am". This is René Descartes's famous statement, originally published 1637 in the *Discourse on the Method*.

It is understandable that he thought this. When using our normal level of awareness, it does seem that we *have* bodies. Almost like in *The War of the Worlds* where we are the little Martian in an unfamiliar world controlling the levers of some powerful, yet clumsy and somewhat unreliable, machine. Sam Harris described it succinctly by saying: "[When you are] giving yourself a pep talk, I mean if you are the one talking, why are you also the one listening, like why do you need the pep talk, and *why* does it work if you're the one *giving* the pep talk", (from an interview on Lex Fridman). He also describes how we can be looking for our car keys and ask ourselves where the keys are, but we already know we are looking, so who are we telling?

Descartes concluded that in a (philosophically) uncertain world the one thing that we can know *must* exist is ourselves. However, in some traditions of Eastern Philosophy (particularly Buddhism), it is proposed that this is a misunderstanding. It would be more accurate to say: "I think, therefore, there is thinking". For me that is the key.

The pronoun "I" is grammatically useful but is not really what we experience if we pay very careful attention; for most people this means uplifting our awareness with meditation, mindfulness, or to be honest, psychedelics. Changing this to the view that we exist more as a *verb* than as a *noun* is more accurate, and importantly, more helpful. We can understand ourselves better as ever-changing processes, rather than persistent entities. As Alan Watts would often say, we think that a verb must be actioned by a noun, but that is a rule of grammar, not a rule of the universe. When you think about it, a *noun* cannot perform a verb by itself. A rock cannot *throw* a tennis ball, even if it had opposable thumbs. You still need some living process or activity.

There are some great examples of this concept from Alan Watts, with my favourite being the ocean wave. If you look in the dictionary an ocean wave it is called a *noun*, so a wave is therefore a *thing*. However, think about it, what really is it? Water, that is all. It is just water in a shape performing an action. The water itself is mostly not traveling horizontally, but there is energy flowing through the water, as if you grab a bed sheet and flick it. Is it a noun, or a verb? The Merriam-Webster dictionary defines a verb as an "act, occurrence, or mode of being". Does that sound like an ocean wave? Yes!

So how does this relate to us? A 2021 Scientific American article called *Our Bodies Replace Billions of Cells Every Day*, states that scientist have determined "about 330 billion cells are replaced daily, equivalent to about 1 percent of all our cells" and that "in 80 to 100 days, 30 trillion will have replenished— the equivalent of a new you". It is a common belief that all our cells are replaced every seven years, however it seems much more nuanced than that. There is an interesting 2019 article on Discovery.com called *Does Your Body Really Replace Itself Every 7 Years?* which discusses that some cells in your stomach replace every two days, your skin every two to three weeks, red blood cells every four months, and white blood cells weekly. Our fat cells last around 10 years, as do bone cells. Some cells do stay with you for life, like tooth enamel and eye lenses. Most of your brain cells don't replace. But you can reasonably say we are *wave-like* overall, with new cells regularly replacing old. We continue to exist, but do so mostly as a *process*, not a persistent unchanging thing. It is easy to say, "of course we change constantly, I know that!". Intellectually we might know this, but if we are honest, we don't really *feel* this impermanence. Anyone over 40 has at some point looked in the mirror and wondered what happened, as we don't feel like we are the middle-aged person in the mirror. We feel like there is an "I" that is trapped *inside* the decaying thing in the mirror.

Why does this matter?

Well one reason this does matter is that you can *attach* something to a thing, a noun, but you cannot *attach* something (literally) to an action, a verb. If we *are* what we *do*, then it makes no sense to ascribe permanent attributes to us; we only need to consider our *actions*.

It took me a long time to finally figure out that quote from *Forrest Gump*: "Stupid is as stupid does", which to me means that we are our actions, and we are not an unchanging identity. Though I still have no idea why life is like a box of chocolates.

If we are our *actions*, then we absolutely *can* change them *at any time*. You might be known as an aggressive or angry debater at work based on your past behaviour, and that might be fair, but those *were* your actions; you can stop doing them at any time. People say that we can change, but we do not need to *change* ourselves, we just need to stop doing the unhelpful action. It doesn't have to be *what* you are: it doesn't to have to be *identity* defining. Well sure, it is not normally *that* easy, and it takes time and work, but you *can* do it. Knowing you could just stop is liberating and it is true. But you cannot stop in the past, and you cannot stop in the future. You can only stop *now*, so now is not only the best, but this is the *only* time to do it. The question is how far away will the *now* that you will stop or start be?

Of all the actions we perform, among the most important are the stories we tell ourselves; meaning how we interpret what happens to us or understand our actions. The stories we tell ourselves about what happens and how that reflects on us, goes a long way to defining the identity we build and rebuild (to sustain), for ourselves. We can define an identity that can be constraining. This pathway is the channel for many of our frustrations as people, strategists, and architects. It feels like an attack on our identity when the business won't invest in, or even listen to, the strategy or roadmap we've defined in a specific business or technology domain. It feels like it is about us when often, it has little to do with us. We can control our actions, but not the outcomes.

If we can let our identities go, or even just create a little space, we can focus on our actions and what we can control. This includes how we interpret what happens. That is all we can really control. We unpack this more in Part 2 by unpacking the game we are in, and therefore what we can and cannot control.

CHAPTER 4

UNDERSTANDING IMPERMANENCE

ANICCA

"It is not impermanence that makes us suffer. What makes us suffer is wanting things to be permanent when they are not."

Thich Nhat Hanh

We *feel* like we are a persistent entity. We *feel* like we are a thing, a noun. We don't *feel* like we are an ever-changing process, like a verb. Yet, as we discussed in the previous chapter, we are much more like a verb than a noun; we are continually changing. Correcting our understanding of this can be liberating.

We believe not only that we are, but that our whole world is, stable and relatively unchanging. We tend to be unsettled when we find seemingly stable things change. On the surface we *think* we understand that nothing lasts forever, and that things change. But we don't really *feel* like that is true; we *feel* like we live in a constant, stable world. We tend to cling to that stability. We are surprised and disorientated when things do change, even though we know *intellectually* that this is inevitable.

Impermanence in cultures

Many cultures around the world embrace the ever-changing nature of things (often called impermanence), as a fundamental truth of life. Beyond simply *accepting* it, they *value* it. Beyond even *valuing* it, they *cherish* it. Impermanence is what makes life worth living. Mostly the deep understanding of impermanence has come from Eastern Philosophical traditions, or at least non-Western, though one notable exception is the work of Marcus Aurelius, Roman Emperor, Stoic Philosopher, and author of the widely revered *Meditations.*

In Buddhist traditions, impermanence is a central concept that is often called Anicca (Pali language). It is one of the three marks of existence; this means we cannot avoid it as a reality of our existence. The overall understanding is that the more we recognise, accept, and value impermanence, the better our lives will be. It is clinging to our identity and resisting the changing nature of life that leads to many of the frustrations we have. Ultimately, we do not control whether things change or not, they just change, no matter what we do.

The Illusion of Stable Entities

Let consider a practical example using an entity - a thing. Think of a company. We will make it a bank with branches throughout a country. What even is this company? If we think about it, we have a collection of people, buildings, paper, cars, and processes, along with computers and computer systems. The bank has recently celebrated its centennial - it has been around a long time. But this bank is in a state of flux; it is not a constant, stable thing. The people change, the cars change, the buildings change, as does the strategy. Even the computers and computer systems change (though frustratingly slowly). The ownership of the bank can change over time, perhaps the ownership structure e.g. demutualisation. Even the name of the bank can change. Nothing is constant, because the company isn't really a thing, it is a concept, a process, an activity, a happening. It is not stable, and not permanent.

Understanding this, deeply, is useful for us in a very practical way. A company is like an ocean wave and our goal should be to surf that wave, not to burn ourselves out trying to swim against it. When we push for a change that we think is logical and necessary by trying to compel the company to do what we want it to do, we normally get resistance. And we can get very tough resistance. But why is it so hard to get change adopted if everything changes all the time anyway? Well, it is to be expected, and in fact it is necessary; you must have some push back for change to happen. It is a bit like Newton's Third Law: Action & Reaction. For every action (force) in nature, there is an equal and opposite reaction. Forces result from all interactions. We need to better understand that companies, divisions, and teams change all the time, and we can understand these flows and the resistance to these changes. Sometimes we are the resistance to change. If you talk to many enthusiastic developers with new novel ideas, they see people in strategy and architecture roles blocking them by asking questions about strategic alignment or technology sprawl. They see us resisting change, yet we see it as managing changes to move towards a desired target.

We need to recognise that impermanence is a feature, it is not a bug. But this doesn't mean it is easy to make any specific change happen.

The Beauty of Impermanence

> "The more a thing tends to be permanent, the more it
> tends to be lifeless."
> *Alan Watts*

In Japan the cherry blossom, or Sakura, is valued and celebrated for its impermanence. The fleeting nature of the cherry blossom symbolises the fleeting nature of life. But it is not only sad. Yes, there is some sadness and nostalgia (referred to as wabi-sabi, which is a nuanced and rich concept), but there is also renewal and hope.

As Shunryu Suzuki liked to say: "It may be so, but it is not always so." This is also the essence of the Persian adage: "This too shall pass". Be it the first date with the love of your life, or lying on the couch with a horrendous hangover, this too shall pass - it is not always so. This is neither good nor bad, it just is.

The Utility of Impermanence

If we deeply understand impermanence, we find we know *something* about *everything*. We have a fundamental understanding of all of the world and all of the universe, which can help us navigate our life. That is a very big statement – yet if everything is impermanent and subject to change, then we have a useful insight about everything that exists. The utility of this knowledge is to learn how to leverage this insight. This takes much practice, and much time, but rewards from the initial insight.

So how do you practice? There are many methods, but ultimately there is no method that is neither necessary nor sufficient. Simply pay attention. That is all there is. Observe.

Impermanence applies to all things, including companies and computer systems, but perhaps the most useful insight we can have with impermanence is that it applies to our feelings as well. Our feelings *are* impermanent. Try an experiment; it will really work. Think of a time when someone did you wrong, and I mean serious wrong; perhaps a relative you no long have anything to do with because of *that thing*. Take some time with it. What was it they did? How did you feel? What were the impacts? Try to take yourself back to that time. Are you *still* angry about it? You can feel that anger, and it probably feels like that anger is *still* there, like an ever-present unbroken feeling. However, this is another illusion, because at the beginning of this paragraph were you feeling angry about it? Were you actively angry before the suggestion to think about it? You are not *still* angry because anger, like everything else, is impermanent. The anger you feel now is new. You have remembered the events and used that to *rehydrate* your anger. You have had to recreate your anger from your memories, and we all do it, all the time. You do not have to do this.

You don't even have to do anything to get rid of your anger, fear, embarrassment, or whatever it is, as that will just happen. Feelings are impermanent and they cannot last. We recreate these feelings, so we *can* stop recreating them. It takes work, and I'm not there yet, but we only need to stop re-hydrating those feelings. Again, any progress on this path will be rewarding. Even just knowing this will be of some benefit; If you practice you will get much more insight and benefit.

To be clear – and this is important – I am not saying we should forget about important things. This is not about ignorance – it is the opposite. Someone might have caused us harm, and we should learn from that, without hate or vengeance, but also without being naïve about it. We might be embarrassed about something bad we did, which might have caused harm, and we need to learn from that. But we can create a little space between that event and ourselves. A gap, that allows us not to keep recreating that unhelpful feeling. Sam Harris of *Waking Up* (who also hosts the *Making Sense* podcast), describes it well regarding feelings like anger. With practice you get better with anger, but you still get angry. It isn't about not having the feeling, but you can reduce the half-life of the anger. Where you used to get cut off in traffic in the morning and it would ruin your whole day, you might now *flick the bird*, and then go about your day without it making you an unbearable ogre for your colleagues, family, friends, and for yourself.

CHAPTER 5

THE CREATION OF YOUR UNIVERSE

"To simply sit here and to know experientially, that this
entire universe is actually a part of me, will not happen to
most people. They'll hallucinate for a few moments, after
that they will get distracted by something."

Sadhguru

A consistent theme in Part 1 is that we are, in many ways, not as important
as we believe we are. This is both humbling *and* liberating.

Sadguru, a contemporary Yogic teacher from India, explains this well:
in the vast Universe there are, as scientifically confirmed by astronomy,
hundreds of billions of galaxies, of which our Milky Way is just one
galaxy; in the Milky Way there are hundreds of millions of stars, of which
the Sun is just one, a tiny speck in the universe, not even a speck - if our
star and solar system disappear tomorrow the universe would not detect a
blip; planet Earth is one small speck in the total area of our solar system;
on planet Earth our city is a micro-speck; and within that micro-speck city,

inhabited by thousands or even millions of other human beings, *you* are a *very* important person indeed!

We have a similar view in Western psychology. A friend told me that when we get to around two years old - the so-called terrible twos - we are reacting to the first realisation of our actual status in the world. Before age two we believe we are at the top — like 4-star generals who can command all around us - but by the age of two we start losing our power, and we hear words like *no* and *wait*, and we realise we are not generals but privates, and far from ultimate power, we have no power at all. We are not happy about this change of status and respond by behaving *terribly*. We spend much of our lives trying to regain the prior position as a 4-star-general; this impacts our family, education, employment, and political interactions.

Paradoxically, we have not only less control over our world than we think, but if we clear up some illusions, we have much more control over our world that we think too. We create our Universe. This is one area where the careful observations of Eastern Philosophy, and the marvels of contemporary science, agree. Interestingly, Western Philosophy's recent work on Phenomenology (within Ontology) also aligns to this viewpoint; a relatively late arrival to the party, but at least it has arrived. There have been others in Western Philosophy that have looked at this topic; famously John Locke, George Berkeley, and David Hume. However, we will stick with the Eastern way of understanding it, because it goes down fewer intellectual rabbit holes.

How we experience the Universe

Our experiences of the Universe are created within us. They are not directly experiences of the world. All our perceived world is made by us using limited information from our sensory perceptions; we do not and cannot *directly* experience our world, and therefore we cannot directly *know* anything.

If we gain a deep understanding of this, as Eastern Philosophy has observed for millennia and now Western Science and Philosophy has caught up with, we realise that we all create our own reality; we can then understand how reality can be slightly different for each of us. That is okay. That is the good stuff of life, and in a way the ultimate diversity.

Think about our five senses. It *feels* like they give us a verbatim understanding of the world; however, do they really? Let us go through the high-level flow for just one of our five senses. When we *see* something in the *real world*, there is light bouncing off the object as light waves, entering the lens of the eye, refracting through a jellylike substance, and due to the shape of it, inverting. Then the waves engage with the retina which can only possibly represent a two-dimensional image due to the eyes structure. The retina sends electronic impulses up the optic nerve to the occipital cortex through two distinct pathways, then processes in the brain are used to reverse (correct) the image, and finally construct what we perceive as reality. In the process, our brain is converting the image to three-dimensions (using edge definitions and other factors), and with what we believe are colours, even though we know they are only variances of light wave frequencies; we can't possibly see three-dimensional images or colours.

We think this image is *real*, but we have fully constructed it in our brains based on limited and selective information. This is why optical illusions are so powerful, they leverage this process, and our brains do the rest. It is also why images in dreams and hallucinations can seems so realistic; in all cases we are creating the image in the brain, so they are as real to us as anything else we see.

I am always amused by the debate about virtual meetings vs physical meetings. We construct a person we physically see in front of us, just as we construct a person we see in a picture, painting, video, or even on a virtual meeting; in many ways there is no great difference as most of the work is done by our brains. The key difference is how light waves are delivered to us. When considering a virtual meeting on a computer, many people say they aren't anything like a *real* physical meeting. But what is really happening here and how different are virtual meetings? Light is projected from a screen rather than reflecting off a surface, which is a slightly different process. We have all had an experience of seeing a space in a mall, bar, or restaurant, that seemed real, only to realise we are seeing a wall that is a large mirror, and our depth perception suddenly gets jolted; we know the mirror is a flat 2D surface, but we had perceived a real scene with all of the real depth such as a restaurant being twice the size it actually was. Computer screens are flat 2D surfaces but have the same potential as the mirrors to show what we perceive as reality.

We should also keep in mind that there are many things we know exist, but which we don't see, such as all the oxygen in the world that enables us to live. We don't see it because it doesn't reflect light, but it is just as real as a table. If we do perceive it visually it is because of something in the air, like dust, that reflects light.

Why would we want to think about all this? It is a stark reminder of how limited and selective our understanding of even the most fundamental aspect of our *perceived* universe is, and how significant our part is in the creation of that universe. It is also interesting when we think about all the abstractions we overlay on top of this limited input. For example, I referred to a *real* table, but 'table' is *conventional*, which is to say it might just be some wood in a particular shape that *by convention* we all agree is to be called a table. Many a philosophy student has gone bonkers trying to unpack Austrian philosopher Ludwig Wittgenstein's writings on this topic.

Do we experience the real Universe?

There is no *real* way that things are. Staying with our sense of sight discussion, think of a rose. Imagine a rose in your mind, or do a quick Google search, we think we see the rose as it really is. For example, the red colour of a rose. But we know that colours don't exist in the way we perceive them. They are, as science confirms, a conceptual construction created by our brains to *represent* light wave frequency in a more assessable way for us. Colour is a useful, if not accurate, concept to allow us to differentiate. It is well understood in the Yogic tradition that this type of concept is part of how the intellect *discriminates*. From an evolution viewpoint we needed this discrimination to allow us to survive, for example when determining safe food. Unfortunately, we decided it was also a way to determine safe people, which obviously makes not sense at all. Why would the frequency of light waves from a person's skin make any difference.

Back to the rose. If we see a red object, it is red because the object's surface does not absorb that frequency of light wave, so the red is the reject; you could perhaps argue the colour of the rose is anything but red, but of course that is not that practical or useful. Pure black objects absorb all light waves - though pure black is hard to find. A few years ago a material named Vantablack was created, which is a coating that absorbs up to 99.965% of visible light. This crazy stuff plays all sorts of tricks on your 3D perception, as there is no edge definition. Google Vantablack to see some really crazy effects. Pure white objects reject all waves of light. Projected light sources such as TV and computer screens work a bit differently but are still mimicking the same effect.

Some other animals see more light waves and therefore see more colours. Going back to the rose, it is said that a bee sees many more nuances of reds than we do, including infrared, and therefore they see a very different looking red rose than we do. A dog sees less variations of red than we do; probably just grey. Beyond just the colour, the entire visual perspective of each species is different. Humans see things with what in photography is referred to as a 50mm focal point but does that make it the *real* perspective? Most birds have eyes on the side of their heads, so that is a hard view for us to imagine. If you look on Youtube there are some great videos showing how various species see or create their universe. Therefore, which species sees reality, and the *real* rose as it *really* is? The bee, the dog, or us? I hope you can see that is a silly question. We construct the rose, as does the bee, as does the dog. I've read that we see more shades of green because it was evolutionarily useful. If you pay attention, you can observe how much richer the variations of green in the world are, compared to reds, blues, or other colours. There is a reason why being out in the green natural world feels so vibrant and rich.

I'm writing this on a Sunday morning in January and have a week 18 game of NFL football on TV. I knocked the housework over early and had a quick shower before sitting down for the game. I do some of my best thinking in the shower and was looking at the colour of the Lynx shower gel. It was a weird colour, kind of blue looking to me, but I know that some people call it green, it is perhaps in-between. Looking at a colour chart, perhaps it is turquoise, or aquamarine. But are they even colours? Not only do we have the consideration of how our brain decodes these light wave frequencies, but we must also then agree on sounds we call words, that match these light waves so we can communicate to other people, hoping that they have the nuanced understanding of what we mean. Who knows if they perceive the colour the same, regardless of what they call it? There are no fixed colours, but a variable pallet that we chop up and define as a convention, and then argue about the definitions we just made up.

Keeping us grounded here, I'm using colours as an illustration of how we discriminate and differentiate our reality, and then make up conventional definitions. I'm using something we think we all agree on, sight and colour, but we can see just how conventional all this is. It all gets much harder when we try to agree on abstract concepts, for example what is the definition of a customer, or getting more technical the difference between a managed service and a SaaS offering. We need to be a little less certain that we understand the one irrefutable reality in all areas. However, we'll continue with our sensors.

But the Universe isn't just visual

We have only had a basic look at one of our senses: sight. But the way we construct the world with our perceptions is similar when it comes to other senses like hearing; except here animals like dogs have a much richer experience. And then there is the bat which somehow uses sound as its primary sense to *see*, which is an experience that we have no way to even conceptualise. All our information about the world comes from the five sense organs, which is all the intellect can use to construct the universe for us. Sense organs cannot perceive all of anything, just a part, and our brains fill in the rest. We perceive our world in a way necessary to survive, and our five senses are fine for this. We all create our own version of the Universe, which differs for each of us.

There are other considerations with the senses we use to build our Universe, because sense organs only work on comparison. You can't know light without dark, or loud without quiet, or sweet without sour. But we also bring a lot of interpretation to this. If someone is six feet tall, then they are tall in Japan, but short in the Netherlands. There is a lot of interpretation in building a Universe, and that is before we start our language and definition games.

Language games

We create the meaning of language in our own minds. We know that as with light, sound is waves of air vibration, and our eardrum detects these vibrations, and our brain construct the sounds we perceive. We seldom detect the sound waves themselves, but we have all heard heavy base, such as at a doof doof event, and we can detect the waves. We define musical notes, however in reality, these are constructions because sound exists on a continuum, but we say that at certain points on that continuum they are distinct notes.

Some sounds have special importance, and these we call words. When people speak, they are just making sound, or more precisely producing sound waves through vibrations. We decode these into sounds, and then denote some to be words. We then play all sorts of language games about what these words mean and don't mean, both individually and in combination, sometimes with subtle variations based on the *tone* of the word. We believe the speaker defines the meaning, but that cannot really be true. We make up the meaning ourselves, not the speaker. We infer what the speaker intended. Effectively all language is conventional. It is an agreement, or perhaps more accurately it is an arrangement. Again, Wittgenstein had much to say about this, if you dare.

THE CREATION OF YOUR UNIVERSE

One language game that really does highlight how key *we* are in *our* interpretation of the universe is with jokes. We've all experienced times when we have found a joke funny and others have not, or they have, and we have not. Perhaps our partner found it funny and we found it offensive, and we cannot see any way it would not be seen as offensive. So funny or offensive cannot be attributes of the joke itself. It must be how it is interpreted. All of our universe is like this. How do we interpret it. Do we have agency in this.

Why does this matter

The above is interesting in terms of how we perceive the Universe. But the real message for me is that it brings into question the most fundamental understanding of reality. For example, I recall my father many years ago being rather sceptical about what the media was saying about politicians; now this was in the 1970s, so well before the more recent fuss (few things are really that new). He said you should work out the truth for yourself, and not listen to other people. Great advice, but how exactly do you do that if you don't personally know the politicians, and perhaps even if you do? Ultimately, you will rely on not only your senses, but a whole array of filtration and selection between what politicians, business colleagues, friends, family members, or strangers say and what you actually hear.

We don't want to lose all trust in the Universe because of this. We perhaps just need to relax a little bit and be open at all times to our misperceptions: what we see and hear and what else we overlay onto this. We can use this knowledge to better create the Universe the way we want it by being more generous in our interpretations. We don't always have to be frustrated sitting in traffic. It might be a nice day, windows down, nice beats on the stereo; just enjoy it - at least you don't have a tooth ache.

If we understand that we create the universe ourselves, and fully control how we interpret all interactions, then we again are the 4-star generals calling the shots. It is harder than that, but if we can glimpse this reality, it can and does change our perception a little. We can build on this, and it can take us a long way.

CHAPTER 6

SADGURU AND THE KNIFE INTELLECT

"Buddhi: This is the nature of the intellect that it will
dissect whatever you give it. The entire modern science
is coming out of human intellect – so everything is by
dissection. What you can know by dissection is only the
material aspect of life."

Sadhguru

The intellect is the most fundamental tool used by strategist and architects
and is also one we often misunderstand. Typically, the intellect is defined as
the key conscious function, or facility, of rationality and reason. We would
generally relate it to the activity of thinking when we are aware of our
thoughts, feeling like we are *in control* of them and directing them.

Within Eastern Philosophy, and specifically the Yogic tradition (i.e. relating
to the activity or philosophy of yoga), we can find a useful understanding
of our intellect; what it does and does not do. We find a balanced view of
the strengths and the limitations of our intellect, along with what we have

given up by elevating our intellect to be the hero of our intelligence. How did this happen? Western societies broke free of the shackles of religious and monarchical dogma with The Enlightenment (1685 - 1815), which was a significant leap forward. However, a by-product was the elevation of the intellect to become the only form of intelligence deemed valuable, or even legitimate. Logic and reason, as useful as they are, have become the dictators of our intelligence.

I want to demystify the Yogic tradition, a little, to help us open up to what its thousands of years of careful observation about both the mind and the body, offers this discussion. When we talk about the Yogic tradition, and therefore Yoga, we are talking about the broader sense of Yoga, including, but not limited to, the form we think of as exercise. The *Ministry of External Affairs* in India defines Yoga as: "essentially a spiritual discipline based on an extremely subtle *science*, which focuses on bringing harmony between mind and body; it is an art and science of healthy living. The word 'Yoga' is derived from the Sanskrit root 'Yuj', meaning 'to join' or 'to yoke' or 'to unite'."

The Yogic tradition is less obsessed with, although it does value, the intellect and conscious thinking; I've heard the comment "think whatever you want, it is not so important". We might not want to go that far, but we might want to open ourselves to leveraging intelligence beyond only our intellect. Yes, in the Yogic tradition the intellect is only one part of our intelligence.

Intellectual thought is recycling data that we have already gathered; that is all. *Nothing new comes from conscious thought itself.* Now this statement probably landed with a thud. But think about it. We are not normally skilled at focusing on *where* our thoughts come from, but if you develop this skill through meditation or mindfulness, or just paying close attention, you will find the original spark of any thought, or a new idea, just appears. We are talking here about the very first seed of the idea. Does it seem to our intellect that it arrives from nowhere? It must. If not, then it must be something you already knew and have recalled, and therefore it must not be new. The intellect might set the scene, but that first spark comes from elsewhere. When we think about a novel problem, we are setting the scene for some other process to solve it. Nothing magical or mystical, it is from some other type of intelligence that we don't talk much about in the West, but some in the West have studied it.

Daniel Kahneman, the late Nobel prize winning psychologist, refers to this in his groundbreaking book *Thinking Fast and Slow.* He talked about System 2 for conscious thought, the intellect, and System 1 for unconscious thought; there are subtleties, but this is the general concept. Our System 2 intellect is slow, serial, effortful, logical, sceptical, deliberate, and self-aware. While System 1 is automatic, fast, implicit, effortless, associative, harder to control, and is not self-aware at a conscious level. He clearly elevates System 1 as the star of the show, and the one that does the heavy lifting, with System 2, our intellect, doing the checking. Our intellect, System 2, is lazy, and tends to favour shortcuts, called heuristics, which can lead to biases. System 2 uses the law of least effort because for most of our evolution energy was limited and System 2 is energy intensive, with our brain consuming about 20% of our energy, which is about 100 times the energy used by a smartphone. These energy saving heuristics often work well but can cause big problems at times. Part of the problem is when it goes wrong, we tend to try to justify the outcome with our intellect, System 2, rather than acknowledging, correction and moving on.

New ideas spark in System 1, and once passed to System 2 we can then work on them consciously, but System 1 also keeps working away in the background feeding new sparks to System 2. The key is to use the strengths of each system. Originally System 1 got called the sub-conscious, which was a term coined by John Norris in a 1708 essay, and later used by the psychologist Pierre Janet in an 1889 thesis. Sub-conscious meant it was below, or subordinate to, the conscious; this was a mistake made in the West, and combined with the enlightenments elevation of rationality and reason lead to the undervaluing of System 1.

There are early references from the pioneering psychologist Carl Jung, and others, indicating that the subconscious, System 1, has off-line storage utility; this is true, but key point that Kahneman highlighted is that it also has *background processing*, to paraphrase in technology speak. It is the combination of vast storage and deep processing that is the power of System 1. It's a bit like machine learning on a data lake; very powerful when used on the right tasks.

Going back to the Yogic tradition, I have greatly benefited from the insights of Sadguru, a Yogic teacher from India. I would highly recommend looking into his videos on YouTube. For me Sadguru not only shares great wisdom from India, but also is highly entertaining, in a way that makes me think of him as an Eastern Alan Watts. In both cases, you can read their books, but there is no substitute for the vocal delivery of their warmth, wit and humour. What has Sadguru got to do with strategy and architecture? For me he helps me refine my systems thinking. There is perhaps nothing more important for our roles than understanding systems, be it technology, people, societies, animals, plants, or ecosystems; I would view a company in its broader context as an ecosystem. We are prone to looking at the optimisation of discrete parts, while losing sight of the impact on the whole. Nowhere is this better highlighted than with his unpacking of the intellect.

So, let's look closer at this intellect.

The Intellect

The intellect is elevated to an *all-powerful* and *all-knowing* level in Western thinking. By the intellect we mean thoughts we are consciously aware of, which are based on available information, meaning direct observations and memories (including knowledge). The scientific method, which is a great tool for humanity, is based on this intellect. However, much of Eastern Philosophical thinking is not centred on the intellect, or more specifically there is a recognition that this is not the only form of intelligence. There are other types of intelligence that we largely ignore, or at least value less. More on that later. First let us understand more about the intellect.

Here is a simple question that Sadhguru asks. Would you prefer to have a *sharp* intellect, or a *dull* intellect? Does anybody want a *dull* intellect?

We have learnt how to interpret the above question even though it seems to make no *literal* sense. Why would the intellect be sharp or dull? But from a Yogic viewpoint it makes sense, because the intellect operates like a knife; the sharper the knife the better. The intellect is a mechanism to divide and dissect. The intellect is discriminatory in nature in that it differentiates things. Have you noticed how good we are at categorising and classifying things? Be it with data, words, shapes, processes, people, or almost anything. When we do this, what are we doing? We are dividing things into groups, types, or sections. We are dissecting, and categorising, often to understand things better. But we at times divide things that really are better understood whole. This discrimination is a key tool for strategy and architecture, which is good, providing we know why we are doing it, and balance it with more holistic systems-based thinking as a countermeasure to excessive dividing. For example, defining microservices based on domain driven design, ensuring well defined boundaries, but also considering how these microservices interact as wider systems.

In science we have divided all things, all matter, into smaller pieces: molecules, then atoms (based on a Greek name meaning they were indivisible), then into nucleus and electrons, and then protons, neutrons, and nucleons, and down to quarks and it continues. Driven by the intellects desire to continue to divide we built the Large Hadron Collider ($9bn) to find the so-called *God Particle* (Higgs Boson), and now there is a proposal to build one three times larger. We take this *dividing* of things very seriously indeed.

This ability to divide is why as humans we are good at (or bad at), dividing people into identities of race, religion, nationality, caste, creed, gender, political leanings, temperaments and even into 16 classifications of the Myers–Briggs Type Indicator. How did we even survive the hunter-gather phase of human evolution without the Myers–Briggs Type Indicator to determine which of us ought to go out and look for new resources?

But this intellect, which to be clear is very useful when used for what it is good at, keeps on dividing everything. We divide companies into divisions, and teams, filled with people who are divided into multiple roles. We get very *attached* to our roles and teams. In technology we often talk about *The Business*, as if there is some other part of the company, called *The Business*, which are in some way separate from us and driven by some other force. These structural divisions can be useful, but they are conventional, they are not *real*.

We get very caught up in most large organisations with endless restructures, but these seldom really achieve the stated outcome. They do create a lot of anxiety, as they put stress on our identity based on the chattering of our intellects. As logical as we try to be as strategists and architects, we are still human, and our identities are in play.

You can only use your intellect from a point of your identity, your ego, and therefore your intellect seeks to protect that identity. Your intellect struggles with the uncertainty in the world, and that things don't stay neatly divided; it clings to certainty. Therefore, your intellect often is impacted by anxiety. Effectively we are controlling a sharp-knife, our intellect, with a very unsteady-hand, our anxiety. As you can see, this can be an unhelpful combination, because in the end, the knife is pointed at us.

Beyond the Intellect

Much of Eastern wisdom, in this case the Yogic tradition, does not come from, or centre itself around, the intellect. It comes from a deeper dimension of intelligence within us. A simplistic example of one other type of intelligence is when we consume a piece of bread, and our body makes it into human cells. You cannot do this with your intellect, you cannot think a sandwich or a banana into a human being. But not just any human being, it replaces part of you. If you are younger, it grows you. This is intelligence, and beyond what even science can do using the power of our intellects. It took centuries for science to work out how this process works, yet any fool could just do it. No thinking required.

If we want to know the point of existence, and to be successful and happy, we need other types of intelligence. The intellect is a knife that cuts, it divides, and with this you can know certain things, such as how a person

47

is a combination of organs. But to know a person you don't dissect them, you embrace them. You talk to them and listen to them. In a way it is similar with a company or organisation. You can't sew with a knife yet that is what we try to do with our intellect by dividing things, optimising them, and then expecting to end up with a whole working system.

By turning inwards, you can *experience* this other knowledge. The Eastern wisdom transcends the limitations of sense perception. It is important to realise that English is not a very good language for talking about the inner mind and experience, it just does not have the words. Many of the translations from Sanskrit and Hindi are not very accurate or precise. In the Yogic tradition, there are 16 types of intelligence, which can be put into four main groups (ironically with our intellect). We've met our intellect called Buddhi in Sanskrit. There is our memory called Chitta, which is very rich and diverse including things like our DNA. Our sensory mind is Manas. Finally, Ahakara is our sense of self.

Now this might all sound rather mystical, but it doesn't need to be. There is no hard-wired difference between Eastern and Western thinkers, just some differences in focus and narratives; if you spend some time listening to Eastern thinkers like Alan Watts and Sadhguru, you find you will *click* to the narrative style.

Much of this interaction between the System 1 subconscious and the System 2 intellect is something we do know; we just don't think about it. I've always known that many of the ideas I have for solving problems, or innovating, just pop into my head, often in the morning while having a shower. I now understand the explanation: System 1 works on problems overnight, and at then times when we are on autopilot, such as showering, shopping for groceries, or doing housework, are good times for our brains to be a little active, but not controlled by our intellect, System 2. These are times when things often pop into our consciousness from seemingly nowhere. In the West we've figured this out with many recent psychology and medical studies using our intellect, and in the East, they got there several thousand years earlier by paying careful attention to their minds. We can stand around arguing about who is right, or who got there first, or we can just learn to blend the strengths of Western and Eastern wisdom and benefit all our futures. As strategist and architects, we need to ensure we focus on whole systems, not just optimising parts, but the good news is that outside our intellect our broader intelligence is inherently systems thinking based.

A final thought from Sadguru - people are getting very worried about AI, and if it will do all the thinking for us, but don't worry. This is one reason why *now* is the right time to learn how to go beyond the intellect and let our full intelligence shine, because AI only does the intellect part. We have a much fuller intelligence, and that is our special power, we just forgot use appreciate it. I tend to think AI ought to be called Artificial Intellect, not Artificial Intelligence! Can AI turn a banana into a child? Let AI do the intellect thinking, have a holiday, and make space for our full rich intelligence.

CHAPTER 7

NON-DUALISM

ENDING THE DUALISTIC ILLUSION

"Really, the fundamental, ultimate mystery - the only thing
you need to know to understand the deepest metaphysical
secrets - is this: that for every outside there is an inside
and for every inside there is an outside, and although they
are different, they go together."

Alan Watts

Non-dualism is a big concept, and there is much debate in Eastern
philosophies around this way of understanding the Universe. We won't
get into the debate here other than to point out it is a common, but far
from a consensus, viewpoint. Non-dualism relates to a number of Eastern
philosophical traditions including a branch in Hinduism called Advaita
Vedanta, highlighted in the Sanskrit term *Tat Tvam Asi* meaning *that thou
art (you are that)*. It is also common in Buddhism, Zen, Taoism, and other
Eastern philosophies. Non-dualism is part of many indigenous ways of

viewing the world, and if you hear the term 'holistic' then that *might* be in the non-dualistic neighbourhood. Non-dualism can be found in the thinking of some Western philosophers (e.g. Spinoza's, Kierkegaard's, some of Nietzsche's), although it is hard to talk about non-dualism with the precise intellectual language required in Western philosophy, particularly in academia.

Non-dualism literally means 'not two'. It points to the fundamentals of the nature of reality, or more accurately our perception and understanding of reality, and what is truly separate verses part of, dependent, or codependent (e.g. an object depends on the subject perceiving it, therefore are they two, or one). Basically, it is a very holistic view of the Universe. That all is 'one', and the 'one' is pure consciousness because there can be nothing outside consciousness; I know this sounds like a very flowery spiritual idea, but it doesn't have to be. I'm hoping that after the previous chapter you can see this isn't necessarily at odds with science, it is just a different way of talking about things. In my view this is where our scientific understanding of perception, consciousness, and knowledge, inevitably leads us. Recall in the previous chapter we found that the intellect divides and dissects everything, and that this has limitations. Understanding non-dualism can only be done if we learn to put it all back together, or more accurately, take a fresh look at everything as a whole without dividing.

> "Those who know do not speak. Those who speak do
> not know."
> *Lao Tsu, Tao Te Ching*

I'll warn you now, it is hard to crack this with logical reasoning; you need to let go and experience non-duality to know it. It relates quite closely to our ego, which underpins our identity as described earlier. Our ego doesn't like to give up the game without a fight, and it uses the intellect to wage that fight. I'm not expecting that you will suddenly fully know the non-dualism of reality here, but perhaps I can make you curious enough to investigate to see if there is something useful to you in this concept.

At a minimum, I hope you will have a more holistic, or you could say systems thinking, viewpoint. This becomes useful in strategy and architecture as we start defining boundaries, establishing causation, and defining our view of interdependencies. We start having a better understanding of the whole sphere, and how much we can influence.

Non-what? What even is dualism

In the West, we tend to put a lot of emphases on intellectual thought, particularly post the Enlightenment with its elevation of logic and reason. To be clear, the Enlightenment has largely been a positive thing; however, there have been some potentially unhelpful side effects. If you are reading this book, you are probably in a role where your intellect is your main tool of the trade. The intellect likes to divide things into categories, and in particular into two opposing concepts; actually, not only does it *like* to do it, but it defines the intellect in the same way that flying defines a bird (nuances aside with flightless birds who have evolved to no longer fly ... chattering intellect still categorising everything!).

Let's consider some examples where the intellect divides opposites, such as: up versus down, inside versus outside, loud versus quiet, near versus far, left versus right (which we somewhat crudely ascribe to the multi-dimensional world of politics). Some of those are potentially judgement free, such as up versus down, but many are not such as: good versus bad, beautiful versus ugly, exciting versus boring. These pairs are co-dependent, as you cannot have only up and no down, or only left and no right. You also wouldn't know what good is without bad, because good has no meaning without its juxtaposition. You could consider that when we do have mostly good and no bad we get more nuanced about what is good and bad, to kind of balance the equation. We will always find finer grain ways to decern things.

When a baby enters *into* the world, or more accurately grows *out of* the world (Where could it enter from?), does the baby judge things as being good or bad? No. It doesn't have the concept of good and bad. It does know pain, but not the judgement of things being good or bad, or beautiful and ugly. It doesn't have the concepts. Duality is something we learn conceptually. We are taught to separate, to decern, as independent concepts. This is okay, and it is often useful, but it is not the only way to perceive things, and it does cause some issues. If you doubt, that consider left and right political parties in your country. Is this concept helpful? Will we ever solve the left verses right political issue? And what has it looked like in history when regimes have tried to solve it?

Now in strategy and architecture consider concepts like target and non-target, or strategic and non-strategic. Even loosely coupled and tightly coupled, or centralized and decentralized. We set these up everywhere, and then we apply judgement. We have principles to help us know how we ought to apply judgement. At the base of our technology discipline, being digital, there is binary, which is simply two states of 0 and 1, or off and on, or anything that can have two states. Binary at least doesn't have judgement, in regard to 1 being better than 0. This dualism is neither good nor bad, it just is. All concepts rely on dualism, to the extent that even non-dualism as a concept is dualistic as it is juxtaposed (dualistic versus non-dualistic). I did say it was hard to grasp, partly because you must use concepts to explain non-concepts. The point of non-dualism isn't to stop using concepts, because you can't, it is just to be aware concepts are made up, and somewhat arbitrary. Don't think you can argue to certainty about the *correct* definition of loose and tight coupling for example. Just agree a *helpful* definition, and accept it won't be perfect, as that is all you can do.

Duality goes further than pure concepts. It also applies to objects in the world, both between objects, and between us and objects – known as the subject versus object distinction. Subject and object as concepts are so engrained that we structure our language around them; we will come back to this in other chapters.

Consider first the separation of objects in the world. To use a really simple example think of a tree, a table, and a rolling pin. Three very different *things*. But they might all be made of wood, or to be clearer the tree *is* wood, so there ought to be no difference between a tree, a table, and a rolling pin. The concept of a table, or rolling pin, is purely conventional; we've kind of agreed that a certain shape of wood is called a table, and another is called a rolling pin. You could even cut some large branches from a large tree and make a table, and then make a rolling pin with the left-over wood, while not even killing the tree. So now you have the tree, table, and rolling pin. How separate are these three things? It is *useful* to call them separate things and that is ok, particularly because the table and rolling pin have different utility. The tree has utility as it can be used for shelter, or for a bird nesting. It can be useful to think of them as different, but don't confuse this difference with some type of base reality. These are purely conventional. We've agreed that a certain shape is to be called a rolling pin. If you gave a rolling pin to someone that had never seen one before they'd probably think it was some type of club.

So, let's make this a bit more challenging and consider the tree and the soil that the tree is growing in. Are these separate things? Do you normally find trees growing without the soil? Can you have a tree without water? Where did the tree come from? Did the atoms that grow into the tree come from nowhere? It didn't grow *in* the soil, it grew *out of* the soil; it grew out of the earth (both as soil, and as the planet), and we've just decided to call the atoms tree atoms. More accurately this new arrangement of the existing atoms is now called a tree. Ultimately it is the same soil (earth) that we came from, as we grew from eating plants that came from the earth, or animals that at some point grew from plants that came from the earth. Sadhguru uses an example of a mango tree that grows out of the soil enriched with all sorts of dead animals and excrement, yet the mango tree grows beautiful, sweet mangos that we crave to eat. Call us all separate things at one level, it is useful, but it is not the only way to look at things. There are at least two profound events with the mango, one being the ability for the tree to absorb the atoms, that perhaps come from cow dung, and grow mangos, and the other is for us to consume mangos and use those atoms to grow (or replace part of) a human. When an AI powered 3D printer, brought with blockchain enabled Bitcoin (of course), can take cow dung and grow a human then come and tell me it is impressive technology. It is as impressive as each and every one of us.

In strategy and architecture, it is useful to stay aware of how we are dividing things, how arbitrary these divisions can be, and how interdependent, or even codependent, concepts really are. I've been in many hours of discussions over the years about what a customer is in insurance. We have a customer entity and a policy entity, but in reality, a policy can only exist if there is a customer, or party to the insurance contract. Are these really separate things? It is helpful to say yes, but just remember it is conventional, and done for convenience. The tricky part of defining a customer is agreeing if you can have a customer without a policy. If they only have a quote, are they a customer? What if they take out a policy, but cancel it before it goes on risk? That is the tricky thing with separating concepts, you get border skirmishes. Sometimes these skirmishes don't matter, for example, putting a record in a customer table for a quote might be okay, but if you need to contact all customers for regulatory reasons about something then it might matter a whole lot. In the end we need to do what is useful, and we shouldn't argue too personally about what is *correct*. It is mostly conventional. We just need to agree, and then agree that we agree (which is the harder part of agreeing).

So, what is non-dualism

"For peace to reign on Earth, humans must evolve into
new beings who have learned to see the whole first."
Immanuel Kant

Very basically, non-dualism is the experience of being aware of the illusion of duality, but without trying to exclude dualism, since it is useful in our lives. I'm not sure someone could survive in a purely non-dualistic manner. As stated, we can't even talk about non-dualism without dualism. The key here is that it is an experience, not an intellectual concept. Dualism is created by, or at least the fundamental language of, our intellect, which is why it is so hard to intellectually understand non-dualism. This is why you find really weird sayings about this, such as Alan Watts saying that "by getting it you don't get it, and by not getting it, you get it". These sayings are pointers, because you can't directly describe it to the intellect. Even when you get it, you don't *fully* get it, you glimpse it; and then you try to focus your intellect on it, and it is gone. It is said that duality is an illusion, which it is, but consider that something being an illusion doesn't mean it doesn't *exist*, it means it exists in one way, but we *perceive* it in another way.

Paradoxically, we already know the non-duality of the universe, we just need to realise we know it. Like the person looking around the house for their glasses only to realise they are on their head; we just need to click, and then chuckle at ourselves. There is nothing to learn, just things to forget. We need to create some space to think in different ways and to relax our addiction to the concepts that are often illusions, and which often constrain us.

This method of realisation is so fundamental I put it on the front cover of this book. The gate on the front cover of this book is the Torii from Japan (outside Shinto temples), which is also found in China as the Pailou, in India as the Torana, as well as other parts of Asia. It has some different meanings, but one, and arguably the original one, is as a *gateless gate*. *The Gateless Gate* is also the name used for a collection of Chan (Zen) koans, which are challenges used to break through the dualistic illusion. It is called a gateless gate as a metaphor because there isn't really a gate, you just need to walk through the open gap (to the realisation). It is very hard to pass the gate until you do in which case it was no effort at all. You cannot pass the gate intellectually; you need to *just do it* (that would make a great product slogan). It is a bit like learning to ride a bike, you kind of just have to get it, and then wonder why it was hard; and like that, it is not about trying harder, it is about letting go of trying.

Non-dualism is often described as refuting the subject verses object distinction. As we have seen in the prior chapter on the creation of our universe, we know that we, as the subject, do create the objects we perceive. This can also be called the mind versus matter duality (I'll avoid that rabbit hole which leads to something adjacent to this called the hard problem of consciousness). If we create the universe in our consciousness, then how can there be separateness if everything we perceive is ultimately in our own minds. This is one of the ways to consider non-dualism; we can be the universe, and the universe can be consciousness. But it goes beyond this. Once you feel it, you find it is pervasive at all levels of consciousness, and from our perspective there is nothing outside our consciousness, it *is* our universe. Nothing mystical about it.

I've always liked the description of a glass that you might use to drink from. It is called a *glass* and is made of *glass*, and it has an inside and an outside. You could say that glass is made of glass and nothing else. Well, if you fill it with water, you find there was more than just the glass it was made of. It only worked as a glass because it had a space where the water could go; it is the form of it that makes it work as a glass. The space is just as important as the material (the glass). Then imagine taking the glass up into orbit and trying to fill it with water. Oh, so you needed not only the glass and the space to fill with water, but you also needed gravity. And we haven't even considered what you need to make glass. The concept of a 'glass' needs much more than just the material.

Another example is to think of an ocean wave: is it separate from the other waves, or from the ocean? Alternatively, try to explain a person running without the concept, implicit normally, of the ground to run on. It makes no sense. You can have a person floating in space moving their legs, but it makes no sense to say that they are running. The ground is just as much a part of running as the runner themselves, as of course is gravity, and they won't run far without the air.

What good is non-dualism

This is a tough question. In some ways it is like the red verses blue pill in *The Matrix* movie. Do we want the illusion, or do we want an understanding closer to reality? In our case we build our own matrix, our own world of illusions through concepts, and we are most welcome to live there.

But if we want, we can look through the illusion, while still participating in it, to just understand how things are. Creating a little space to relax a bit more into our lives.

Perhaps even more importantly for strategy and architecture we can understand that we are even more deeply in this world of illusionary abstractions than most. If you work as a truck driver, or gardener, or surgeon, or soldier, then you are much more in touch with reality, and spend less time with concepts. We spend our days with frameworks, definitions, diagrams, roadmaps, endless PowerPoints, and all sorts of other abstract concepts. Remember a few years back when big data was the buzz; everyone knew they had to have it, they just didn't know what it was. Data is fertile ground for concepts that nobody agree on, with data warehouse, data lake, lake house, data mesh, data fabric. This is before you get anywhere near the definitional issues around the manically hyped area of artificial intelligence.

So, understanding non-duality is a useful counter-measure to help us understand that we are only dealing with concepts. In lean thinking managers and people like us are told to go to the Gemba, the real place of work. Go and see. This is grounding us and breaking us out of our concepts just a little.

We can still debate definitions and frameworks and roadmaps, but perhaps we can create just a little space for our own wellbeing. We ought to see these things as important, but perhaps just a little less serious. We might need a definition of customer, but getting others to agree might not need to be a die-in-a-ditch issue. Accept that there is always a bit of arbitrariness to concepts. Any fans of the Western Philosopher *Ludwig Wittgenstein* will recognise some of his concepts echoing here.

How to get into non-dualism

Going back to the gateless gate analogy, there is nothing stopping us just *getting* it. Ultimately, this is an experience, and you only get it when you just get it. But we tend to need to do work to get it. Meditation is probably the main method, thought this is not the only use for it, and it doesn't have to be sitting down in a classic meditation way. Think of this meditation being mindfulness, and it can be done while doing other things, like walking; for me this is the best way. Psychedelics are also a pathway to at least see the possibility, though obviously not recommended as it can cause so many other issues, not least of which is the desire to stay there and then frying your brain. The tricky thing is, you can't get it via a purely intellectual path, though that isn't to say there is no point thinking about it.

Some schools of thought say it is a gradual chipping away, like chipping at a rock with a chisel, while other schools of thought say it must be a sudden breakthrough, like hitting a large rock with a sledgehammer where it looks like nothing is changing, but it suddenly breaks open; this could be the first strike or thousandth strike.

Personally, I tend to think it is sudden, but you can get glimpses of the experience along the way. The analogy I most like is the mirror. Your consciousness is like a mirror, it doesn't judge if things are good or bad, or attractive or not, and it doesn't cling to things, so it isn't worrying about an image once it is gone; it accepts all without holding. And our beautiful mirror consciousness is there for all of us if we remove the dust and grime covering it.

Finally, if you get nothing else from this chapter, you can at least understand the famous non-dualist in-joke: "A Buddhist monk walks up to a hot dog vendor and says: 'How about I make *you* one with everything'". Some versions have the hot dog vendor saying the hotdog was $4, and after the monk gives him $10 and waits, eventually asks where his change is, the hot dog vendor explains that 'change must come from within'. The Zen tradition has much humour, which serves a purpose, because in the end we spend our lives discovering we are deluding ourselves, and that there was nothing to find in the first place.

There is no definition of customer. There is no customer. There is only the naming of the concept customer.

> "The Tao [Way] that can be told of is not the eternal Tao
> [Way]; The name that can be named is not the eternal
> name. The Nameless is the origin of Heaven and Earth
> [Universe]; The Named is the mother of all things."
>
> *Lao Tsu, Tao Te Ching*

CHAPTER 8

UNDERSTANDING TIME AND

CAUSATION

"Space and time are the framework within which the
mind is constrained to construct its experience of reality."
Immanuel Kant

We need to talk about time. We have let all of life be completely defined by time, and in the corporate world this obsession with time translates to urgency. We are all pressed for time. We have limited time. We have no time. Often in our line of work (strategy and architecture) we are dealing with impact horizons of years, yet need answers in days, hours, and sometimes minutes or even seconds. But we can make a strong case that time is an illusion. It is a very compelling illusion, and even a very useful illusion. I do mean an illusion in terms of time existing, just not in the way we perceive.

Don't worry, this isn't as disorientating as it might seem. There are very practical uses for changing our relationship with time. It will still be there for us. You won't miss out on your birthday cake. We are just going to make it work for us rather than always controlling and limiting us.

The illusion of time

> "What is time then? If nobody asks me, I know; but if
> I were desirous to explain it to one that should ask me,
> plainly I do not know."

St. Augustine

There is no future and past separate from now, there is only now. It has only ever been now, and there only will be now, which is not *really* controversial if we think about it. We generate ideas of past and future. We can plan now for the future, and we can remember the past, often not verbatim, however we can only do these now. We can even remember having remembered in the past, or remember planning for the future in the past. But we cannot access anything other than now, and therefore we don't need the concept of now, or past, or future. We don't *need* the concept of time, or at least we don't need to be ruled by it. Mindfulness is gaining popularity and is described as staying present, which is good, but when you get deep into it you find you don't have to do something to stay in the present, you just are present, there is no other option. Mindfulness is really about being mindful about your attention, and this is very important indeed. Time isn't really limited if you think about it, but attention is. When we say we shouldn't waste our precious time, we could make a better point by saying we shouldn't waste our precious attention.

"If we take eternity to mean not infinite temporal
duration but timelessness, then eternal life belongs to
those who live in the present."

Ludwig Wittgenstein

However, we must admit that time is a sticky concept. We really struggle to let it go. So, what is it? Many philosophers and physicists in the West and the East have spent much time (attention), on this, and I'm not digging around in that here as you can easily find some great descriptions on YouTube or elsewhere. I would say that it does seem to be closely related to space and movement. It gets very hard to talk about distance without time and speed of movement. The other driver of time, for humans, does seem to link to our extensive memories, which our intellect relates to positions in time, and our imagination, where we can freely move between past and future. As any police officer or judge knows there is no bright line between our memories and our imagination, and often we cannot tell the difference.

Overall, the biggest impact of our misunderstanding of time might be how it encourages a misunderstanding of causation.

Our backward view of causation

"Freedom is not freedom from causation. It's freedom
from causation that is not your own. What could be more
obvious?"

Mike Hockney, The Sam Harris Delusion

We tend to have a backward view of causation, and this does us a disservice. We are fixated with the idea that events in the past *cause* events that occur now and will impact events in the future. Alan Watts describes this as how we feel we are driven forward by past events.

However, when we think about it, the opposite happens. Events happen now (when else could they happen?), and they fade into the past. It is now that *causes* the past, not the other way around. This might feel paradoxical. It makes sense, but we still want to say one event *causes* another event later in time. A nice Alan Watts analogy is the question, does the wake of a ship in the ocean *push* the ship and *cause* the ship to move? No, the ship (i.e. now) causes the wake (i.e. past) to flow from it. The source of the paradox isn't the causation, the paradox is the definition of the boundaries of the *event*. Recall that the intellect divides and discriminates. We do this with everything, including not only graduations of colour (e.g. the blue green boundary), but also when we define a specific occurrence of an event. We'll go back to Alan Watts for an example, which I have extended somewhat.

Let's consider World War II. When did it start? Well, the official answer is September 1st, 1939, when France and the UK declared war. Officially, you could say the invasion of Poland by Germany was the *event* that *caused* the war. But it is a World War because it involved both hemispheres and Japan invaded China in 1937 with horrific impacts for Manchuria, so perhaps that is the start of the war. Some say it was the rise of the Third Reich who came to power in 1933 that caused it; however, the rise of the Imperial Japanese Empire seems to be mostly independent. Many point out that the Third Reich wouldn't have risen without the impacts of the Treaty of Versailles after World War I, so maybe it was caused by, or a continuation of, World War I.

So maybe we've found it. We have just one World War from 1914 to 1945, starting on 28 June 1914 with the assassination of Archduke Franz Ferdinand in Sarajevo. But the cause of the assassination traces back to the Bosnia-Herzegovina annexation by Austria-Hungary in 1908. Before we start tracing this back through the history of the Ottoman Empire, we could take a shortcut and just accept that to some degree, looking for prior causes and pushing back the start of the event will take us back to the Big Bang, which of course was ultimately caused by the previous Big Bang. It is turtles all the way down.

Ultimately, trying to explain events now from past events, is in a way, refusing to explain them at all. Now don't take this too far. This is to jolt our understanding. This allows us to consider events and causation more holistically. It allows us to break out of the causative cycle that can be very limiting. Take the example of the bad behaviour of a teenage being blamed on their parents, who might blame their parents, who might be dead now, but even if they weren't, they had a terrible upbringing, and it was hardly their fault. Again, we end up at the Big Bang, and turtles all the way down.

Causation is very real in physics. If you throw a rock in the air, then due to gravity, the throwing the rock event will cause the rock to fall. It is foreseeable and causative. The problematic part is assigning causation in the same way to human action, in terms of behavioural psychology. That is not to say there are not real reasons for behaviour, as there clearly are, but there are also choices. I can say a person's parent hit them and that is the reason they hit their child; however, that isn't the cause. The cause is that the person decided to hit their child. This is not predetermined. When we blame causation for our actions, effectively saying everything is a *reaction*, we are trying to absolve ourselves of our decisions to take the action. This isn't to say we are irredeemable either, it is just to say we need to make other decisions and there is nothing stopping us from doing that.

> "You're under no obligation to be the same person you
> were 5 minutes ago."
> *Alan Watts*

Why does this matter for strategy and architecture?

This can all get very esoteric, and that is not what we want to do here. This chapter is intended to nudge your thinking and allow you to free yourself from the shackles of time and causation, while not abandoning these concepts as they are clearly very useful, and foundational in our modern Western world.

I gained some insight on how causation works (in practice), being at a large financial services organisation for a long time (22 years). There were many urgent initiatives that didn't succeed, only for people to move on, and then others to come along and try something very similar. It is hard not to get cynical. You know the rhetoric: move fast, limit scope, no gold-plating, out of the box, best-practice, foundation phase with value add to follow. Some of the biggest issues for the business and its customers came from the supposedly *successful* programs, that delivered on-time and on-budget (or within a disgruntledly tolerated margin), and were claimed as successes, but just cause more pain. We seem to forget in the heat of battle the original reasons for doing the program, and elevate delivery of the program as success, rather than solving the business need or problem. Outcomes another story, and Chapter 9 talks to these.

My observation is that there is often more time than we think to take good actions. There is normally more money than we think as well, if we get the narrative right, and have a strong focus on business outcomes. This ought not to be *just* to get new shiny technology. Breaking problems down into chunks that deliver incremental value is very important, but not with valueless foundational phases with value phases to follow. It is very hard, but we must find ways to add business value at each increment, or at least in parallel, e.g. mixing in architectural epics with functional epics.

As a strategist or enterprise architect, our time horizon needs to be focused on years, even if measured in the popular performance *game* of quarters. Now we will have some short term focuses, but we need to ensure they serve the medium-term game. There are plenty of roles around with shorter time horizons, so we need to do our job and keep the pressure on the medium term. But we also need to ensure we know it is actions now that will make that strategy come to life.

Causation is an interesting one. For example, having been on many very large core system replacement programs, I know that the demand for requirements from 'the business' can be an endless point of frustration for all involved. In a well-established company with well-engrained processes executed on legacy applications, the expectation often is that 'the business' has documented, or at least a logical understanding of, *their* processes now and what that ought to be; this is unrealistic. Often the business and the legacy system have grown up together, in what can be considered *co-dependant origination* (using a great Eastern philosophical term). Often when asked what the logical process is the business say to look at the legacy system to find out or ask the *sage status* aging technical SME. Don't expect that however it works today was ever really what anyone wanted. The business might have asked 25 years ago for something like monthly payments of a premium to work a certain way, and due to system, budget, or time constraints it may have been implemented a different way. Over the years people move on and nobody recalls what was originally envisioned. Tweaks are made, with similar constraints. People might know that they find the process frustrating but might not know what would be better. Or they have a belief, but that might not actually *be* better. Tracing the causes for how things work, and what processes ought to be, is hard.

We also have challenges where delivering the program is under such pressure that the reason for doing it gets lost. There are some well-known countermeasures that can be employed, and I really like the ethos to *ignore sunk costs*. This makes good sense when deciding what to do next, which might be to stop, or pivot. Just remember that what we might see as a financial decision, just might be a career decision for a sponsor who can't so easily say 'let's just write off the money spent to date, it's not worth proceeding'.

Many long-established companies have very complex legacy technology environments. This can be seen as a cause of increasing cost of ownership and lack of agility, and this is often true, though that premise does not always mean the best course of action is to consolidate technologies. You might be able to automate or use other countermeasures. Sometimes this complexity is the result of mergers and acquisitions; however other times, particularly outside the core systems, the actual cause is incomplete efforts to remove complexity. We have all seen intelligent and motivated colleagues introduce a new technology to replace all the existing technologies, but in the end, we just add one more technology to the mix because we can't fully replace the legacy technology. Replacing an integration technology is a good example. It can be prohibitively expensive to have one project replace all existing integrations, and so we do it *opportunistically*, but that never finishes before we add the next generation of integration tool, and we keep growing our technology duplication.

It is hard. Stay grounded in now, and what action can be taken now. Stay focused on your time horizon relevant to your role, and let others worry about short term initiatives, which isn't to say you don't support them, just take care of where your focus should be. Don't take the easy answer on causation, and a good rule of thumb is that if it is a clear and simple explanation, it is probably just wrong. Also, be humble and remember you are laying the groundwork for future causation postmortems, which people will also misunderstand. It is important to understand why things have happened, but only because it allows you to take an action now.

Your *current* action is what matters.

> "I have realized that the past and future are real illusions,
> that they exist in the present, which is what there is and
> all there is."
>
> *Alan Watts*

CHAPTER 9

A LESSON FROM THE

BHAGAVAD GITA

"When doubts haunt me, when disappointments stare me
in the face, and I see not one ray of hope on the horizon,
I turn to Bhagavad-Gita and find a verse to comfort
me; and I immediately begin to smile in the midst of
overwhelming sorrow. Those who meditate on the Gita
will derive fresh joy and new meanings from it every day."

Mahatma Gandhi

You have probably heard of the *Bhagavad Gita* recently if you have seen
the Oppenheimer movie. If you have a connection to India or Indian
based philosophy, then you probably know of it. I have gained much
insight from reading many versions of this very practical and usable work.
There is a lot of context that is useful for interpreting the Bhagavad Gita;
however, as stated, I am not writing an academic book or essay on this
text. I'll give a brief context, but then focus on what (for me) is the central

lesson. Despite this, there are many lessons in the Gita, so what is the most important lesson will differ for people and will change at different points of life, when we have different challenges.

> "Actions do not cling to me because I am not attached to
> their results. Those who understand this and practice it
> live in freedom."

> Krishna-Dwaipayana Vyasa, The Bhagavad Gita

The lesson is well captured in the quote: "Actions do not cling to me because I am not attached to their [outcomes]. Those who understand this and practice it live in freedom." This is particularly useful as a countermeasure to our modern corporate quarterly goal-based anxiety. I will warn you though, it tends to be hard for modern executives to comprehend as it seems to pull the rug out from under their bonus grounded feet.

Very brief context for The Bhagavad Gita

> "[The Bhagavad Gita is] the most systematic statement of
> spiritual evolution of endowing value to mankind.", "[It
> is] one of the most clear and comprehensive summaries
> of perennial philosophy ever revealed; hence its enduring
> value is subject not only to India but to all of humanity."

> Aldous Huxley

The *Bhagavad Gita*, often affectionately called the *Gita*, is an episode recorded in the *Mahabharata*, which is an epic Sanskrit poem. The name is generally translated to *The Lords Song*, or *God's Song*, though either of these names would be misleading to most Westerners, and I'd recommend thinking of it as *The Universe's Poem*. The story itself is in the form of a dialogue between Prince Arjuna and Krishna - an incarnation of the god Vishnu - on the eve of a great battle, where Arjuna is struggling with the idea of fighting his family members in the opposing army, and his charioteer happens to be lord Krishna, who councils Arjuna on his duty. This story captures much of the wisdom of the *Upanishads*, which is a core text in Hinduism. There is much more nuance here as Hinduism is a very big tent indeed, also the authorship and timeline of the writing of the *Gita* are somewhat debated. For this chapter, I won't dive deeper, as one click down would be an entire book in itself, one which I would not be the person to write.

Importantly, there are many English editions of the *Bhagavad Gita*, but these are interpretations and commentaries. There is only one *Bhagavad Gita* and that is in Sanskrit. Recall in earlier chapters we discussed how we create our universe, well there are many layers of interpretation between the original text and what we read. That is okay. I've read many editions of this commentary, and there are nuances, but I largely take the same lessons from them. This is just something to be aware of.

According to *Gaur Gopal Das*, a renowned Hindu monk in India and a former HP electrical engineer, the *Bhagavad Gita* is not a religious text but is a guide on the way to live life, particularly around the actions you take. However, that said, I'm sure many do consider it a religious text. Defining what *is* religion is hard in Western culture, but I think overlaying Western concepts of religion is an unhelpful way to look at many Eastern cultures and beliefs. Regardless, I think most people who are familiar with the text would say it does also provide great value if read as a non-religious text.

Actions verses Outcomes

> "He who is ever brooding over result often loses nerve
> in the performance of his duty. He becomes impatient
> and then gives vent to anger and begins to do unworthy
> things; he jumps from action to action never remaining
> faithful to any. He who broods over results is like a
> man given to objects of senses; he is ever distracted, he
> says goodbye to all scruples, everything is right in his
> estimation and he therefore resorts to means fair and foul
> to attain"

> *Mahatma Gandhi, Bhagavad Gita According to Gandhi*

Karma is basically action, and not as often misunderstood in the West as some type of retribution of the universe. The law of Karma is that every action is both a cause of later actions, and an effect of prior actions. Therefore, the way to change outcomes is to change the actions in the only moment you can: the present. The web of causation is very complex and the fact that there are causes and effects doesn't mean we can know how they interact, let alone take specific actions that we know with certainty will lead to particular outcomes. Fixating on these outcomes will lead to endless correction and overcorrection, in a kind of screeching feedback loop.

The real power is not in the physical actions, but the actions of the mind. If we take craving, perhaps for that slice of baked New York cheesecake (my favourite), the seed of eating that slice which we wanted to resist didn't happen when we bought it, but when we first had that thought. Perhaps seeing it in a cabinet, reacted to that thought, and then clinging to the thought. Controlling, or more accurately letting go of that initial seed of thought is where the chain of Karma can be broken. Obviously, this is a rather simple example, but it might lead in combination to becoming obese and all manner of related *Karmic* health problems over time. We can, after all, only gain weight one bite at a time, which is to say it is the result of many interdependent actions.

Often in Indian philosophies, thoughts are understood with the analogy of planting seeds in soil. These seeds start very small, but will grow anywhere with the right conditions. These might become plants we want, or plants we don't want. We need to take care of what thought seeds we let grow. We can leverage the seed analogy further, as when we do want seeds to grow into plants we water them, shelter them. Ironically, we perhaps add manure, to grow beautiful flowers. We cannot just pull at the young plants to get the outcome of flowers, we must focus on the process and not the outcome. The outcome will be what it is, as we probably can't know for sure what type of seeds we started with.

There are many other gifts of wisdom in the *Gita*. According to *Gaur Gopal Das*, some of the other gifts include: we are more powerful than we think and can achieve more than we dream, we need to stay focused on our key purpose and not get caught up in distractions of life, and our mind is very powerful if we can keep it on track and use it right.

Applying the lessons in our work

> Repeated: "Actions do not cling to me because I am not
> attached to their [outcomes]. Those who understand this
> and practice it live in freedom."
>
> *Krishna-Dwaipayana Vyasa, The Bhagavad Gita*

The lessons have been profound for me in my work. The key lesson is the part where we do not focus on outcomes. I use the word *outcomes* rather than *results* because corporate vernacular has gravitated in recent years to the term *outcomes*. When we say we are not *attached* to outcomes, that should not be considered to mean we *ignore* outcomes, or that we are indifferent to outcomes; we just don't *grasp* for them, or *cling* to them.

We should know what the outcomes we believe we want to achieve are, notice if we are heading towards them or away from them, and finally determine if we do or don't achieve them and why we did or didn't. But there is a little space. A gap. There are some reasons for this, including that we seldom have all the needed control of actions to ensure we get the outcome, and we might along the way find that we ought to pivot from *that* outcome to another one. We might also find that by getting the outcome we *thought* we wanted, we create a bad outcome in another way.

How does this work with quarterly planning and performance payments? I don't think it does work very well with it, but that is the system we typically find ourselves in. And to be honest, if given the chance, I'm still grabbing the cash. The best move in a bad game.

The good thing is that when we create less attachment to outcomes, we do actually increase our ability to achieve them. It is like the rugby kicker having an 80th minute kick to win the World Cup, or an NFL kicker in the Superbowl. Often, a kick they could make 9 out of 10 times becomes extremely difficult because they are attached to the outcome. You often see kickers focus on very specific rituals, so their attention is focused on the action, not the outcome. Those that do this well are often the top clutch kickers. In the NFL, if a kicker misses the game winning kick in a Superbowl or conference championship game he will be remembered in team folklore for decades. Literally his children and grandchildren won't get invited to birthday parties because of it. But worrying about it while kicking won't improve the situation. At least he can say he played in a Superbowl.

"This is the unmistakable teaching of the Gita. He
who gives up action falls. He who gives up only the
reward rises. But renunciation of fruit in no way means
indifference to the result."

*Mahatma Gandhi, The Bhagavad Gita According to
Gandhi*

CHAPTER 10

KEEP YOUR BEGINNERS MIND

"If your mind is empty, it is always ready for anything;
it is open to everything. In the beginner's mind there are
many possibilities, but in the expert's there are few"

Shunryu Suzuki, Zen Mind, Beginner's Mind

We wrap up part 1 with a short chapter unpacking the above quote from *Zen Mind, Beginner's Mind*, which is a transcript in book form of teachings by Shunryu Suzuki at his Zen centre in Los Altos, California. The book was published in 1970 and is highly revered in Western Zen circles, and for good reason.

Suzuki's original name, or at least birth name (Zen in-joke), was Toshitaka Suzuki, and who was also known as Suzuki Roshi, with *Roshi* being a nod of respect meaning *old master*, or *venerable old one*. This book is a very easy read relatively speaking, as are all his books. Just don't confuse him with *D.T.* Suzuki who is a different Zen teacher who was famous in the West during an overlapping time period.

"The goal of practice is always to keep our beginner's
mind."
Shunryu Suzuki

One of the most endearing things about Shunryu Suzuki was his clear but simple explanations. This is a very simple concept, being that if you know everything and are an expert, then you probably won't see all the potential possibilities. If you are a novice, you might look more freely at options, but even then, only if you have the right beginner's mind. This is not about saying novices are better and experts ought to be ignored, that is not the point. It is simply saying keep your mind open to new things by creating space for them. That is it.

Paradoxically having a beginner's mind or an expert's mind doesn't necessarily correlate to being an actual beginner or expert. You can be a beginner with the orientation of an expert, and we have all met that person. You can also be an expert in one sense, while never giving up the openness of the beginner, and if you have been lucky enough to meet such a person, they are a wonderful joy to be around.

One of my personal concerns with many of our education systems is that we seem to stomp on this beginner's mind very early. We teach to the test, and very early squash the beginners natural wonder and curiosity by filling them with *facts*. This is one of my hopes for Generative A.I. technologies. Perhaps when there is less need to just regurgitate *facts*, we can get back to *thinking* and creating.

There is another quote, below, which is another way to leverage this emptiness. The concept of emptiness is important in Zen. For example, as we previously discussed, it is the emptiness that makes a glass useful by allowing you to put water in it. In a similar way, how do you acquire more ideas, or even knowledge, if you have already filled you brain with expert facts?

He had some useful guidance for us in our corporate world, and for life in general, and it is a fitting way to end part 1 on getting out of your own way.

> "When you listen to someone, you should give up all
> your preconceived ideas and your subjective opinions;
> you should just listen to [them], just observe what [their]
> way is. We put very little emphasis on right and wrong or
> good and bad. We just see things as they are with [them]
> and accept [them]. This is how we communicate with
> each other. Usually when you listen to some statement,
> you hear it as a kind of echo of yourself. You are actually
> listening to your own opinion. If it agrees with your
> opinion, you may accept it, but if it does not, you will
> reject it, or you may not even really hear it."
>
> *Shunryu Suzuki*

PART 2

UNDERSTANDING THE GAME

"This is the real secret of life - to be completely engaged with what you are doing in the here and now. And instead of calling it work, realize it is play."
Alan Watts

CHAPTER 11

UNDERSTANDING THE GAME

"I am always sincere, but never serious."
Alan Watts

Having covered some possible ways to understand better our place in the universe we can now seek to understand better the corporate, or organisational, world we spend our careers in.

As stated in the introduction: there are other good (and some not-so-good) books about technology strategy and about enterprise architecture. Therefore, I'm not trying to cover either topic specifically, but I am talking about how we interact with these as people. Likewise, I'm not giving a comprehensive view of how corporations and organizational activities do or ought to work. In Part 2 of this book, we split concepts into chapters to allow clear demarcation between those ideas. We look at some of the observations I've had about corporations and organisations, and we can blend our previous learnings. For example, in the next chapter, we look at the business case game with some insights for you to consider, but without fully describing or prescribing how business cases should be done; it is more about how to feel about the activity when it gets tough, and it does.

It is helpful if we understand the game and don't get too caught up in it at an emotional level. Ultimately, it comes down to creating a little space, a gap, between you and the situation. Releasing our attachments to our ideas. Not clinging so tightly to how we think the corporate world ought to be.

Looking around various world philosophies, the one concept that most resonates with me for understanding the game is the Hindu concept of līlā (Sanskrit), which you can pronounce lila or leela. According to the non-dualist view of līlā it describes the reality of the universe: Brahman. Līlā is generally translated as "play" or "drama". Therefore, we can consider all the political happenings in an organisation or company to be like a play, or drama, perhaps even a sport or a dance, and we simply have a part in that theatrical production. What we do in our careers is important, and we want to be authentic and sincere, but we need to keep a little space. We need to enjoy the show. Relax a little. We might find we are more effective.

In the end, what we do in our careers is serious; it is just not very serious. Don't take this too literally. We are just going to be more effective in the end if we are confident, and if we enjoy the game by not taking ourselves too seriously all the time.

Alan Watts has a great analogy of looking all around the house in a huff trying to find your glasses, only to realise they've been on your head the whole time. There is nothing to do but chuckle at yourself. This is the way.

CHAPTER 12

THE BUSINESS CASE GAME

"All the world's a stage, and all the men and women
merely players. They have their exits and their entrances,
And one [person] in [their] time plays many parts."

Shakespeare, As You Like It, Act 2, Scene 7

We can now take a brief look at one of the most prolific games going on in the corporate world, which is the business case game. It might be more of a sport than a game, and it has aspects of a play, but either way, it is certainly dramatic. Different people tend to interact with business cases in different ways.

There are all sorts of unspoken rules that we must-work out along the way, a bit like some strange type of initiation or rite-of-passage. These are my observations on the business case game and how to navigate it while staying sane.

The positions and the roles

It took me some time to realise that the business case game is different for various individual people involved in it. What I mean here is that multiple games are being played on the same field at the same time, with sporadic interactions between them, with different rules and different definitions of winning. The variations of business case development processes and roles involved are extensive, but in general, I think of the following roles, which are mostly just my informal names for each one.

There is almost always a *visionary*, who is the person who wants the initiative or has the vision, which could be a small project or a large program. Normally, this is about profitability (i.e. increasing revenue, reducing costs, or both). However, the business case might be about risk management, customer experience, or compliance. It could also be a vanity project that someone just wants to do. The intended change might or might not be known up front, meaning it could be to achieve an outcome without knowing what to change to achieve it. It could be to implement something like new software or services, a new offering, a change in capacity, a merger or acquisition, divestment, perhaps a new business partnership, operating model changes, or something else. This visionary might or might not be the *business owner*. Often, the visionary will talk in audacious, bold statements, with the classic John F. Kennedy example from 1961 being, "I believe that this nation should commit itself to achieving the goal, before this decade is out, of landing a man on the moon and returning him safely to the earth". However, they might get even bolder, saying they will replace all the constraining legacy core systems with next-generation cloud-enabled smart digital platforms. These big, audacious statements don't always have a whole lot of real strategic thinking underpinning them. That is normal, and part of our role is to help tease out the strategy and roadmap implications. Ironically, JFK went 1 for 1 on achieving the moon shot, which far exceeds the successes of core replacement programs.

The *business owner* is typically the key stakeholder who is *accountable* for achieving some outcome that the business case will deliver or enable. In the end, they tend to be the ones pitching the funding request to the budget approval body, which could be a leadership team, executive team, board, or even a government body. They will often end up feeling like there is a gun held to their head, but we'll get to that.

The *salesperson* is often someone who sees this as a game, with winning defined by getting the business case over the line. They might be a business owner, but more often, a program or project manager or management consultant. They might hold some non-program or non-project title and might even head up strategy. For them, it is often the thrill of the chase to see if they can get the hit when they get the final approval. There is nothing wrong with this; it is an important role; we just need to have checks and balances. This role works well when others do their jobs and keep the sales pitch valid.

The **penholders** could be internal or external, sometimes a management consultancy or some other external party. The pen holder could be the visionary and, in rare cases, even the business. Regardless the penholder, which could be a small team, is the one that writes the business case. Often, they just love the intellectual challenge of storytelling and could include strategists and architects. They tend to work closely with the business owner and reach out to the next role for information, who are the expendables.

The *expendables* have walk-on parts. They are the people who help to build the business case by providing information to the penholders. This might be requirements, risks, assumptions, estimates, or other information. Often, they are part-time in the business case development and will be involved in implementation if the business case is approved. These people can get quite frustrated by the process and can often end up having limited time to provide information. That information will get filtered and sometimes manipulated and, later in the post-mortem, be deemed inaccurate or incomplete. Strategists and particularly architects can find themselves in this group. When I say they are *expendables*, I am not talking about them being expendable as people, but their role in the business case and opinions and views just seem to get discarded if inconvenient; their input is *expendable*.

Building the business case

There are various ways we see business cases come together, and often, this varies by the context of the appetite for change and funding pathways.

If the business case is very large and going to the board (or other high-level governing body), then they are probably going to want a logo on the business case from some external partner like a management consultancy. The Big-4 accountancy firms are often favoured, particularly for financial services like banking and insurance, and at times government, so Deloitte, KPMG, PwC, and EY. There are also the Top-3 strategy players of McKinsey, BCG and Bain (the Big-4 and Top-3 are mutually exclusive), and the Top-3 seem to be quite strong choices in digital transformation. McKinsey has also had a large impact on management consulting with thought leaders like Barbra Minto. I'm not going to unpack the differences here, other than to say the Big 4 often have very strong relationships between their *partners* (senior people who own stakes in the firm) and the client company executives. Often, company executives and board members are ex Big-4 partners. Also, the Big-4 do push hard to cross-sell their other service offerings, such as with system integrator or governance services. Now, many companies say that if one of the Big-4 does the business case, they cannot also do implementation, but that all feels rather self-serving in such a small cohort. Other players in the management consulting space provide increasingly less air-cover for boards, and these include IT specialists such as Accenture and IBM. There are some specialised boutique players like Willis Tower Watson in the insurance space or independent consultants, and finally, some companies have internal management consultants.

It is common for internal strategists and architects to be quite cynical about management consultants, and the classic line about them is "borrowing your watch to tell you the time". This comes from the tendency for them to tap into internal expertise and then bang out some smooth-looking slides with the company's own content. There is some truth to this, but also, using techniques like the Minto Pyramid, they can be experts at telling cohesive stories to executives by knowing what to include and exclude, which can be the difference between a good concept being supported or not. Also, if you can tap into their top global experts, they really can have a wealth of experience from around the globe that can save you many millions of dollars in going down false pathways. I've had examples of that with general insurance packages and considerations like instances per geographic jurisdiction. That said, you find that if you sign up for them as a system integrator, you probably don't get to keep the top-shelf people involved post-signing on the dotted line unless you have secured named resources from them.

But for boards, the reason for having the Big-4 or Top 3 involved is simple. It helps manage the accountability risk for boards, and in modern public companies, that can mean very real personal financial risk to board members and executives. In some countries, it could extend to jail time if the negligence is deemed serious enough. Having a Big-4 logo on the business case advice goes a long way to providing cover or at least plausible deniability. So, this is a big part of the game. The boards don't make the rules; they just need to play by, or at least within, the rules. The boards also have institutional investors leaning on them, such as BlackRock and Vanguard, and if you doubt this, look at the shareholdings of any large company. You need to understand the way the game works if you want to avoid needless frustration.

The management consultancy will have a very specific statement of work (SOW), and it can be frustratingly hard to get them to look at necessary areas outside that scope, but these firms are working to a budget, which is large, and need to manage their own professional risk. They will stick to the SOW.

It is common with large business cases for the business owner, visionary, and salesperson, to have been given an indication of what type if investment envelope would be palatable. Often, the business case must fit within that envelope, and it seems like this envelope is not deterministic. All sorts of pressure and manipulation get applied to get to the saleable figure. On the other hand, with something like a core system replacement, there isn't much chance of changing the scope to fit. This can set things up poorly from the outset.

The sell

The sales pitch varies depending on who approves funding, but often, the hard work is done in advance of the main sell. Generally, the business owner and visionary, along with the salesperson, are working on building consensus. If the Big-4 are involved, then often a partner from there will be doing a lot of the consensus building. Watching how experienced management consultants work to build consensus and get support is impressive. Unfortunately, they seem as effective at getting both good and bad business cases over the line.

I read a book some time ago that talked about how large agreements are made at Toyota. Many of the final decision-making meetings are effectively ceremonial, with agreement and consensus being worked through in advance to ensure everyone truly understands and will fully and actively support not just the decision but the realisation.

As part of this consensus building at modern organisations, there can often be a lot of *horse-trading* amongst executives or relevant budget holders. It might be mutual support for each other's business cases, *quid pro quo* style, or it might include some scope items they want in the business case scope. It could be a longer-term trade, so support my case this year, and I'll support yours next year - wink. There are all sorts of backroom deals that most of us will never see.

I even heard of a situation many years ago on a program I later joined where the CFO was *knocked-off* by the CIO with the help of the CEO in order to get an ERP investment across the line. By *knocked-off*, I mean they left the organisation, though how this was achieved was not clear to me. That same CIO would chat openly with me about political techniques over morning coffee on my way past his office. It was great *coaching in the moment*. With the same business case, he described how it was necessary to create not just a compelling case but a real sense of the 11th-hour urgency for the board. He said that if they could possibly just defer the decision and hope someone else had to deal with it, they would; this technique reminds me of a quote from Sam Harris that it would be "the best move in a bad game".

Sometimes, the real driver from the business owner is not necessarily to get approval, but to defend against non-delivery of some business outcomes they are accountable for, as they can say that the outcome was not achieved because the funding was not approved. If they have not made a request for funding, then they cannot really play this card, as they would just be told that they never brought a fundable business case to the table.

Other times, the pitch might be to open the narrative, and test the water, and help clear the pathway for a future business case. This is why we ought not to get too caught up in the outcome. We just won't know all the angles. Do your job well and do it with integrity.

The aftermath

The business case might not get approved. This might be a good outcome and much better than investing in the wrong initiative. A CEO at a customer-focused mutual insurance company had a great saying about evaluating insurance claims, "say no when no is the right answer". His point was to do it quickly and accurately for the wider good of all customers if no was correct, in this case, because the policy didn't cover that particular loss. If the business case doesn't get approved, but the decision is sound, that is a good outcome; even then, there might be further activity in the future to re-pitch a revised case. It might even be a good business case and a good investment, just not at the top when ranked against the other good business cases on a constrained investment slate.

I've been on some initiatives to build business cases for a particular business partnership where it didn't even get to the pitch. It was because the opportunity fit wasn't good, and the timing wasn't appropriate, and the plug was pulled. It was correct to consider the business case, and it was right to stop when we did. This is a good outcome. This is a success. Don't get attached to success being approval.

Sometimes, the business case gets approved with appropriate funding, scope, and timelines. Unfortunately, this seems to be the exception for large programs.

Often the approval comes without all the funding realistically needed. This seems to be when the salesperson and business owner get very keen on the thrill of the chase. Now, this can be all part of the game. They pitch to what they think they can get funded or adjust to the size of the envelope, with the knowledge that they can come back and ask for more money later once they are too far in to stop or have proven some success. The board will often know this and think the end cost will be plus twenty or more percent or some other contingency.

There are a few risks with this game for technology-heavy initiatives. First is that the scope of the business case might be fixed, in which case there is little possibility of managing it to meet the budget, and the quality ends up impacted. System replacement is an example of this. Replacing an aging core system that was hand-crafted for the business over decades will, without doubt, throw up many surprises.

The other problem is that commitment, loyalty, stakeholders, shareholder demands, technology, and even capital availability can and will change over time. For example, the hardening capital market post the covid pandemic has caught many by surprise, and going back for more capital investment is out of the question for many publicly listed companies. Other governments and not for profits are also struggling with inflation post covid, so capital all around is under huge pressure. Typically, many programs in such environments are told they must cut-to-their-cloth, which, of course, is tough if you didn't start with nearly enough cloth, to begin with.

What does this mean for strategists and architects

> Repeat: "Actions do not cling to me because I am not attached to their results. Those who understand this and practice it live in freedom."
>
> —*Krishna-Dwaipayana Vyasa, The Bhagavad Gita*

This is a great example of where the wisdom from the Bhagavad Gita can help us, specifically the quote above. We need to leverage the ability to create a little space between our actions and the outcomes. Now, outcomes matter, as we have said, but we can avoid getting caught up with unhelpful attachment to the outcomes. We need to do our job; we need to fulfil our role. We cannot control all the factors in the business case game, and we cannot personally ensure the approval or not of the business case or the realisation of the resulting program.

We have an important role supporting the visionary as a trusted advisor, and that might even be prior to the business case by helping foster the desire and formulating the vision; this is to say we can be a catalyst for a business case, using our stills with narratives to help foster a vision. Part of our ability ought to be *the art of the possible*. We do need to help turn the vision into an actionable strategy and roadmap and we should carefully lean into that, being mindful not to try to do too much at the business case phase. For example, in insurance initiatives with distribution partners like brokers, underwriting agencies, or third-party administrators (who manage claims), then it might be useful to use a level 0 or 1 capability model to clarify what the demarcation between what capabilities our company does and the external company. This might materially impact the high-level estimate and risk profile to an extent it needs to be considered at business case time. I've always found that trying to get overly methodical about this will just scare people off, and it is better to subtly poke and prod, trusting your intuition and only digging down where there is a real need at this early phase.

Keep your focus on the real business outcome. With rare exceptions, it is *not* about the technology. Even if this is highly infrastructural or enabling, and the business owner is the technology exec, they still need to frame it from a business outcome viewpoint. If it is a highly technical initiative perhaps around nonfunctional requirements (NFRs) like cyber, disaster recovery, or availability, then it still is only done for the business benefit in the end.

The business owner can find themselves caught between a rock and a hard place. Often, they are formally accountable. We need to support them and try to avoid just offloading impossible choices to them, overly relying on using risk acceptance, for example, which is where it can feel like they have a gun held to their head. The owner is there to make tough choices, but we need to support them and help protect them as well. Ultimately, they ought to be held to account for how they make decisions, not necessarily on the outcome, as if they only take sure bets then the company isn't going to be very competitive. They need to be able to defend their decisions and how they did what they could to get the right information, and that is often where we come in.

It is important that we don't get caught up being the salesperson for the business case; in my view, that ought never to be our role. If we end up doing this role, we ought to clearly recurse ourselves from our strategy and architecture advisor role. You simply cannot be an objective salesperson; that is an oxymoron.

If you get to work with an external, or for that matter, internal management consultancy then don't start with a cynical perspective. It can be frustrating to see how that logo makes such a big difference to how what seems to be a prettier subset of your message gets received. But often, if we keep our ego under control, we can learn a huge amount from them about the subtle art of effective executive communication. McKinsey, for example, are a highly respected advisor to executives for a very good reason, and much of that is around their ability to use methods like the Minto Pyramid to communicate complex concepts in a clear and concise manner. Their ability to work through to a consensus is often very impressive. Our role is to try to ensure that what they sell so effectively will actually be achievable. For a long time, I was highly critical of management consultants, but then I got to work in a team with internal management consultants who had come from the Big-4 and Top-3 and seeing how the sausage was actually made was wonderful. These were among the smartest and most professional people I'd ever worked with, and they genuinely valued my extensive domain knowledge in insurance as respectfully leveraging expertise is key for them and a great skill for us all to learn. I got exposed to workshops and other training on the underlying methodologies used, and it was a real a-ha moment. I realized that for years, I'd been turning up to executive pitches with no chance of success; I was turning up to a gun fight without even a knife but a sticky note.

The best advice I can give during business case time is the wise words that my first great enterprise architecture mentor, Bernard, once gave me. He said with an Australian twang, "Yeah, mate, just make sure you play with a straight bat". This cricket reference means do your job and be straight up and honest. I've had situations where people have leaned on me to rachet down estimates or soften risks, but I always say they can change it if they wish, but I'll call it as I see it. It is well worth getting anything you say down in emails or documents that are *discoverable* (i.e. for legal discovery purposes).

We can ensure we provide the best information we can regarding estimates, risks, and assumptions. We need to take smart measures to protect ourselves and ensure there is an audit trail of what we provide. It is important to support our colleagues, and as seniors, we should coach, mentor and support those around us.

Most importantly of all we need to ensure the focus of the business case, to the extent we can influence, is to get a good decision regardless of if it is that it gets approved, deferred, or declined. Accept the answer from the accountable decision-makers. They have factors to weigh up that we won't know about or understand.

Finally, if things end up going badly, there is just no upside to saying, "I told you so". Be humble. Take the learnings.

CHAPTER 13

LEVERAGE NARRATIVES

"The single biggest problem in communication is the
illusion that it has taken place."
George Bernard Shaw

I think I've always had an innate ability to notice narrative tendencies and word choices in conversations. That is not in any way to suggest I have a gift for words, just that I do seem to notice what are key words for people and link that into my conversation, often without consciously thinking about it. There is probably some psychological term for this, but I've not investigated it.

Another thing that I've always done, and these days it is something I need to manage, is to pick up on accents and start using them when talking to people. I don't intend to do it, nor am I conscious of it, but it just happens, and it happens very quickly. Sometimes, this has caused offence, though not normally to the person with the accent, but to others who think I'm being disingenuous. Interestingly, we all have accents, and there really is no *normal* accent.

I first became conscious of my word awareness while studying computer technology. Words that lecturers used often or with emphasis stuck out to me, and when answering questions and completing exam papers, I knew exactly which words and phrases tick the box for individual lecturers. I noticed that if you hit those words and avoided tripwire words and phrases, you got good marks. Humans use heuristics, which are cognitive shortcuts, and it seemed to me that when marking multiple papers, I could make it easy for the lecturer to save time or cognitive load and quickly identify my work for a high mark. Win for them, win for me.

Moving into the corporate world, this seems to work even better. The busier the stakeholder, particularly execs, then the better this works. That said, it is nuanced, and the tripwires are much more prevalent.

Key-words that turn locks

The words you use matter. Getting the narrative right is key, as well as ticking the box on keywords and phrases the stakeholders want to hear or, perhaps more accurately, are comfortable hearing. This is more important the busier stakeholders are, and the more abstract the level they operate at is.

To find the keywords, read and listen carefully to everything you can from your stakeholders and *their* stakeholders, right up to the board or government if you can. Share market presentations for publicly listed companies are the ultimate, as this is what they are saying to the investors of the company. If it is a government organisation, mutual, or privately owned company, be creative and find what you can, where you can. What words are emphasised or repeated; these might not be technology words, but words like 'seamless', or 'frictionless.' Other words like 'efficiencies', and of course 'growth'. Sometimes, these words are euphemisms, such as 'service rationalisation'.

There will be industry language, as well as company language, and words will find and lose favour over time. If you can find what outcomes stakeholders are on the hook for, then this is gold. One company I worked at had everyone's performance goals centrally located and available company-wide. It was a masterstroke from the CEO. I was amazed at how few people leveraged this valuable asset.

Focus on a concise, logical narrative that fits tightly together, hitting the keywords and phrases, but don't overuse them. Never use them inappropriately, as that will backfire badly for you. For example, don't say that "the addition of the architectural review board will ensure frictionless delivery"; it might, but you would need to do a lot of work to justify using the word *frictionless* in that context, and you won't get that much time with an exec.

Remember, it is not about proving what you know or even proving you are right; it is about getting the funding, approval, or support you need. Never sell past the close. Leave your ego at home for this one.

Tripwire words that slam doors

Often, there are words that work as tripwires, and if you stumble into one of these, the door can quickly slam shut. This slammed door might even impact you again in the future in a completely different context. You *must* identify and avoid the tripwire words and phrases. This is not just an inconvenience; this is a key part of your job.

Identifying tripwire words is an art, and you need to be savvy to find them, as these are typically words or phrases that don't appear *anywhere*. People just need to know not to use the word. So how do you find them? If you have been at the company or organisation for a long time, you should be aware of things that didn't go well, or phrases that were trendy then suddenly just died. Sometimes, these are industry words. If you are newer to the company, then ask around about projects or initiatives in your area of interest that people don't want to revisit. Often, you can find old business cases or reviews. Stakeholders probably won't want to talk about such things, but there will be some old-timers who love telling you the story.

I've even been known to drop an old disastrous project name into a conversation with a stakeholder but hiding it as a normal use of the word, kind of a dog whistle, to say discretely that we don't want to repeat that. This can be powerful but is an advance technique and can easily go very wrong, so probably something to avoid unless you have a good understanding of the stakeholders. They were somewhat peripheral to the disaster, and you just love the challenge of it.

Find out if there are any tripwire industry or technology terms, such as a disastrous customer master data management implementation (C-MDM), either at the company or elsewhere for the key stakeholder whom you want to be the sponsor; if so, pick a different term, for example, just call it a customer record. Perhaps they got burned trying to implement a decoupled digital layer at a bank, so you need not emphasize this aspect. Obviously, you cannot lie about what you want to do, but that is not what we mean by a tripwire. It is literally a term that makes people's stomach turn.

In terms of finding stale industry terms, you can use tools like trends. google.com, which will show you search term usage over time. For example, worldwide the term *big data* has been trending since 2011, peaking in 2018, but still common. The term *microservice* is still very strong, as is API, yet *SOAP* had its heyday in the early 2000s. No surprise that *A.I.* has exploded since 2022. Don't confuse notoriety with popularity; you need to apply some interpretation to this. For example, people might be searching for ways to move away from *microservices*, though I don't think so. Beyond search trends, you can also use Ngram viewer to find word usage trends in books.

Cliché words that are tacky and boring

We've all heard them, and we all roll our eyes. Terms such as *best practice, disruption, visionary, new normal, pivot, synergies, low-hanging fruit,* and *think like a startup.* I'm tempted to put *technical debt* on this list, but I know I'll get disinvited from the architects' society.

It is best to find new creative ways to say these things if they must be said at all.

Introduce narratives and see them flourish

Finally, don't be afraid of sowing the seeds of narratives, by which I don't just mean the whole story, but also words and phrases. If you avoid the tripwires and clichés above, then you can start to carefully introduce your own useful terminology and repeat it with stakeholders. You would be amazed at how often you can find this bouncing back to you down the track. Don't try to claim it; just smile at yourself and get on with the job.

CHAPTER 14

UNDERSTANDING THE ROLE

"As complexity rises, precise statements lose meaning and
meaningful statements lose precision."
Lotfi A. Zadeh

The various technology architect roles, particularly that of enterprise architect, are relatively new and relatively immature disciplines compared to many other professional roles. For example, the role of a building architect is much more mature and typically involves specific qualifications. The role of technology strategist is also relatively immature, though often this role is one part of another position, such as architect or consultant; sometimes there are specific technology strategist positions.

I've presented at enterprise architecture conferences, participated in and moderated enterprise architecture discussion panels, and have attended or watched many other such events. What I noticed is that many of the presentations at these conferences are about what enterprise architecture even is, what is the value of it, and why it should exist at all. Surprisingly, after all these years, we are still trying to justify and even define ourselves.

I'm not going to tell you that I can solve this, but I have a view of where some of the challenges are, and I think a more useful way of thinking about the essence of the various architecture roles.

To some extent we end up with strategists and architects, specifically enterprise architects, focusing too much on technology detail because we misunderstand the roles, or at least what these roles could be. We at times, attract people into these roles when, if we all understood the game differently, we would see some of these people might thrive elsewhere, which can be better for them and better for the company or organization. This comes from a misunderstood role hierarchy that people aspire to climb.

There is a view that strategists and enterprise architects are more *senior* than domain architects, solution architects, or technology architects and *higher* than specialist roles like data or integration architects. All these architects are often seen as more senior than engineers, who are more senior than developers and testers. This is the wrong view. Individuals might be more senior, but it should not be because of the abstraction level of the role. Correcting this view can help us to get more satisfaction operating at the level of abstraction we enjoy and excel at.

I've been encouraged to see a positive trend in recent years being, the rise of the status of technology engineers, driven largely by the success of digital native companies and platforms built on engineering excellence. Notable examples, of course being AWS, Google, Azure, Netflix, Uber, Facebook, and there are many others. There are various types of engineers, including software, DevOps, security, data, integration etc. We also find a number of thought leaders that act as bridges between engineering, development and architecture with Gregor Hohpe and Martin Fowler being notable examples. To a large extent, what we call people is less relevant than what they do.

In the abstract

"The menu is not the meal."
Alan Watts

The key difference between strategists, architects, engineers, and developers is the level of abstraction they both enjoy and excel at dealing with. Some people just prefer working at a more conceptual level, a more abstract level and some people much prefer keeping close to the implementation, keeping in mind that all software and data is an abstraction at some level. This preference can change over time and can correlate to age, which can correlate to seniority and leadership focus. However, there are exceptions, with people who prefer to work at an abstract level early in their careers and people who prefer working with code late in their careers. People mostly know what they prefer, and that is okay.

Perhaps this tendency by many to deal more with abstract concepts as they age relates to something in an article by the American Psychological Association. It describes that semantic memory (the ability to recall concepts and general facts that are not related to specific experiences) continues to improve for many people as they age; this refers to changes as adults and not the development of abstract thinking earlier in life. Now, this is a developing area of scientific study, and some believe it might be more about abstract reasoning not deteriorating at the same rate as we age, and given our experiences through life and our ability to deal with uncertainty, we become more effective at abstract reasoning.

However, the level of abstraction people prefer ought not to define their importance or worth. High-functioning architects, engineers, and developers are all as important as each other, though the market rewards them differently due to availability. It is tempting for technologists to chase the money of some of these highly abstracted roles even if they don't prefer them, but in the end, it is unlikely to lead to a more satisfying and productive career. It is a hard choice, but until the game becomes more balanced, it is how it works, and we must still make the best choice for ourselves.

> "If you say that getting the money is the most important
> thing, you'll spend your life completely wasting your time.
> You'll be doing things you don't like doing in order to
> go on living, that is to go on doing thing you don't like
> doing, which is stupid."
>
> *Alan Watts*

By gaining the correct understanding of the role of seniority versus actual value, we can ensure that people can do what they love and excel at. The worst thing we can do is to have a high-functioning developer or engineer move into solution architecture if they don't really love it just because they have been led to believe this is the natural progression. Engineers are gold, and high-functioning developers are still the fundamental building block of technology; you don't want these people wrestling diagrams, getting bored in endless meetings, playing email games, and manicuring a flood of

PowerPoints. Of course, they should make their own decisions on what they want to do, but let's not nudge them into something they don't really want. And let's not in any way make them feel lower in the pecking order because they are good at something closer to the real work. Often, people think that architects get more power and say in how things are done; well I don't know many architects that feel like this is so. This also applies to technology strategists if these exist as separate roles.

The analogy of the physical world architect

For this discussion I'll just use the example of enterprise, domain, and solution architects, but these roles vary at different organisations. We also have more specialist roles like data architects or integration architects.

With all these roles it generally comes down to depth and breadth, the level of abstraction, and the time horizon. All this needs to be tailored to the organisation, for example, a multinational with a hundred architects or a mutual with just two architects. It also comes down to the mix of individual architects, and the strengths and aspirations of individual people. Let's use the analogy of buildings, campuses, and cities to work this through.

My apologies to any physical world architects who find my analogy inaccurate; it just seems intuitive enough to be useful.

The solution architect is the building architect

The solution architect is often the real workhorse of the architectural practice, getting deeply involved with projects and interacting closely with delivery teams. They often have a wide variety of skills and experiences and can have a lot of contextual technology and business knowledge. They can fulfil domain responsibilities if the domain role isn't explicitly defined. They also are the place where you are most likely to find contractors given the strong delivery focus. The building architect is a good analogy, where a key focus is often the design of a specific building or part thereof based on specific requirements for good functionality. They get dropped into a variety of situations, including coming in on contract and picking up where someone else has left things or situations where things have been very ad hoc without a specific architect on board until things got tricky. The time horizon is relatively short, being months to a few years, depending on the scenario.

Questions a building architect (solution architect) will consider include: What are the needed functions? What is the needed capacity? Where on the campus or site does it go (where in the enterprise landscape)? How do we need to integrate with other buildings (applications)? What is the design of x, y, z, features? How do we ensure users like it? What building products (technologies) are we able to use?

They will work closely with the campus architect (domain architect) or planner (enterprise architect) if applicable, particularly around concerns like where on the campus or site it goes and how it integrates with other buildings. They will need to understand various guidelines in that city, such as hight limits.

The domain architect is the campus architect

Where the role exists, the domain architect will focus on a particular business capability or function or a particular technology capability. Their key focus is the high-level target state, roadmap, and strategic-tactical balance. Analogist to the campus architect who is responsible for long-term designs of large campus sites like hospitals, airports, ports, universities, and large corporate campuses. The time horizon is medium long-term, being 5 to 10 years, depending on the scenario.

Questions a campus architect (domain architect) will consider include: What is the campus (domain) layout going to be to support the long-term strategy of the organisation or business? What capacity do we have, and what will we need, when? What buildings (systems) are end of life or non-compliant? What is the investment envelope? How can we continue to function while we renew incrementally? Are their big bang opportunities like building on a new site (new application)?

The campus architect will be working closely with building architects (solution architects) to ensure the roadmap is realised. They will also, if a significant city capability, have some interaction with city planners (enterprise architects).

The enterprise architect is the city planner

The key focus of the enterprise architect is the long-term investments supporting business strategy and operating models, business case input, and coordinating with other architects, particularly domain architects or equivalent. This is analogist to a city planner for a city, who will focus on the long-term vision for the city, including its resources, opportunities, threats, and constraints. The time horizon is long to very long.

Questions the city planner (enterprise architect) might consider include: Where should the CBD be (core systems), how big (scale), and how many (platforms or specific)? Do we have a port, where, and what sort? How does the city define itself, and how does it create employment (capability mapping)? Is the focus on industry, entertainment, tourism, a combination, or something else (business model)? What roading is needed over time (integration capabilities)? Where do we put the airport? Where do we put hospitals? How many?

What we need to know

The key for architects is to keep within an appropriate level of abstraction, and responsibilities of the defined boundary of concerns.

Building architect - "I need to know how many sinks there are, what type, and where are they?" OK, that seems like something you might need to know in some situations.

Campus architect - "I need to know how many sinks there are, what type, and where are they?" Well, maybe you need to know; you might want to standardise, negotiate contracts etc, but with limited details.

City planner - "I need to know how many sinks there are, what type, and where are they?" No, you don't! You really don't!

For a city planner, sinks ought not to be your concern. Although you could theoretically map down to them and maybe dream up a useful scenario or even wow the mayor with a drill-down diagram, it really is not something to focus on. Any concern is handled with building codes and inspections if needed, but that is not a city planning concern. The mayor ought not to get involved ever, but someone closer to the detail ought to care; if the mayor needs to be concerned something has gone very wrong.

Enterprise architects ought not to get into detail but evolve guardrails and provide context to determine the domain/platform boundaries of concern, which enable domain/platform, and solution decisions. This isn't to say the enterprise architects should become aloof. It is important for enterprise architects to connect at all levels and to listen much more than they speak.

All architects can play conservation or restoration architect

When it comes to older buildings and other structures, conservation or restoration architects are the specialists. Often, they are involved in restoring a structure, and this can mean investigation. Now, for buildings, there can be protected heritage statuses and buildings of historical significance. For technology, we luckily don't tend to have protected heritage systems, but sometimes they might as well be due to interdependencies or investment constraints. Sometimes, we need to find ways to modernise or cope with the aging architecture. In some situations, the bigger financial reality of the company means that this is the exact right thing to do. We need to recognise this by building trusted and respectful relationships with long-serving development team members to find opportunities and provide options to stakeholders.

The time horizon is relatively short, being months to a few years, depending on the scenario.

I've seen a very old legacy system with index file data storage, so pre-RDBMS, where the team was using contemporary devops approaches, and importantly delivered multiple functional releases each week, with test automation, toggle switches, etc. It is a mind shift and might not be your ideal, but if it helps the business then why not?

Does knowing this help

In my experience knowing the level of abstraction we ought to be operating in is important to understand our roles better. We need to be able to work with and trust each other, and that comes down to understanding our role and that of others. Knowing where our expertise is and were that sits with others. Not only the *expertise* but also the responsibility and accountability.

Sometimes, we need to get our egos out of the way and let others make the call. When I say 'let' others, I really mean the decision sits with others, perhaps less senior than us, and we need to take a step back. Companies need to have a flow of people coming through the ranks, and for that to happen, people need to be able to make decisions. Not all these decisions will be perfect, but that is okay.

We can always help guide others in both less and more senior roles, and that works if we are respectful. Ideally, we'll offer to help but then wait for the invite before offering our so-called *wisdom*.

CHAPTER 15

THE THEORY OF THE BIG BANG

"Technology is destructive only in the hands of people
who do not realize that they are one and the same process
as the universe."

Alan Watts

Most of us know about the big bang theory. Not the T.V. show, but the physics theory that describes the expansion of the Universe from a concentrated mass of only millimetres to what it is now. Apparently, this expansion has taken 13.77 billion years. NASA.com rounds this up to 13.8 billion years, while space.com rounds it down to 13.7 billion years. What's a hundred million years among friends? Even I can estimate delivery timelines within that margin.

There is also a theory that the Big Bang is followed by a Big Crunch, which reverses this expansion and is a time of contraction, back down to millimetres, and then that is again followed by another Big Bang. This continues and is called the Big Bounce. There is a significant similarity to a concept in Hinduism described in the Nasadiya Sukta, part of the Rig Veda, originating over 3000 years ago.

I don't know about all the logic the supports the Big Bang, Crunch, and ongoing Bounce, but I do know that an ongoing cycle of centralising and decentralising is a fundamental part of the evolution of information technology. For us, there are implications for hardware and networks, applications and data, integration and security. Even more impactfully, at a human level, there are implications for operating models and organisational structures.

For us as strategists and architects, understanding these cycles can help us to keep some objectivity and humility, and allow us to manage some of our frustrations. Nothing is new. And *nothing* is unchanging.

Let's briefly remind ourselves of the cycles of centralisation and decentralisation in information technology and consider some of the implications for how we go about and think about our work.

Hardware and networks

Anyone reading this will likely be familiar with the highly centralised mainframe world, with the advent of the IBM System/360 in 1966. Although this was highly centralised, it was *less* centralised and a lot less expensive than the custom-built computers prior to this phase. But still it was large companies that could afford to buy and run these mainframes, so these were centralised technologies and operating models.

Personal computers emerged with the release of the Apple II in 1977. IBM PCs really ignited that market in the 1980s, and we all know about the rise of related companies like Intel, Microsoft, and others. This allowed decentralization of processing power, data, and technology operating models; in the case of the last one quite a dramatic change.

Servers, as a concept, is a pattern where one computer serves other computers, and this pattern was around with mainframes in the 1960s, with the typical capability served (a service) being around processing or data storage. But generally, when we think of servers, we think of PC based servers, for example, in a typical 3 tier architecture with a database server, an application server, and clients. These PC servers became very powerful. Often, these were in data rooms in company headquarters and offices. In both cases, the pattern relied on connectivity between computers, initially in local networks (LANs) and then in wider networks (WANs).

These servers (data and processing power) were geographically centralised again into data centres (via WANs), which were typically shared in metropolitan areas or perhaps states or provinces. As we know, this has changed in the internet age morphing into cloud data centres, and the reach has got much wider now, with much broader geographical regions. You can kind of look at cloud data centres around the world at a global level and say they are centralised, but you can also tilt your head and say they are spread out around the globe and decentralised.

Either way, with the heating up of the geopolitical global picture and all major geopolitical players having the capability to cut undersea cables, countries are quietly moving to in-country cloud regions, for example, with AWS, Azure, and Google building data centres in small, isolated countries like New Zealand.

Overall, we continue to see centralising and decentralising cycles with hardware and networking, though with important nuances and certainly a lot of abstraction from detail. The driver for this is often economic, though governance, risk, and NFRs like latency are all factors as well. There is a lot for strategists and architects to stay ahead of in this ever-changing and highly nuanced bouncing.

Applications and data

To a significant extent, applications and data have been impacted by the hardware and networking centralisation and decentralisation.

Back in the days of mainframes it made a lot of sense to have bespoke applications coded to the specific diverse needs of the company. For example, an insurance mainframe might address capabilities for customer data, policy data, quoting, pricing, billing, cashiering, claims management, insurance printing, and potentially even reinsurance management. Beyond these unique functions applications also took care of reference data, authentication, management reporting and more. So, applications in the mainframe world were almost inherently highly centralised, even with the early LANs and WANs.

That said, you can also argue that the applications being bespoke were decentralized out into individual companies, as there were very few general-use packages in the early days. Looking again at insurance, one of the early business adopters of computers, Policy Management Systems Corporation (PMSC) started selling the first commercially available policy management system in 1974. Even then, there was a lot of customisations required, but you could argue the *base* software was standardised and centralised.

The adoption of PC based client-server models and 3-tier architecture did enable a lot of functionality to be decentralised; the data could, of course, decentralise with it. ERPs changed the picture again in the 1990s, centralising the base code with a lot of configurability, and most of the customizing being around integration to other applications and businesses. With the internet we then started to see the growth of CRMs and other applications that, with the rise of cloud, we would now think of as SaaS. A key concern is the centralisation of data, which both makes it more secure, and less secure, depending on the tilt of your head. Data sovereignty has become a big issue with the centralisation of data into cloud data centres, which are at the same time decentralised around the world from a global perspective. Oddly globalisation of data has been more closely scrutinised than the globalisation of finance and supply chains. However, I'm not sure the sovereignty implications and risks are less than they are with data.

Data has taken a related but different journey, with centralised database servers, replicated databases, data warehousing, data lakes, Hadoop, NoSQL and more. The combination of data and APIs has allowed data in one way to be decentralised, while from another viewpoint being centralised into master data and reference data API services.

Overall, we continue to see centralizing and decentralizing cycles with applications and data as we do with hardware, though with even more important nuances and abstraction. For example, edge computing to reduce latency, mobile applications, thin clients, fat clients, web applications and single page applications. The drivers for this are again largely economic, though governance, risk, and NFRs like latency all being factors as well.

There is much for strategists and architects to stay ahead of in this ever-changing, fragmented, and highly nuanced abstracting of concerns while centralising and decentralising. Generally, it could be said with all this that we are *moving* the complexity, not *removing* the complexity. I always try to figure out where the complexity has gone and what the implications are. Who does it impact, and, importantly, do they know? What it means for optionality, particularly around business and operating models, but also future functional changes. We cannot just go along with group think, we need to question everything and ensure these changes make sense in context.

Operating models and organisational structures

We all know that large organisations are addicted to restructures. We tend to be most acutely aware of the organisational structure changes around team structures, reporting lines, and role disestablishments, as these are the areas that impact us and our colleagues and generate a lot of angst. It is hard to know what the driver for many of these restructures actually is. It can, at times seem like the people in power at very large companies like to exercise that power given very limited control on other factors due to shareholder pressures, regulation, market realities, and other factors (e.g. being human). Perhaps when they move people around, it makes them feel like they are in control. Maybe I'm being harsh, but I see it causes a lot of stress to a lot of humans that I care about, so unless convinced otherwise, it often seems rather unnecessary and unhelpful. I do know many leaders do dread having to *execute* these restructures, and they are often adversely affected themselves.

There are certainly people who believe that the underline restructuring ethos, at an economic theory level (i.e. neoliberalism), is to ensure worker insecurity because insecure people will work for less and are generally easier to control. I'm not going to head down such rabbit holes here, but I would observe that many people do indeed feel very insecure. I'll let other people debate if that is a bug or a feature of many modern large organisations.

However, changes in operating models can be the difference that makes an organisation thrive, combined, of course, with other key factors like strategy and culture. Therefore, some organisational structure changes and restructures can be well conceived and necessary.

An example from the country where I live, New Zealand (NZ), is capital-intensive financial services. With a population only recently exceeding 5 million people, it has been hard to have enough capital to support a choice in banks and insurance companies. Most of these companies have been purchased by multinationals, and the majority by Australian companies cashed up with Australian superannuation funds. This has often been done with an approach of reducing duplication in functions, and this has led to operating model changes and restructures. You could argue that the centralisation or concentration of some functions like call centres has not been necessary, but other functions like reinsurance and supply chain in insurance companies really have enabled huge buying power that has benefited customer affordability and shareholder returns in what is still a risk-based investment (e.g. you really can lose your money in a catastrophe, and very quickly, so you want a return).

This move towards multinational ownership has not gone unnoticed by the public in these countries. In NZ, the media are very quick to jump on stories of excessive profits by overseas-owned and controlled companies. In NZ we do have some local companies, not being able to rely on massive economies of scale, who have been able to become very efficient and use the local status as a significant differentiator. Many are also able to carefully evolve very strong employee cultures, largely free from excessive restructuring.

Another common type of operating model change is of course, outsourcing, offshoring, or any number of euphemisms for moving roles outside the organisation. I'm largely not a fan of this. However, it happens, and perhaps sometimes it is necessary or at least beneficial. What I have noticed is that this also seems cyclic.

Outsourcing can be necessary if the capabilities are not available inhouse. For example, many insurance companies outsource some of their actuarial capabilities, particularly if they are small or medium-sized insurers. At the other end of the spectrum, a large company might run its own cafeteria and decide it is better to outsource it to a professional catering company, or perhaps they outsource nursing services to a manufacturer as having enough cover inhouse can be very hard. But when we think outsourcing, we are probably thinking about key value stream functions; for example, with insurers they can outsource the key function of claims to a third-party administrator (TPA), where there are a number of large specialist companies in this space. This can make a lot of sense strategically, even if it is just for a period of time.

Offshoring is really about the difference in cost between employees in the country the service is being consumed, and the cost of typically outsourced and offshored partner employees. It seems that plays around cost reduction drive the move of functions outside the company, and improved service drives the return of function back inside the company. Sometimes the narrative is not this, but it is hard to see this other narrative making sense. Often it seems executives are rewarded with performance bonuses for the changes in both directions. Perhaps for companies, as with NFL quarterbacks, the best trait is to have a short memory. Finally, even if operating functions are not offshored, the possibility they could be probably impacts pay negotiations.

What do these cycles mean for strategists and architects

Often, these endless cycles of centralising and decentralising can seem like a pointless waste of time and money. But consider this: as long as companies keep changing their minds, we still have careers. If they ever decide that it is better to just tick over as they are, then we are done-for. Don't panic. There seems to be little chance this is happening any time soon. That said, we ought to do our best to advise when these changes are beneficial and when these are *nervous jabbering*; just don't call it that. We especially need to advise care when these changes adversely impact real humans without very real and significant business benefits.

After starting my IT career with several 2-year stints, I spent 22 years at one organisation, and during that time, I got to see a lot of leaders come and go and a lot of change cycles go around and around. I went through a rather cynical phase but determined that this cynicism didn't help the company, the leaders coming in, or my colleagues. Most if all it didn't help me. I learned to be generous to the people trying the same things that didn't work before. Maybe they could get it right, or perhaps the context had changed. One of the smartest observations I've seen was from a McKinsey article that said that technology shifts tended to take much longer than predicted but tended, where successful, to have even bigger impacts than imagined; the ecommerce driven dot-com bubble of the late 90s arrived over a decade after it was predicted to, but two decades later the extent of the change could hardly have been imagined at the hight of the bubble.

To a significant extent the decentralising and centralising of hardware is driven by cost. The cloud is all about commoditising, from high-end servers and appliances to cheaper computing power. This ultimately drives down computation and storage costs. The natural culmination (so far) is cloud, with connectivity still producing cost and latency challenges, but edge computing is starting to address this. Being flexible is a key consideration for us, specifically preserving optionality for the company. Cloud providers have moved costs from CapEx to OpEx. Relatively low upfront costs but creeping operational costs. This fits very nicely with the typical corporate friction with up front capital funding and all the planning process and political challenges. We just add the services we need, which is easy to approve if we are enabling cost-out or growth benefits. But this all adds up over time. The reduction of total cost of ownership (TCO) or total controllable expenses (TCE) is becoming a key concern. The challenge is that it is normally easier to reduce the initial implementation costs while adding run cost (or reducing service levels) over time. It looks good initially as some business outcome is achieved, and the initial cost increase might be relatively insignificant, but it adds up collectively. Our job is to impartially tell the story, but we need to develop defendable projections to prove this.

We also need to tell the story around potential service cost increases from cloud providers. In theory, there is plenty of competition, and if you can stay cloud agnostic, you can play vendors off each other. In reality, this doesn't work very well, as staying cloud agnostic means using only the most generic services rather than the real differentiators. Nobody really knows how this will all play out, but it is a risk that ought to be acknowledged.

One big issue that doesn't get enough focus in corporations because it is inconvenient is geopolitics and its impact on NFRs (e.g. ocean cable cutting). This is added to the privacy issues, concentration of risk and other factors. Keep an eye on regulators and industry bodies and stay ahead of regulation; pay attention to the narratives and language they use. Mostly, regulations are brought in because companies aren't acting appropriately, and then aren't getting the hints to up their game. Don't wait for regulations to hit to do the right thing. For example, banks often have regulatory rules saying they need to be able to run operationally independently from an offshore parent, but other companies, like insurance companies, might not have this regulated. However it is just good business practice to ensure you have operational independence, so it ought not need to be regulated. If the regulators bring in rules, it is because companies are not acting appropriately, which they should be. We might not have the final say, but we ought to be making the case for good risk management in this area if we believe it is in the long-term interest of the corporation, shareholders, employees, public, industry sector, or even country. A final consideration is that many companies in regulated industries take short cuts because they don't have time to consider such prudent factors. However, a lot of that activity can be catching up with regulations that they could have kept ahead of by doing the right thing initially and that longer-term foresight ought to be in our wheelhouse.

Our strategy and architecture challenges go up the stack to applications and data, with a few nuances. The centralising and decentralisation will continue based on flexibility and economy of scale. Getting more well defined modularity is important as then we give better optionality. The interplay with abstraction is key, as we often don't abstract as many concerns as we pretend that we do, for example latency. Not everything that looks good on an abstract diagram will run well in production. Lean governance is one of the best tools if aligned with good modularity, NFRs, engineering expertise, and ownership.

At most large organisations, operating model and organisational structure changes are a big factor for strategy and architecture. Attaching our architecture to organisational structures is very tempting, given the stakeholder power, funding pathways, and politics, but doing so is very risky as we'll never keep up. Organisational structures can move much quicker than architectures. We need to look through this distraction and focus on the business strategy, operating model and capabilities. I get a lot of value using MIT CISR operating model quadrants as defined in the seminal book *Enterprise Architecture as Strategy - Creating a Foundation for Business Execution by Jeanne W. Ross, Peter Weill, and David Robertson*. CISR is the Centre for Information Systems Research at MIT and has been providing IT thought leadership for over 50 years. The 2006 *Enterprise Architecture as Strategy* book has aged somewhat; however, it still provides valuable guidance for enterprise architects, strategists, and other technology leaders.

The empirically identified CISR operating model has four quadrants, which go from the locally flexible *diversified*, where operations are not standardised or integrated between organisation units (teams, brands, divisions, countries, subsidiaries etc), and at the other end *unified*, where the operations are highly standardised and integrated. *Coordinated* covers high integration and low standardisation and *replicated* being high standardisation and low integration. The beauty of this model is that no quadrant is inherently better than any other; each quadrant has its own strengths and weaknesses. *Unified* can drive down costs by standardising not just operations but also technology; however, it can stifle local innovation and slow down decision-making with broad governance processes. *Diversified* can allow greater variation in operations and technology, potentially leading to quicker decision-making and more innovation; this is particularly useful if geographies have a lot of market or regulatory variances. Often, there is a desire to drive down technology costs via standardisation, which can, under the right circumstances, be easier with a *unified* approach, but even with a *diversified* approach, we can use a careful *replicated* technology approach to drive costs down. This isn't the data replication, but the likes of governing that all countries in a multi-national use SAP for their GL, getting the best licence cost negotiations, and sharing expertise, even though each country might still have separate implementations targeting local regulations and practices.

These operating models can be thought of as *unified* being centralised, and *diversified* being decentralised. And again, this can be cyclic, going centralised to drive down cost and decentralised to improve innovation, then back around again.

Now, we are probably all aware that technology overall and strategy and architecture, are not immune to operating models and organisational change. The interplay between the wider operating model changes and technology is nuanced, but certainly, architecture can go from being highly decentralised to centralized and increasingly to federated (decentralised with coordination).

Enterprise architects are more common in centralised and federated models and not really applicable in highly decentralised models unless each 'node' is big enough to warrant them. All these models have their merit. Centralised can standardise and can provide some cost reduction, particularly when reducing complexity with a big stick approach; centralised can also be useful for very large program execution. Decentralised can be more flexible but tends to fragment technology and lead to higher costs. Federated can be a good balance if executed well, and that is not easy. Also, there are reasons to oscillate. Each is, in a way, a cure for the other. If you are highly decentralised and think federated is optimal for your organisation, then getting there is almost impossible if you do not go through centralised for a time to standardise and face into some intense battles, then relax back out to federated, leveraging governance, principles, standards, and patterns. As people, we are going to get caught right in the middle of these changes. There was a reason that Part 1, getting out of your own way, was at the front of this book; it might help you to navigate all this change on a personal level, specifically around letting go of attachments, letting go of yourself, understanding impermanence, and not forcing.

In the end, much of this oscillation between centralised and decentralised, including hardware, application, data, operating models, and organisational structures, is driven by some trendy metanarrative.

Metanarrative: An overarching account or interpretation of events and circumstances that provides a pattern or structure for people's beliefs and gives meaning to their experiences.

Definition from Oxford Languages

So, metanarratives around what offshoring can provide certain industries, moving to the cloud, going cloud agnostic, or throwing all unstructured data into a data lake. These ideas get often introduced innocently enough but then take on a life of their own until the metanarrative changes. Our role is not to get caught up in the hype. Understand and respect that stakeholders get caught up in it, but we need to work through the value and risks calmly and logically. Importantly, it often comes down to timing.

As I write this, there is a lot of hype about large language models, and it seems like experts in this emerging paradigm have appeared from everywhere. Almost all stakeholders are talking about it, and a lot of employees are hearing about it on the nightly news or social media, and are feeling the end of their livelihoods is near. We need to lean into this and be mindful of the right time and way to advise our companies to embrace this. If the McKinsey advice is correct, the change will take longer than we think, but the change will be even bigger than we imagine. These changes need to be navigated carefully with sound advice. And that really is in our wheelhouse.

CHAPTER 16

BIG SHORT MOVIE

ABSTRACTION AND DATA

"It ain't what you don't know that gets you into trouble.

It's what you know for sure that just ain't so."

Ascribed to Mark Twain

(however, the original source is debated)

The above quote, regardless of its source, beautifully summarises the essence of the movie *The Big Short*, based on the book *The Big Short: Inside the Doomsday Machine* by Michael Lewis. This is the story of how Wall Street's best and brightest managed to destroy $1.75 trillion of wealth in the subprime mortgage markets. It was the main cause, or at the very least the trigger, of the Global Financial Crisis (GFC), costing almost 9 million US jobs and $13 Trillion of value from household's net worth in the US alone. In the US 6 million people lost their homes. It was the worse financial crisis since The Great Depression of the 1930's. The human cost in the US and around the world was devastating.

When Michael Lewis wrote his book, he didn't want to focus on the CEOs of Wall Street's big investment banks; they had no clue what was going on *while* it was going on. He told the story by focusing on a small number of people who were looking through the illusion Wall Street created for itself. These colourful characters bet against the subprime mortgage bubble they perceived, using something called *shorting*, hence the name: *The Big Short*.

When I watched *The Big Short* while flying back from Sydney to Christchurch on an Emirates A380 in 2018 (ironically bumped up to a very comfortable business class), the story was illuminating. It was just the analogy I longed for. I had never heard of the movie or the book, and I just happened to click on the title and thought I'd give it a go, as I like Brad Pitt and Christian Bale. It was at a time when I'd been listening to a lot of Noam Chomsky's lambasting of neo-liberalism, so seeing the misbehaving of Wall Street, regulators, and politicians fitted that narrative nicely. However, I had also been spending a lot of time unpacking lean and the Toyota way. What really struck me the most was the way the movie depicted going to the Gemba, the real place of work. I loved the various ways the key players looked through the abstractions and into the facts behind the data.

Mortgage-backed security and CDOs

There are a couple of financial instruments in the movie that need to be understood a little. The movie, which is a comedy-drama, has a wonderful technique where various cameos jump in with definitions, like Selena Gomez explaining synthetic-CDOs, with a little help from Dr. Richard Thaler, the father of behavioural economics. You'll have to watch the movie to see the magic of this, but I'll explain a couple of basic concepts.

Mortgage-backed securities (MBS) are bundles of home loans and other real estate debt issued by banks and brought and traded by investment institutes. They are effectively collateralized bonds and have the safety of the aggregate mortgages and assets underpinning them. Because of the pooling of independent risks, they are perceived to be very secure, or at least they were before the GFC.

The specific type of MBSs in the movie are called Collateralized Debt Obligations (CDOs). These have multiple pools, called tranches, of mortgages. These tranches each get their own credit ratings, so investors, in theory, understand the risk of the pool of individual mortgages.

Subprime mortgages are explained through the movie, but essentially, for our purpose, they are, as Investopedia defines, a mortgage that's normally issued to borrowers with low credit ratings with a greater-than-average risk of defaulting.

The synthetic-CDOs get much more complex again and include credit default swaps, which we'll get to later, but they are described as the financial instrument equivalent of an atomic bomb and add to the precarious *greed-fuelled* house of cards that collapses, but for our purpose, we'll stop at the MBS and CDO level of abstraction.

One click down

> "These outsiders saw the giant lie at the heart of the
> economy, and they saw it by doing something the rest of
> the suckers never thought to do: They looked."

Jared Vennett in the movie The Big Short

Perhaps the most fascinating person to feature in the movie is Dr. Michael Burry. A one-eye'd Californian physician with Asperger's Syndrome, Michael found he could avoid having to deal with people by starting a hedge fund called Scion Capital.

According to the movie in 2005, Michael Burry dug into the top 20 Mortgage-Backed Security bonds and analysed the individual records about each one of the thousands of mortgages in each bond. He particularly looked at the credit risk. This was a time consuming and detailed activity that nobody had done, but everyone assumed someone else had. Burry doubted executives at investment banks understood them, but they understood the profit they generated. It would be common for a bond to be rated 65% AAA, meaning that the majority of the loans in the bond were very secure. Bond rating agencies supposedly ensured these ratings were correct. Burry believed the banks had started to fill these bonds with higher percentages of variable-rate high-risk subprime mortgages once they ran out of low-risk mortgages. Many of the mortgages were negative amortizing interest-only loans, meaning you not only don't have to pay the principle, you also don't have to pay the interest; it just keeps increasing the debt. What could possibly go wrong?

He anticipated that when variable interest rates increased, many would default. By his calculation, once more than 15% of the loans defaulted the entire bond would become worthless. Michael Lewis believes that this excentric and brilliant hedge fund manager was doing the first real analysis of the creditworthiness of the subprime borrowers. Lewis nicely summed it up as these subprime homeowners being "one broken refrigerator away from default."

Burry predicted the subprime market would collapse in 2007, and he wanted to bet big on it.

The shorting

> "Wall Street is able to delude itself because it's paid to delude itself. I mean one of the lessons of this story is that people see what they're incentivized to see. If you pay someone not to see the truth, they will not see the truth."
>
> *Michael Lewis on 60 Minutes*

In the movie, Michael Burry goes to various investment banks, starting with Goldman Sachs, and asks them to create a new instrument for him called a Credit Default Swap, which were an inexpensive insurance contract on the securities that would payout if the underline subprime filled bond failed. He wanted to bet against the housing market. He is told that it would only pay out if millions of people didn't pay their mortgages, and that has never happened in history. They agreed to create an instrument, but if the value of the bonds went up, he would have to pay a monthly premium.

The movie depicts these investment banks smarting at the thought of free money being bet against a sure thing: AAA mortgage-backed securities. Burry ends up putting most of Scion Capital's liquidity, 1.3 billion, into these credit default swaps. Scion Capital's investors are shown as being more than a little nervous about this investment. He is under a lot of pressure.

There is quite an intense drama generated around this in the movie, but this isn't the part we need to focus on in this chapter.

However, investment banks like Goldman Sachs aren't in the business of taking risks, and they convinced AIG to insure $20 billion worth of AAA rated subprime mortgage securities. Michael Lewis describes that AIG didn't bother looking into them in detail. Overall, ensuring credit default swaps would end up costing AIG $30 billion. In the end, AIG was deemed *too big to fail* and was bailed out.

The bandwagon

The movie depicts a number of other players finding out about Michael Burry's prediction of the collapse of the subprime market and the investment in credit default swaps on CDOs. Only Michael Burry's character (played by Christian Bale) is a direct representation, and by the sounds of it reasonably accurate in the key point according to History vs Hollywood. They also say that Burry spent around 12 hours talking to the actor Christian Bale.

Jared Vennett (played by Ryan Gosling) is shown as the first to take an interest in what Burry is doing, and he is based on Deutsche Bank bond salesman Greg Lippmann. Jared decides to purchase credit default swaps himself after assessing the quantitative analysis of the subprime-based mortgage bonds and CDOs. Looking to offload some of his credit default swaps due to increasing premiums, a misplaced call gets picked up by FrontPoint Partners (a wholly owned subsidiary of investment bank Morgan Stanley) and gets brought to the attention of a fiery fund manager, Mark Baum (played by Steve Carell) based on Steve Eisman, and his team of sceptical critical thinkers.

Steve's team got curious when Jared Vennett said on the phone he wanted to short housing bonds. Because Steve's team was so sceptical and critical, they couldn't resist looking into it. It is all dramatically depicted, but the basics of the story do happen. They reached out to Jared Vennett to find out more.

Jared Vennett had used quantitative analysis to prove out the risk of the CDOs. At this stage, the movie uses a world-famous chef, Anthony Bourdain, to describe CDOs, and it is fantastic. He describes how the higher risk unsold levels of the bond are bundled into CDOs that are analogist to putting unused old seafood into a seafood stew, creating a whole new product out of items that probably ought not to be on the menu, or at least people wouldn't consume if they knew what they were.

The other players depicted in the movie are a couple of guys from Brownfield Fund. However, for this chapter we'll stay with FrontPoint Partners. The team were sceptical about Jared Vennett's offer to sell them credit default swaps. Mark Baum, in the movie, says, "Is he right about the mortgage market? Let's find out, let's find out." Mark frames up the hypothesis to be tested, "Look, it's two very simple questions. Is there a housing bubble? And if there is, how exposed are the banks?"

Go and see

In lean thinking, they talk about the Gemba being the real place of work. The place where you can see what is going on. FrontPoint goes to the equivalent of the Gemba for the housing market. They go to Miami, Florida.

It seems that the movie is reasonably accurate about this trip, with a little dramatization. They visit people from various aspects of the housing market to see what the reality behind the numbers is. They visit the tenant of a landlord who is overdue on his mortgage, in this case, over 90 days overdue. Importantly the movie makes sure to put a lens on the human aspect. In the visit, they depict that the landlord filled out the mortgage using his dogs name; who knows if it is true, but it makes the point. Other houses they visit are abandoned. Some subdivisions are sparsely populated.

They talk to a real estate agent, who describes that the market is in "an itsy-bitsy little gully right now". House prices had been skyrocketing for some time, but now it was tightening up, and there were a lot of job losses. It seemed there were a lot of motivated middle-class sellers in the market.

Next, they talk to some mortgage brokers. Business has boomed in the last few years. One broker says, "I was a bartender, and now I own a boat". Again, who knows, but it makes the point. The brokers they talk to think that about 90% are adjustable rate mortgages and point out that their bonuses for selling them have also skyrocketed. They laugh when asked if any applicants ever get rejected; one broker says they just leave the income section blank if they want to. Another broker says he focuses on subprime lenders, specifically exotic dancers, as they tend to have poor credit but lots of cash.

So they talk to exotic dancers and get told that they tend to have multiple loans on their houses. They put down around 5%. The movie shows Mark Baum (though in the book, it was someone else in his team) explaining that after the 'teaser rates' go up on the mortgage the repayments could go up double or triple. The dancer explains she has 5 houses and a condo.

The movie combines various conversations and activities in the book to make it work on screen and add a bit more drama and humour, but it seems the key points are accurate. The conclusion that Mark and the team from FrontPoint come to is that there is every reason to think that there is a housing bubble and that it can't last.

Defying gravity - the watchdogs and the end game

> "Never attribute to malice that which is adequately
> explained by stupidity."
> *Robert J. Hanlon, known as Hanlon's Razor*

Mortgage delinquency hits a new high. This flashes across an electronic billboard as the housing market starts to tank, yet subprime mortgage bond prices are still rising. This is where the credit market starts defying gravity, and our credit default swap investors start to realise just how derailed the market has become. They have made, to use a phrase from Sam Harris, *the best move in a bad game*, but it is still a bad game.

This is not a movie review, and I'm not going to disclose how the entire drama plays out, as you need to watch it unfold. For the purpose of this chapter, I do want to touch on the credit rating agencies. As the delinquencies continue, yet the bonds containing them don't lose value, they start to wonder why the rating agencies, such as Standard and Poor's, and Moody's are not downgrading the CDOs and mortgage bonds; they are still rating them AAA. The banks are the customers of the rating agencies, so there is motivation for the rating agencies to keep their customers happy. Not described in the movie, but something Michael Lewis talks about is that the CDOs were so complex that the rating agencies didn't really understand them, so the experts at the banks that wanted the rating helped the rating agencies to understand them.

143

The U.S. Securities and Exchange Commission (SEC) as depicted via a poolside character who is probably made up, and they describe how they don't have the resources to investigate housing bonds. The depict a close relationship between people working at the regulators, and people working at the investment institutions, for example, people moving from one side to the other without constraint.

What might strategists and architects take from the movie

For me, this movie has lots of rich advice for us, summarised nicely by the opening quote, "It ain't what you don't know that gets you into trouble. It's what you know for sure that just ain't so."

We are told that the CEOs of Wall Street's investment banks and many experts had no clue what was going on while it was going on. All of us have cognitive biases; it is hard-wired into us as humans to ignore information that doesn't fit what we believe. We all do it; we just don't all run large corporations. However, in our roles we do advise people who do. It is worth considering that of the thousands of mostly smart and ethical people who could have known, only a very few actually did. And don't forget that in other situations, the outliers that *knew* something other people didn't, were normally wrong. We need to bring our humility as we are far more likely to miss these things than to see them or to see things that aren't there.

The movie gives us a master class on storytelling, keeping a very complex topic simple and using just a small number of people who were looking through the illusion Wall Street created for itself. It is a big story and they only had 130 minutes of movie to tell it. This is relevant for us as we also get very little time to tell stories. Try getting 130 minutes with an executive;

good luck with that. For that matter, try getting even 13 minutes of quality-focused attention from an executive to explain something complex and nuanced. These are very busy people, and they get hit with a lot of big problems to consider. We should not blame them for not giving us the attention; it is our job to package it in a way that *they* can consume. As a side note, it is very important to build good relationships with executive assistants as they are the gatekeepers to the executive's calendars; they also tend to be awesome people and have a tough role, so be respectful.

Digging into the details of abstract data is a good lesson for us. We are not normally experts in quantitative data analysis like Michael Burry but we can find people who are experts in our company, and we can learn enough to be able to poke and prod the numbers. We can be a little sceptical of the common wisdom of the crowd. We need to be respectful and humble while also listening to our instincts when things don't *smell* right. So perhaps it is the growth or cost-out projections or estimates around the total cost of ownership. What assumptions are being made? How reasonable are these?

The misplaced call that gets picked up by FrontPoint Partners was pure serendipity. Apparently, that really happened. We need to be awake enough to roll with chance opportunities.

There is a great lesson for going to the Gemba; the real place of work. Look through the abstractions and into the facts behind the data. You probably can't check it all, but you can sniff test some representative data. In the movie, Mark Baum frames up the relevant questions as "it's two very simple questions: Is there a housing bubble? And if there is, how exposed are the banks?". We can come up with appropriate questions in our areas. Then, we can work out how to find the answers, as they did by going to Miami, Florida, and talking to tenants and landlords, including seeing abandoned houses in subdivisions, talking to real estate agents, mortgage brokers, and end customers, in this case, exotic dancers. Some interesting points shown in the movie are that they sometimes didn't even know what questions to ask, like the dancer saying she had 5 houses. These are all good lessons for us. Talk to people close to the real place of work; testers, developers, support people, SMEs, business managers and team leads, and frontline staff. Ask who else would be good to talk to. Always show respect. Never offer to solve a problem unless you really can and will. If it is an industry like insurance, talk to your friends about their experiences.

There are important lessons for us about misaligned incentives. Standard and Poor's, and Moody's, are depicted as not downgrading the CDOs and mortgage bonds once mortgage defaults start rising. The banks are the customers of the rating agencies, so there is motivation for the rating agencies to keep their customers happy. We get this all the time. Perhaps we need to recharge our work internally, and at some companies, that can be rather stressful for us. If a program manager gives us a recharge code, then it can get hard to charge them for the time we are spending, forcing them through governance hoops or delaying them with risk assessments. But we need to do our job. Typically, the program manager or PM will be long gone while we are still dealing with the fallout of bad decisions. It is tough. But that is the role.

The other interesting aspect of rating agencies shown in the movie was that CDOs were so complex that the rating agencies didn't really understand them, so the experts at the banks that wanted the rating helped the rating agencies to work them out. We are often on both sides of this challenge. Sometimes we need people to explain complexities to us and want candour. Other times, we need to explain complex concepts to businesspeople, program managers, steering committees, and others. We can often explain things in a way that favours the outcome we want; for example, we can downplay the complexity and risk of implementing an asynchronous messaging pattern we want to try out. But we need to consider our long-term credibility, and we need to always act with integrity. Remember, we need to be *trusted* advisors.

An interesting observation in the movie is that there are a lot of very intimidating terms in the investment market, like CDOs for *collateralized debt obligations* full of *tranches* of *mortgage-backed securities*. This means most outside people avoid asking very many questions. The movie suggests that this is by design. Obviously, technology has a lot of terminology that also makes it hard for outsiders to understand what is going on. And, of course we love our acronyms, TBH. So, we need to be careful about how and where we use these terms. I'd recommend briefly defining these terms in any material being circulated to people who might not understand them so they can discreetly review what they are. Often, senior leaders are hesitant to ask what terms mean, particularly in meetings that include their pairs.

We also need to be wary of using euphemisms, and we see these in the movie. Synthetic CDO. Really, why does that term need to exist? Even the term *subprime* mortgage is a euphemism. It isn't just terms either; it can be phrases, like when the real-estate agent describes that the market is in "an itsy-bitsy little gully right now". One phrase we use in our world is technical debt. I could write another book on what is wrong with that term. One approach the movie uses with complex terms is when the world-famous chef describes CDOs as being like seafood stew made of leftovers. We can get creative to explain concepts. I often use a phone call to describe synchronous messaging and texting to describe asynchronous; sure, it isn't that simple, but it helps businesspeople get the basic idea.

The movie depicted a close relationship between people working at the regulators and people working at the investment institutions. As a card-carrying introvert, I've never been that motivated to go out to drinks or dinner with vendors. There have been times I have, and there have been people working for vendors I've considered friends. However, we do need to carefully consider the appropriateness of going out socially with people our company is buying services from. Many companies have policies around financially benefiting in such situations. The world has moved on, and there are all sorts of reasons this is no longer appropriate, including that certain demographics of employees are not easily able to, or ethically willing to, play this game and, therefore, from a diversity viewpoint, are disadvantaged from a career perspective.

Overall, the movie combines various conversations and activities in the book to make it work on screen in the allotted time, and it adds drama and clever humour, some self-abasing, to get the message across. We can learn a lot from it.

I want to leave you with a final exchange in the movie that does also applies to us in our work at times. Michael Burry is under pressure about how much he invested in credit default swaps and if he really knows more than all the experts, and he says, "I may have been early, but I'm not wrong". He is told it is the same thing. When we get our timing wrong about when a company should invest, then being early or late is the same as being wrong. Often, it is the executive that needs to make the decision and be accountable for this timing in the end. Not easy.

CHAPTER 17

A VERY COMMON TRAGEDY

"For that which is common to the greatest number has the least care bestowed upon it. Everyone thinks chiefly of his own, hardly at all of the common interest, and only when he is himself concerned an individual. For besides other considerations, everybody is more inclined to neglect something which he expects another to fulfil..."

Aristotle, The Politics, 4th-century BC

The term *The Tragedy of the Commons* was the famous title of a 1968 essay by ecologist Garrett Hardin. It has become the metaphoric label of a concept dating back to at least Aristotle in the West, with a significant work from Oxford economist William Forster Lloyd in an 1838 pamphlet. The term relates to how people are motivated to behave when sharing a common resource; basically, our near-term self-interests can take precedence over the common good, including our own longer-term interests, if we mistakenly believe someone else will deal with the issues.

The tragedy of the commons gets quite detailed and complex in modern academic studies including economics, ecology, psychology, politics, and science. It is generally considered a subset of game-theory, but for our discussion, we will keep the concept simple. Where it is different from other types of game-theory, like the prisoner's dilemma, is that it is based on positive effects being specific to the decision maker, while the negative effects being dispersed among a wider population, meaning the decision maker gets a big upside and a relatively small downside. The tragedy part of the name comes from it working as long as most people don't do it, yet it is often obvious to everyone that they are better off doing this, and therefore, in the end, everyone gets a large downside.

Hardin indicated the countermeasure to the tragedy of the commons was for societies or other collectives to make some type of social contracts, such as agreements, legal contracts, or legislation, with a modern example being fishing quotas to limit the depletion of fishing areas. However, Elinor Ostrom shared the Nobel Prize in Economics with her extensive work on how various societies have managed this problem with a wide variety of countermeasures for hundreds of years, and not just the countermeasure suggested by Hardin.

Although the tragedy of the commons is best known in economics, ecology, and other sciences, I think we can observe such behaviour in technology strategy and architecture; it is just harder to notice it for what it is. We can also look at some principles from Elinor Ostrom on how collectives successfully manage this problem, as these might help us. But first, let's work on a typical scenario so we are clear on the concept.

Counting Cows

> "Ruin is the destination toward which all men rush, each
> pursuing his own best interest in a society that believes in
> the freedom of the commons. Freedom in a commons
> brings ruin to all."

Garrett Hardin, The Tragedy of the Commons

Examples of the tragedy of the commons normally go something like this. Consider 15 farmers grazing cows on common land, where the land can optimally support 150 dairy cows. So, it seems obvious that each farmer should keep 10 cows, assuming they want to play nicely. However, one farmer, let's call him Barry, realises that if he adds an additional cow, the total number of cows on the land-only goes from 150 to 151, so not much less efficient for all farmers, but a big relative gain of 10% more milk production for him. Barry adds another cow, so he has 12, and the overall total is 152. Barry gets 20% higher milk production, with little personal cost to him and a small, shared cost for the other 14 farmers. This is smart. Barry is smart. But so is Steve, one of the other farmers, and he comes to the same conclusion: it is an idea he'll bet on with 10 extra cows and a promising young yearling. But the same conclusion, without the yearling, is reached by farmers Bernard, Peter, Keng, Mehdi, Andy, Kane, Prabhat, Nikhil, Nick, Nathan, Jono, Adam, and Hieu. Suddenly, by everyone making the smartest individual decision, there are over 200 cows on land that can only support 150 cows, and the small individual cost envisioned by each person becomes a catastrophic cost to all, hence the tragedy of the commons.

There is a lot of debate about the reality of this scenario, given that with a little bit of communication and some social rules, it could easily be avoided. For example, when Barry added extra cows, Steve could have named and shamed Barry out on the Farmbook social media platform.

But for our discussion we can leave the many debates on this concept behind and just consider where we might see similar behaviour in technology. If you have a small piece of land with large cows, then coordinating might be easy, but in the complex world of technology it is often hard to even know this tragedy of the commons is happening.

Shared resources and BAU

One area where we might see this happening is with shared resource models of various types. I tend to look at what behaviour is being incentivised either explicitly or implicitly.

Perhaps your company has some type of recharge model, where resources working on initiatives are recharged to the requesting business unit. I'm not a fan of it as the company ends up doing business with itself; it is a bad game. But sometimes that is what you must deal with, and to be honest you need some type of limiter and prioritisation approach, or the tragedy just gets worse. Often, a company will realise it is impractical to charge for every small change, so perhaps there is a common pool of time for business-as-usual changes (BAU) under a certain complexity or cost. The common pool often also covers basic technology upkeep tasks like software upgrades and delivery improvements like DevOps.

However, people are smart and realise the best move in this bad game is to chop their changes up into small requests that, therefore, count as BAU and are *free*, meaning the cost is hidden and shared by all, so a relatively big upside and very small downside for each requestor. Of course, if everyone does this smart move, then the whole BAU resource gets overwhelmed, and worse, there may be no time for upkeep tasks. We shouldn't confuse this with a sensible product approach, with a Kanban, where teams in small units pull through work; that is a good approach and different from the BAU scenario above.

Technical debt

> "The rational man finds that his share of the cost of the wastes he discharges into the commons is less than the cost of purifying his wastes before releasing them. Since this is true for everyone, we are locked into a system of 'fouling our own nest' so long as we behave only as independent, rational, free enterprises."
>
> *Garrett Hardin, The Tragedy of the Commons*

Importantly, the tragedy of the commons is not only relevant for resource usage but also for pollution of the environment; for example, if you discarded your personal wastewater into a local stream, it wouldn't likely cause an issue, but if the whole town made the same decision, it would. Therefore, there are laws prohibiting such behaviour.

For strategy and architecture, particularly architecture, this is a good analogy for technical debt (tech-debt). As architects, we tend to talk a lot about tech debt, though I'd question if we really have a clear and coherent understanding of what it is. It is not the tech part; it is the debt part. At best, it is mostly a *doubtful* debt, but if your starting position is a doubtful debt, then it is probably just a bad loan. Also, if you don't have a choice about the loan, that they won't pay back, then I think that might just be a robbery. It is a thought-provoking analogy. There are times when people personally profit by incurring tech-debt that allows them to meet incentive targets. Incentives can lead to undesirable and unforeseen outcomes. Be careful how you raise this issue. Often people are behaving in a logical manner given the situation. It might be, for them, the best move in a bad game.

Anyway, let's just go with the idea we want to minimise technical debt. I think we can agree we don't want to pollute our system with bad architecture. However, we do often get pressured by business stakeholders and project managers to accommodate tech-debt. Now, I often argue that, at times, it makes sense to accommodate tech debt, and if it does make sense for the business, then is it really tech debt? But for this discussion, we are talking about the many situations where individuals are incentivised to get their tech-debt accepted so they can get their initiatives in cheaper or quicker. The accumulated effect of everyone doing this does indeed pollute the system and does lead to system instability, cost, and lack of agility.

Better countermeasures

Elinor Ostrom shared the Nobel Prize in Economics with her extensive work on how various societies have managed this problem for hundreds of years using a variety of countermeasures. Ostrom looked at what these independent societies did and defined 8 principles that describe the characteristics of these various management practices.

Some of these principles will feel familiar to us, but some probably won't, or the nuances of them can be unpacked, and we can refine our approach.

Principle one certainly should resonate, and that is to define clear group boundaries. Now, there are many levels at which this can apply, but think of it in terms of resource allocation and environment management (including the architecture of the environment, system, or ecosystem). For architecture, the delivery of true microservices mapped to a product ethos seems to fit well. Ideas like team topologies can be useful, and clear architectural domain boundaries. These boundaries must include consideration for business stakeholders, funding, and prioritisation.

Principle two is easier if we get the first principle right, as this principle is to match rules governing the use of common goods to local needs and conditions. This is basically ensuring that the rules match the intent of the boundaries for resource allocation and environment management.

Principle three is to ensure that those affected by the rules in principle two can participate in modifying the rules. Again, with microservices and a product ethos, we talk about self-governing teams, but it is hard. The wording here is that people can *participate*, which doesn't mean we need a consensus, as that is just not realistic.

Principle four requires high level executive support as it is to make sure outside authorities respect the rule-making rights of community members. That means these rules need to be part of a wider technology strategy and governance approach. This is because we can't just go it alone within our team, as the corporate pressure will build from outside.

Principle five requires us to develop a system, carried out by community members, for monitoring members' behaviour. This can be done with governance, but it goes further as it is also a culture of holding ourselves and each other to account. It is important to find a way to not allow this to create technology verses business friction or architecture verses delivery. This is where cross-functional teams can really help.

Principle six might not be easy to apply as it prescribes using graduated sanctions for rule violators. The key here is to tone back on the word *sanctions*. That is probably not what we need in most corporations, although in some regulated industries, there can be very real sanctions for certain technology missteps, so this can flow down. But generally, we'd be using softer approaches like nudging, mapping to performance measures, and other methods to encourage appropriate behaviour.

Principle seven will be applicable as it is to provide accessible, low-cost means for dispute resolution. In this regard, the low cost would be in terms of time and effort and political repercussions. This is probably going to look something like an architectural review board, but it is important to minimise how often this body or person needs to make a disputed final call. Disputes can be viewed as coaching opportunities because, to the extent possible, you want teams to self-govern within guardrails of appropriate decision-making.

Principle eight rounds this out to an enterprise scale by building responsibility for governing the common resource in nested tiers from the lowest level up to the entire interconnected system. This is certainly a key area for enterprise architecture to add value, which, of course, needs to be linked to a clear strategy.

No magic

The eight principles above can help avoid the tragedy of the commons in terms of behaviour in decision-making. However, it doesn't magically make decisions easy, or trade-offs evaporate. The eight principles help to allow the hard part of the decision to be brought into the open, but it is still hard. If you have a compliance change to a legacy system and to meet the timeline you have to add more technical debt, then that is still likely to happen because it might still be the only feasible trade-off. No magic.

CHAPTER 18

THE DARK SIDE OF REMOVING

COMPLEXITY

Complexity is often *public enemy number one* for technologists in large corporations, and rightly so. Let's forget about good versus bad complexity and focus on the latter. Okay, so I often use other people's quotes, but here is an original (as far as I know):

> "Complexity is resilient and difficult to remove, but it is
> often easy to move; therefore, when projects or people
> say they are removing complexity, they are typically just
> moving it onto someone else, such as development teams,
> frontline staff, or customers."
>
> *Michael D. Stark, author of Surviving Strategy and*
> *Architecture*

Think about the times you have seen complexity being *removed* and about the flow on effects from a holistic *systems-thinking* viewpoint. Was the complexity really *removed*?

The anecdote

Many years ago, I was involved in an ERP implementation in the public mental health sector, and I remember some simplification decisions during the program. After going live, unit managers were complaining very loudly about having to click a couple of extra buttons on a screen as part of a common process in a high-dependency unit; we sat in our office, which was an old operating theatre, and worked out it took about an extra 20 seconds, which they needed to do a few dozen times a shift. Clearly, this was not a big deal and not worth *customizing* the package, which would add *complexity*, impacting upgrades.

I decided to go out to this unit to talk to them and see what was really going on. I went to the gemba: the real place of work. This changed my viewpoint forever.

The little office they had the computer in was in the middle of this high dependency mental health unit, with big glass windows and two corridor openings. There were highly animated people everywhere and it was a very confusing and unpredictable environment; I really did feel exposed and uncomfortable. For those people who were working there, often understaffed, taking your eyes off the situation for even a few seconds exposed patients, yourself, and other staff to potentially significant risk. We thought we had *removed complexity*, but we had simply *moved the complexity* and moved it to a place that put people at risk.

I went back to the ex-theatre office, sucked back some oxygen, and registered the ERP module for customization.

"Go see, ask why, show respect."
Fujio Cho, honorary chairman of Toyota Motor Corporation, referring to going to the Gemba (the real place of work)

Complex verses complicated

Some systems theorists believe that we confuse *complex* situations with *complicated* situations, and although a definitional rabbit hole, in the end, there is a logical difference, and the difference matters a whole lot in architecture. An iPhone, for example, is *complicated*, having many different components and extensive software, but this is all hidden by the user-centric design, so for a user, it is generally not *complex*; this is because most people find iPhones highly intuitive, predictable, and easy to use. Personally, I don't, so I use an Android!

Complicated problems are deterministic and, therefore, can be solved logically in a reasonably accessible way, whereas *complex* problems tend to be more multi-factored and interrelated, with many unknowns, making outcomes harder to predict. If you look at managing *complicated* software engineering problems, then typically, a well-structured logical approach will solve it, and once solved, they tend to be open to automation techniques.

A *complex* engineering problem, however, is not easily *worked out* using logical thinking and whiteboards; even sticky notes can struggle here. Leading approaches use things like lateral thinking, systems thinking, HCD, design thinking, etc. Typically, you come up with a hypothesis and then experiment to find out if it works, adapting to feedback and pivoting. It is easier to observe actual behaviour and adjust rather than to try to predict behaviour accurately.

"Complex situations do not lend themselves to a solution, and it is folly to spend the time, energy, or effort even to attempt to create solutions. Yet this is exactly how the complicated way of thinking works."

Dr. Rick Nason

We need to look beyond simply how *complicated* something is when determining *complexity*. A great example of a *complicated* solution is a modern passenger aircraft. An Airbus A380 is made up of about four million individual parts produced by 1,500 companies from 30 countries around the world. Their software executes over 100 million lines of code. These awesome machines are most certainly *complicated*, but if they were *complex* and therefore unpredictable, we wouldn't travel in them. Generally, they are highly predictable given the pilots training and industry processes, and therefore are safe.

In comparison a rugby ball has significantly less than 4 million parts. Basically, an inner bladder and an outer synthetic layer. However, ask any rugby player, and they'll tell you that relying on the bounce of the ball is highly risky; it can bounce in any direction. Technically, it must be deterministic, but given the number of variables and decision-making time, you cannot reliably predict it; perhaps this is chaos theory related, but I don't want to go there. Effectively, in the context of the game, this is *complex*, even though it is not *complicated*. This is similar to the story of the button in the metal health unit, where the *complexity* is in no small part due to the context of usage.

You may or may not agree with this definition of *complex* verses *complicated*, but to avoid an etymological debate, let's just agree that *complexity* is nuanced, and an understanding of the full context is necessary to understand if something is *complex* in practice.

We care about distinguishing the *complicated* from the *complex* because we don't want to remove *complications* that can be handled logically and end up creating *complexity* elsewhere in the wider system that cannot, including people, processes, and technology.

> On complexity – "Think 'manage, not solve'"
> *Dr. Rick Nason*

Solving the complicated

It is probably *complicated* if it is intricate with many parts, components, modules, lines of code, actors etc, and reasonably predictable behaviour in context. Approach with *solving* techniques like logical determination, such as decision trees, structured testing approaches, documented execution processes, and test automation.

Avoid treating it as *complexity* that must be removed, where attempting to remove it may actually create real *complexity* elsewhere. An extreme example would be removing the Ground Proximity Warning System (GPWS) from an A380 aircraft to reduce the amount of code when the GPWS is there to remove complexity for the pilot in keeping the plan safe.

The *complicated* can bloat and morph into *complexity* over time as many interrelated *complicated* systems almost certainly become *complex*.

Managing the complex

It is probably *complex* if it is hard to predict its behaviour in context.

Note that often, it will be intricate as well, but it may not be e.g. the bounce of the rugby ball. Approach with management techniques like defining hypothesis, testing, observing, and pivoting. You might find that advanced analytics may provide benefits. Carefully determine if the technology *complexity* is buffering people and processes from additional *complexity*, particularly where that might add operational cost or risk to your businesses or more importantly, expose customers to pain.

Things to avoid include trying to solve *complexity* with logic alone or simply pushing the problem to others with assumptions and risk acceptance. If you do decide you ought to remove the *complexity*, ensure it is truly being removed and not just move to another technical domain or worse, onto the business, partners, or customers.

A note on systems thinking

It is beyond the scope of this chapter to unpack systems thinking, but this is a great area to explore to gain a more in-depth understanding of how things interrelate in broader systems, and the various complicated and complex challenges. Thought leaders include Russell L. Ackoff, Ludwig von Bertalanffy, or for a more contemporary view Donella Meadows book, Thinking in Systems, which is an excellent read, particularly around feedback loops. I'd argue that Lao Tzu was the earliest documented systems thinker with his work the Tao Te Ching.

CHAPTER 19

RISE OF THE INTROVERTS

"Don't think of introversion as something that needs to
be cured."
*Susan Cain, Quiet: The Power of Introverts in a World
That Can't Stop Talking*

Susan Cain changed my life forever.

In January 2012, Susan released her book *Quiet: The Power of Introverts in a World That Can't Stop Talking*. If you are an introvert and have not read or listened to this book, you should do so. Many people in strategy and architecture roles are introverts, as introversion traits are beneficial in these roles. If you are an extravert who knows and cares about introverts, perhaps a spouse or a child, or colleagues, or even stakeholders, then this book could change your relationships. If you are an extrovert but find social gatherings fun but exhausting, then you are probably an introvert, so again, read the book and stop pretending. This book has had a huge impact on how introversion is understood. For example, prior to the book, Google searches for the word *introvert* were about 7-10 times more than for *extrovert*, but this shot up post 2012 (release of the book Quiet), and now searches for *introvert* are 50-60 times more than for *extrovert*. Google books Ngram viewer shows *introvert* mentions in books overtook *extrovert* mentions in 2012.

I found Susan's book around 2015 and originally borrowed it from the library, then brought a paperback, then a hardback, then audiobook. I can't see them releasing a movie, but the 2012 TED talk is a good teaser, as is the Google talk during the same year.

I had been managing depression for several years and had made some good progress, but this book really did answer many nagging questions. I'd had some stomach (gut) challenges between 2008 and 2012 that had severely drained me, or more specifically, my serotonin levels, and had highlighted the link between the gut and the brain and the correlation with energy levels. Then, in 2011 my city, Christchurch, New Zealand, was wiped out by and earthquake that caused the demolition of 90% of the CBD floor area. At the time of the quake, I was on the 10th floor of an office building where the peak ground acceleration was over 2g, mostly vertical, meaning the building was being pulled back down at double the speed of gravity. I had no doubt at all I was going to die; but I don't think I did. This earthquake also caused the mutual insurance company I worked for to need a financial bailout from the government and was subsequently sold and merged into an international insurer. Then, while out walking one frosty morning in 2012, before my daughter's netball game, I found a homeless man hanging from a tree in a disused stockyard. The accumulation of all this was very draining, and the world got very dark for some time; it was a battle to get through it.

It took time to get to my new baseline. My family were amazing. My employer at the time also provided great support, and post-quake, a lot of people needed support. The entire city started talking about *resilience*, which isn't a term I use. I prefer willow tree strength over oak tree strength. That said, we need to be the tree we are.

I'm a better human for the experience of depression, and I owe a lot to cognitive behavioural therapy (CBT) and later to Buddhist and other Eastern philosophies. What I did learn from my gut and depression challenges was how close the link between energy levels and mental wellbeing are.

Introversion is also all about energy levels, and there are potential correlations between introversion and depression; more on that later. Reading *Quiet* was lifechanging for me in that it allowed me to understand it is okay, and absolutely *normal*, to be introverted.

The Introvert-Extrovert continuum

> "Shyness is the fear of social disapproval or humiliation, while introversion is a preference for environments that are not overstimulating. Shyness is inherently painful; introversion is not."
>
> *Susan Cain, Quiet*

Introversion and extroversion exist on a spectrum, which I tend to prefer to call a continuum, but I think the *expert* term is a spectrum. There is a normal bell curve distribution, and in the middle of the bell curve, you are defined as ambivert. Nobody is entirely extroverted or introverted, but in the tests that I have done online, I am highly introverted at 85-90%, or

10-15% extroverted (as the supposed norm), which does match my lived experiences.

This spectrum is based on how you recharge your energy, with high levels of sensory input invigorating and recharging *extroverts* while draining *introverts*. This is not to say it is unpleasant for introverts, just the duration of preferred exposure to sensory input differs. For me, noise is probably the most draining; rooms full of talking people, particularly rooms with poor sound absorption, and where I cannot find a corner or wall so I can limit the directions the sound hits me from. My wife is highly extroverted, which is a common couple mix, and we both enjoy social occasions; it is just that I prefer one a week and am done after two hours, whereas my wife might still be enjoying all the vibrant activity 6 hours later. It has taken time to figure out how to balance this, but we are doing quite well with it now.

When introverts naturally prefer corners and walls, it is not about shyness. Introversion is not shyness, nor is it about autism, which is where I find the term spectrum does confuse things further. You can be a shy introvert or a shy extrovert, and I'd imagine the latter is particularly tough to manage, but I don't live that one. Introversion is not an affliction, and it does not need to be fixed. Introversion is healthy in a balanced society. We do not need to *get out of our shells*.

It seems the main *mechanical* difference is how sensitive, or receptive, our brains are to sensory input. More extroverted people are less sensitive to input, and so they gain energy from more sensory input, like a noisy social event, whereas people who are more introverted are highly sensitive to input and find such events draining after a shorter time and beyond a point quite overwhelming. There is a lot of detail, but the key to the scientific understanding was the development of neuroimaging technologies, including functional magnetic resonance imaging (FMRI), and the scientifically supported, quantitative evidence indicating there are structural differences in the brains of extroverts and introverts. It seems extroverts respond more to the neurotransmitter dopamine, and this drives reward-seeking behaviour, like risk-taking, novelty, or social engagement: carpe diem. Introverts do take risks but are more likely to risk assess and proceed with care. Sometimes, the opportunity is lost by the time introverts act, but sometimes the disaster is avoided. Introversion and extroversion are neither good nor bad; they are just a trait. Interestingly, all species seem to have a balanced population of these traits.

Introverts respond more to the neurotransmitter acetylcholine, which is associated with favouring turning inward, and the find this calming and satisfying. Introverts have longer and more complicated brain pathways, and extroverts have shorter and simpler pathways, leading introverts inwards and extroverts outwards. There are functional brain activity and structural differences that have been identified, which is complex but leads to introverts being more easily overstimulated and therefore avoiding stimulation, and extroverts seeking stimulating environments. There have also been differences found in the prefrontal cortex, and researchers believe this leads to introverts favouring abstract thought.

However, there is, as always, a nature verse nurture factor. What society you are born into and the social interactions you have also impact where you both are and appear to be on this continuum. There is some indication that people can shift where they are on this continuum throughout their lives, though I'm not so sure you can deliberately do this beyond just appearance.

Most importantly, there is no right or wrong place to be on this continuum. What matters is that you know how to manage this for yourself and that you are considerate and accepting of where other people are on this continuum.

Discrimination

> "Extroversion is an enormously appealing personality
> style, but we've turned it into an oppressive standard to
> which most of us feel we must conform."
>
> *Susan Cain, Quiet*

The biggest issue I find is that introverts are told to try harder to be more outgoing, to be more extroverted. It is good for them. It will fix them. Do we tell women to try to be more male? Well, we do in subtle ways; at least we are starting to call it out and change it which is a good thing. We blame introverts for being introverted, and then we disadvantage them if they don't conform to extraverted ideals of normality. It is not just extroverts that blame them either, it is often introverts, including those pretending to be extroverted, that are the harshest critics of introverts.

As I discussed in the introduction to this book, I am not trying to *prove* anything, and therefore, I am not formally citing sources as proof. However, I will refer to one paper by quoting from the abstract summary.

"A growing body of information suggests that core or underlying personality is a significant concomitant [(natural accompaniment)] of depression and suicidality. Introversion (i.e., low extroversion) is especially promising in its relationship to the phenomenology and outcome of depression and may represent an underlying heritable trait of etiologic [(contributing)] significance. Furthermore, the presence of introversion has implications for differentiating unipolar and bipolar depression. It is likely that introversion acts in concert with other core personality variables, including neuroticism and having a feeling-type personality to influence depression."

Janowsky DS, Introversion and extroversion: implications for depression and suicidality.

As per the Jaowsky paper quoted above, it does intuitively make sense that there would be a statistical correlation between introversion and depression. Interestingly, introversion is described as low extroversion, which sounds a lot like *extroversion* is deemed *normal*, and therefore, to use a post-modern term, *introversion* would be *other* than normal; language matters. Also, it is always on a continuum, as stated, and therefore, to use another post-modern term is non-binary. The paper largely using the Myers Briggs Type Indicator (MBTI) and compares this to unipolar and bipolar depression. I'm not at all qualified, or more importantly, I don't have the knowledge or desire, to appropriately critique this paper, but I would note that it makes no mention of introversion and depression not existing in a vacuum, which is to say there are many complex factors interacting in this correlation. I find myself wondering if depression has a direct relationship to introversion or if it is how society treats introverted people that is the link. I suspect the latter is a big part of it, and largely based on introverts having to behave like extroverts, or at least to exist in environments optimised for extroverts. In both cases, the overloading of sensory input and depletion of mental energy can be significant, and I'd have thought this could be the causal link, but I'm not an expert; I'm a beginner.

It is the still-hidden diversity and inclusion issue of our time, and it impacts all cultures and genders. The studies vary, but it seems at least 1 in 4 people are more introverted than extroverted, and it could be 1 in 3 or even half, but this does vary within and between populations. Also, in any company or career, it can vary, e.g. lots of introverts like to get lost in computer code but do suffer the standups at the scrum or kanban board. And then, from an intersectionality viewpoint people may fit into other disadvantaged categories in addition to being introverts.

Many creatives are introverts. Philosophers also tend to be introverted, given that *doing* philosophy is largely about contemplation, even though there is a lot of talking about philosophy, which is less so. Western societies of late have come to value action over contemplation, but nature says there is a place for both and that these tendencies are complimentary. Many of the most important creative, scientific, political, and financial works have come from introverted thinkers, including Abraham Lincoln, Albert Einstein, Warren Buffett, Gandhi, Steve Wozniak, Elon Musk, Charles Darwin, Steven Spielberg, Issac Newton, and many others.

Most importantly, there have been some powerful mixed partnerships, with perhaps the most famous in recent times being Steve Wozniak (introvert) and Steve Jobs (extrovert); without this balance, you quite possibly wouldn't have the smartphone you have in your pocket today, because there quite possibly wouldn't have been Apple computers. Had Wozniak been on his own, the Apple Computer company might not have happened, and the Apple II and Mac might not have made it into production.

Old societies were character over personality, but now, in the West, and increasingly elsewhere, it is personality over character. The preference is toward displaying the ability to influence quickly rather than building long-term credibility. I would note that in some societies, being extroverted has been a disadvantage, to be fair. If you were born into the Brahman caste in pre-colonial India, then I'd have thought introversion would have been the advantageous temperament.

It is not only extroverts that need to work on changing this. The balance of power is tilted towards extroverts, but this is not a free pass for introverts to get all self-righteous, either. Introverts do need to work to accommodate extroverts as well.

> "Introversion- along with its cousins' sensitivity, seriousness, and shyness - is now a second-class personality trait, somewhere between a disappointment and a pathology.
>
> *Susan Cain, Quiet*

Superpowers

Introverts are all different because introverts are people, so I don't want to over generalise. Many of the characteristics ascribed to introverts are described as limitations, but there are many that can be considered superpowers, though often there is both advantages and challenges with each. These are what I see as the most interesting strengths.

Deep thinking and intense focus: We spend a lot of time in our heads, and are very comfortable there, giving us a great ability to focus. We can be good at problem-solving, risk assessments, and innovation. We also might enjoy deep philosophical challenges and excel at abstract concepts.

Hyper-observance: Our brains are hard-wired to absorb much more of the input from the external world, and if we practice, we can be very good observers. The challenge is filtering the noise and seeing the key information. This can, for example, allow us to pick up on subtleties of language usage with stakeholders.

Good listeners and deep connections: We don't tend to like small talk and much prefer deep connections and meaningful conversations. Often, we prefer one on one connections or small, intimate groups. For example, when I'm working on strategy, operating models, or business cases, I much prefer to do one on one discussions with stakeholders and subject matter experts. I don't tend to get much from large workshops with Post-It notes and don't get me started on the whole Miro board fad. There is a place for workshops, and I know some people prefer them.

Independent and autonomous: By our nature we are often independent thinkers and are happy to operate autonomously. Introverts often get encouraged not to do this, for example, by being pushed into work groups because it will be *good for us*. Also, we can be prone to overthinking things, and then there can be a lot of time spinning our wheels, so working independently but with checkpoints can be a good balance.

A bit stoic: There is a renewed interest in stoicism, and in general, introverts seem to align quite well with this. The virtues of wisdom, courage, justice, and self-discipline are common for introverts. In particular courage in a cause that they care deeply about. Focusing on what can be controlled is also a tendency I see in introverts, which includes accepting external events, like the weather, and just curling up with a good book. This gap between themselves and external events helps endurance in the face of challenges. And finally, we can be sure Lao Tzu (Tao Te Ching) was an introvert, as we often love the peace of nature.

Self-awareness: Given the tendency for introverts to introspect, they are often self-reflecting and, therefore, are often self-aware. This can, at times be problematic as they are prone to overthinking past events, which they can't change, and future events, that often won't happen anyway. Many introverts do find their way to tools that help manage this, which can vary from art, sport, and hobbies to more spiritual growth or religious practices.

Compassionate and good leaders: As with self-awareness, self-reflection can also manifest as compassion for others, which can make them good in leadership roles, regardless of having management responsibilities or not. Their ability to listen intensely is also a huge benefit in this area.

Noisy when it matters: A superpower that surprises many is that introverts are very noisy and energetic about topics they know well and are passionate about. Their intensity at such times is hard for extroverts to match, particularly as it tends to be a surprise to extroverts.

Work style

> "Do not do unto others as you would that they should do
> unto you. Their tastes may not be the same."
> *George Bernard Shaw*

There are lots of ways workplaces can be more introvert-inclusive, and work from home (WFH) has been a game changer. I remember during the COVID lockdown, which were extensive in New Zealand, people at work would say they missed the in-person interaction. I'd pop down to BP for a coffee once a month, and that was all the in-person interaction I needed. That was at a time when I was spending most of my day in video meetings.

The most important thing for both introverts and extroverts is to trust they know what work style is best for them and most efficient. It is good to be aware that introverts often do not prefer large team meetings or workshops, though they can like these for topics important to them. The key is to have these sessions well organised and for them to stay on track. Also, think carefully about having long multiday sessions as these are very draining. The worse scenario for me is flying early to a workshop, particularly if poorly organised and without good contextual information shared in advance, and then expectations of a social outing at the end of the workshop such as dinner, drinks or axe throwing (the combination is to be avoided). Speaking of axe throwing, perhaps for strategists and architects axe catching would be a more appropriate pastime.

If dealing with introverts, for example, having key introverts involved in a workshop, then it is important to give them as much context as possible in advance so they can think through the material. If you don't, then it is common for introverts to be relatively quiet in the workshop, and then the host will receive a long well, thought out email from the introvert a day or two later. I've been known to have a pre-meeting with key introverts prior to the group session so I could give them as much context as possible a couple of days ahead of time. It works well.

Travel

For many introverts travel can be challenging depending on the mode of transport. For local travel, cycling or, if close enough, walking might be preferred as it allows a lot of quiet time. Private vehicles might also be agreeable for introverts. However, public transport, most often trains or buses, can be quite challenging and draining for introverts as it involves being around a lot of people, even though you probably don't have to engage with them. There are some things that can make this a bit easier, and for me, the sound is the key draining factor, so using noise-cancelling headphones (now earbuds) helps a lot. Some people prefer music, but for me, audiobooks and podcasts are a bit of an addiction and allow me to have something else to focus on.

The bigger challenge is often with air travel, with international travel being particularly challenging. One year, at a prior employer, I travelled from Christchurch to the Auckland head office 25 times, mostly for a week each trip. It was an 80-minute flight, with a need to arrive 30 minutes beforehand and another 30 to 60 minutes to get from the airport to the city office. So approximately a 3-hour door to door trip, mostly surrounded by people with all the audible and visual input. And of course, the travel is for a reason, so once you get to the office, you have meetings, workshops, and endless coffee catchups to network, which is important and very rewarding.

At the end of the day, there might be drinks or dinner and breakfast with people the next morning.

This is amplified with international trips; for example I've taken many trips from Christchurch to Sydney and to Melbourne. The flight is up to 3 hours, and the airport throughput is tougher with customs queues and a lot of people in very close proximity. Door to door the trip is about 6 hours, and to get to the office by 9 am it means leaving for the airport around 3:30 am.

Generally, these international trips are tiring for everyone but utterly exhausting for introverts. It would often take me several days to return to any useful human state after such an overseas trip. Therefore, you would be away from your family for several days, and then what returns to the family afterwards is barely human and not much use at all. In my case I have no anxiety about the actual flying in terms of safety, just of being crammed into a toothpaste tube with a crowd of other people and navigating the airport process. It is tough, but there are tricks that can ease it a little.

Start by trying to book your own flights, as it gives you more control over timing and other factors. For international travel, I got to the stage where I would advocate hard for flying the day before I needed to be in the office to avoid the early start, and to manage the sensory input with a break after the flight. It made the trip much more useful. When booking flights, I tried to get on the largest plane possible as that tended to have more space, and for the Christchurch to Sydney flight, there was an Emirates A380, which often was half empty on that leg.

I've always been inclined to get isle seats, so that is easier if you can choose your own, and eventually, I started personally paying a little extra and, where possible, getting a seat at the front of the bus. For A320 domestic flights, I was often able to get the front row, which meant you didn't really see many other passengers, and it made a huge difference for me. The one thing to note is that you want to board close to the last; otherwise, you have hundreds of people nudging past you, which is awful.

Noise cancelling headphones for airports, planes, trains, and buses are a saviour for me for sure. The caveat there is that I have also missed flights as I've not heard the last boarding call, and of course, you need to be careful wearing them around trains and traffic for safety reasons. When appropriate, sunglasses also reduce the sensory load for some strange reason. Another approach to use instead of headphones, or at the point necessary, is to get some high-fidelity earplugs, which reduce the volume without reducing the quality of the sound, and the good ones also reduce voice less; I brought some Etymotic Research ER20XS High Fidelity Earplugs, but there are a number of good options. These ear plugs are great in bars, noisy restaurants and cafes, and of course, can be awesome at music events.

One of the last tricks for me was just keeping a limit on coffee consumption, as that impacts your sleep.

Virtual Meetings

Virtual meetings can be good or bad for introverts. It is nice not having to travel if you are working from home. If in a noisy environment, it is important to use headphones that limit background noise, and of course, the extra expense for noise cancelling can be well worth it. I think for introverts, having the best quality audio possible is helpful. If in a quiet environment, you could try bone conductor headphones, and I use Shokz

OpenComm, which don't block your ears at all, and for some reason, I find these much better for all day usage.

Even in the office, I tend to join virtual meetings from my desktop rather than going into a meeting room with virtual capabilities because I find the sensory input in these rooms difficult, particularly if there is unclear audio, along with my tendency to prefer a louder volume than others in the room.

Finally, something that I heard Susan Cain recommend in a recent videocast was to consider turning off your self-view as seeing yourself is quite abnormal, adding self-consciousness and a lot of sensory input.

Group think

Group working is highly promoted these days. It is considered good for us from school, even preschool, right through to universities, and of course, the workplace. I've even seen this in older persons rest homes. Group working can be great for extroverts and, at times, for introverts, but many people don't thrive in a group thinking environment, and this is ok. One size does not fit all.

This group work ethos seems to be at least partially behind the fad of open-plan office spaces. Working from home has at least saved us from this. Back when many people had their own offices, there were opportunities for them to manage their space by having open doors when they could be interrupted, closed doors if they wanted focus time, and even partially open doors to indicate that they were available if it was important.

Introverts do need to accommodate some group work for practical reasons. If work can be framed in a group session, then people can focus on individual aspects and then have group checkpoints. Another useful tool is group chats, which are still group-orientated, but because they are asynchronous, you still get a bit of space and can manage interruptions.

Executive games

Often, executives seem to be keen to push back to office agendas. I do think that quite a few executives are introverts, but let's face it, the trade of the executive level is often in building in person relationships and working the political angles. I think they find work from home hard as they can't really ply their trade. They can go back to the office themselves, but it probably feels strange being at the top of the hierarchy in an empty office.

All I think we can do as introverts are to continue to advocate for people to have more rights to work in a way that is best for them, provided they can get the job done.

Home Life

The key concern with regard to being an introvert and balancing work and home life is being aware of not burning yourself out with work interactions and having nothing left in the tank for your family. It is very hard, but we must work out how to get the right balance.

CHAPTER 20

DECOMMISSIONING STINKS

A STORY

"Sometimes people don't want to hear the truth because
they don't want their illusions destroyed."
Friedrich Nietzsche

Most of us have had exposure to the remains of some system replacement
that didn't quite finish decommissioning the legacy system. Perhaps it
still performs some current functions or is simply used to access historic
or run-off data. Perhaps it is not a business core system but some other
platform like an integration platform or warehousing system.

We often feel this is problematic and the result of a lack of commitment.
We feel like people don't get how logical and important fully replacing
legacy is, but is it always the most logical choice? I find this story a good
way to think differently about the decision, even if it doesn't clearly tell you
how to deal with it.

The analogy

A good friend of mine told me a story, or perhaps a legend, told to him at the shipping company he was working for. It just completely captures the essence of the decommissioning problem.

Like all good technology analogies, it starts with a consignment of frozen Mackerel.

As the story goes, there was a shipping container full of frozen Mackerel (Fish) that was being shipped from Ghana, West Africa, to a customer in Europe, passing through some very hot areas, including Dubai, on the way. At the Port of Jebel Ali, Dubai, someone noticed a rather unpleasant smell and, upon inspection, found that the refrigerator had been turned off. This was potentially a major headache to deal with properly, and it wasn't their bad, so they simply turned it back on and sent it on its way to Europe.

Arriving at the Port of Amsterdam where it was scheduled to transfer to a truck, it first needed inspection. Customs crack the container to check it prior to it being cleared for entry into the Netherlands. The container was one massive block of frozen rotten fish. A blend of water from what was the packing ice, Mackerel, and mangled cardboard. The door was quickly closed again so it could be returned to the sender, as the regulations for disposing of such cargo meant it would be an expensive and very messy task for the port to do.

During the elapsed time of this journey, the fishery company in Ghana that had sent the container of Mackerel had gone bankrupt, and so the port could neither send the rotten frozen fish back to West Africa nor let it into the country to send it forward to its intended recipient. This was a massive headache for the manager responsible for dealing with it, whose targets didn't accommodate the time and cost of this cleanup. Then, one of the team pointed out that they could put it out back in an unused corner of the port and just leave it plugged in. No cost and no real downside for the manager. Job done. A couple of years later, the manager had moved on, and then one hot summer day a couple of years after that a worker noticed a rather foul smell coming out of the container. The refrigerator motor had seized. Nobody knew what the container was even there for at first, but one of the cynical old boys did remember it.

Opening the container only to be hit with a wall of foul smell, the new manager quickly closed the door, and it took them less than a minute to determine it was much quicker and cheaper just to fix the refrigerator motor. The same exact thing happened 5 years later to a different manager, with the same outcome: just fix the motor and leave it alone but with one difference. He was a more diligent manager and wanted to do the right thing, so he organised for regular maintenance of the refrigeration unit.

According to the legend, the container is still humming away some 25 years later. True or not, does anybody doubt that this is a perfect analogy for the non-decommissioned legacy system?

Picking the eyes out

This strange expression is quite common in New Zealand and Australia but apparently not so common elsewhere. It basically means picking out the good bit and leaving a carcass of little use.

The analogy about the rotten Mackerel in the container needs no further explanation in regard to how it applies to the psychology of what people do in such situations. It is all quite logical with rotten fish and hanger-on legacy systems. If we can kick the can down the road, then why wouldn't we? But how do these systems get like that?

Well, typically it is all about bringing the value forward during system replacement programs. It makes good sense. Aim for the high value first and pick the eyes out. What you are left with is a few functions that typically don't have a very strong ROV (Return of Value) for a replacement business case. With a lot of old mainframe systems, it is common to move them to a low-cost Windows platform, which makes sense. But this further reduces the business case for completely decommissioning it. Few of us are able to get a case for a 20-year ROV horizon approved.

As architects, we get frustrated with these old systems hanging around, particularly from a *systems-thinking* viewpoint, when we can see the accumulative impact on the overall enterprise. But assuming people act logically given their current conditions, then it largely makes sense and is almost inevitable when you add it all up from a business viewpoint. So, what is the answer? What are we to do?

The best way to deal with this situation would be to ensure the original program has a governance gate for success that includes the *full* decommissioning of the legacy system. But to be honest, in the heat of battle, when sponsors are under pressure, this is likely to get traded away with perhaps a risk assessment and the good old sponsor risk acceptance trick.

"To predict the behaviour of ordinary people in advance,
you only have to assume that they will always try to
escape a disagreeable situation with the smallest possible
expenditure of intelligence."

Friedrich Nietzsche

Alternatively, if you have lots of these old containers full of rotten Mackerel out back you can push to get a strategy endorsed at a high enough level that individual business cases to decommission are not needed. So, make it a strategic *business* priority if you can.

I don't know the answer, but perhaps the logical thing to do is to find a cool, dark corner out back, plug in the refrigerator container, and let it be. Just don't forget a bit of maintenance if you don't want to stink the place up. Sorry, but in the end, given the condition we operate in, it often makes sense.

PART 3

THE OTHER STRATEGY AND

ARCHITECTURE SKILLS

"The sign of intelligence is that you are constantly wondering.
Idiots are always dead sure about every damn thing they are
doing in their life."
Sadhguru

CHAPTER 21

THE OTHER STRATEGY AND ARCHITECTURE SKILLS

"Problems that remain persistently insoluble should
always be suspected as questions asked in the wrong way."
Alan Watts

We have considered how to get out of our own way, and we have looked at the way the game works in our corporate world. In section 3, we look at some of the less often discussed aspects of strategy and architecture.

It is of course, important to gain solid groundings in core strategy methodologies if you are focusing on that area and core architecture and technology patterns and methodologies to various depths, including engineering, depending on your specific area of focus. For example, if you are a solution architect, you'll want solid knowledge of concerns like microservices, event sourcing, various synchronous and asynchronous integration patterns, digital patterns, and data patterns.

CHAPTER 22

KNOW THE BUSINESS INSIDE-OUT

"The only way to make sense out of change is to plunge
into it, move with it, and join the dance."
Alan Watts

It is not about the technology. Our organisations are trying to achieve something else; something human. We need to recognise this and keep aware of it in our professional work. Britannica defines technology as "the *application* of scientific knowledge to the *practical aims of human life* or, as it is sometimes phrased, to the change and manipulation of the human environment". The world of IT has got very large and bloated, and as that has happened, we've started spending a lot of time and energy talking about ourselves; but we need to focus on the aims of the organization we are in. Technology is a tool and, therefore, a means to an end.

Some companies focus solely on technology pursuits, and there are some roles that focus only on technology concerns; however, most strategy and architecture roles cannot do this if they are to be relevant to most organisations.

Of all the architecture roles, the enterprise architect needs to keep one foot on the business side, and this is also, of course, true for strategy roles. Personally, I prefer to take the view that where roles like solution architects might look from technology to the business, the enterprise architect and strategist should generally look from the business side towards technology. The strategist or enterprise architect should be an ally to and advocate for the business and its concerns in technology matters, and therefore, they must fluently speak the language of the business.

The purpose and strategy of the organisation

Most organisations today work hard to define their purpose. Hubert Joly, former chairman and CEO of Best Buy, describes the corporate purpose in NBR as "the ultimate goal of the business, the essential reason why it exists, and how it contributes to the common good".

We need to ensure we not only know the stated purpose, but also how leaders at various levels of the organisation describe it. Focus on the specific words people use and how the organisation intends to measure progress towards achieving its purpose. There will be key words that you can use to *say you are really on the team*. Look for external communications like those to shareholders or stakeholders, as well as internal communications to employees. And of course, pay attention to how this purpose is communicated to customers.

We also need to unpack the corporate strategy. This can vary greatly depending on the organisation. There is a lot we can say here about good strategy and bad strategy, to use the title of the book by Professor Richard P. Rumelt, who is the author of Good Strategy, Bad Strategy, and The Crux. I'd recommend reading those two books, as Richard is scathing in his evaluation of what passes as a strategy in many corporations. Often, corporations tend to state organisational goals rather than clearly describe how they will solve problems, focus on priorities within resource constraints, and actually achieve those stated goals. As Richard explained in a 2022 McKinsey podcast, "Many companies treat strategy as a way of presenting to the board and to the investing public their ambitions for performance, and they confuse that with having a strategy". Richard brings this home, stating that "Executives end up saying, 'Our strategy is to achieve these results,' but that is not strategy". Does he say what strategy is? Yes, "Strategy is problem-solving. It is how you overcome the obstacles that stand between where you are and what you want to achieve".

However, good strategy or bad strategy, strategy is not easy, and we need to deeply understand it and be careful about criticizing it in front of our business. By deeply understanding the objectives, areas of focus, and actions described, we can talk the relevant business language; if we do this well, we might get brought in early to strategic conversations. Once we get in early, we can be a truly trusted partner and start to nudge or even drive strategy for the company.

Listen to anything you can find where senior leaders are talking about the strategy. Presentations to shareholders can be highly valuable because if leaders are making commitments to the market, then they will be very focused on achieving these; also, they are probably measured and rewarded based on this. It is now common to find presentations online, both in packs and often videos. Watch and read it all, and focus on the commitments, strategies, and tactics described. The language they use to describe this, identifying any key words. Depending on the organisation, this might filter down into the middle and lower levels of management.

The industry dynamics

We need to deeply understand the dynamics of the industry or sector we are in if we are to be of value to our organisation. What are the common business models, operating models, political pressures, economic pressures, and regulator factors? Also, what is the typical verbal fluff that gets regurgitated? How, fundamentally, does the industry or sector work? Are there industry or sector bodies that can provide information? Look also for what people don't know about the industry; often, people who have worked for a long time in the industry know some areas well, but they might have limited knowledge in other areas of it.

I've spent a couple of decades in the insurance sector, specifically at a large property and casualty (P&C) general insurer and more recently at a mid-sized P&C insurer. It took a few years to get interested in the fundamentals of risk and risk transfer. Understanding how insurance contracts, coverages, perils, customer risk profiles, and asset risk profiles work. Then there is the pricing, with technical prices, probability and severity of losses. The levers for adjusting risk through optional coverages, exclusions, limits, and excesses. Then you get into the terms and conditions, the regulatory concerns, billing and payments. Claims and supply chains are significant concerns, with 50-70% of every dollar of premium paid in claims depending on the product class. Eventually you go wider and get interested in all the reinsurance models around treaty and facultative, and other reinsurance models. Product design and legal concerns are significant. There are actuarial activities around reserving, pricing, and capital modelling. Regulatory compliance and remediations are unavoidable and can be good leverage for strategy and architecture if we understand the landscape well. If you've only focused on personal line products, there is a whole new world with commercial products and some very complex risks, along with a lot of margin pressures at a product and broker portfolio level. Distribution models come into play, with direct models, partnerships, referrals, and the whole broker side, with its many nuances. You also have Managing General Agencies (MGA) and much more. There are other factors like acquisitions, divestments, and, of course, trusty reorganization.

The whole insurance industry lives or dies on capital, something that became painfully clear when perils events increased in many regions, along with repair cost post-pandemic, and insurers suddenly found themselves in a hard capital market impacting reinsurance cost and availability. Not only do companies have to be concerned with the size of *their* slice of the pie, but the industry must worry about the overall size of that pie. And it goes out beyond insurance as if you can't insure it, you can't borrow against it. It impacts society and real people's lives.

My point here is that this is just general insurance, and it is complex, nuanced, and if you dive into it, rather fascinating, or at least interesting enough to keep you entertained. And all the above applied equally in the 1950s before you even had computer technology, so you need to understand it all conceptually and practically at a business level in addition to the technology. Every industry and sector will have its own nuances, its own fundamentals, and a whole language you must be able to speak if you want to be relevant to the business.

There are often internal training opportunities and external resources for learning about the industry, including online learning platforms. There will be the fundamentals, the standard knowledge sources, and your colleagues, who often will love talking about their work. I find podcasts often have some great niche stories about the reality of an industry. For example, I found some great podcast episodes going into the war stories of commercial underwriters, which you don't find in the normal sources. The more you understand the nuances, the more useful you will be. Be brave enough to engage in business conversations, but don't go in and tell them how to run their business unless asked, as that never builds respect and trust.

We must have a relentless focus on the business side of any problem or opportunity because, in the end, it is not about the technology.

Invest in relationships at all levels

Technology is all about relationships: human relationships. We noted earlier that Britannica defined technology as "the *application* of scientific knowledge to the *practical aims of human life*". Looking at Cambridge Dictionary, they defined an organisation as "a group of people who work together in an organized way for a shared purpose". When we try to solve problems with technology, it is directly or indirectly about people. It is not just about getting the business case approved, securing funding and the required prioritisation. Ultimately, success or failure comes down to the impact on people and people at all levels, including customers, employees, and other stakeholders like shareholders or, potentially, the general public.

There is no better investment the strategist or architect can make than to build relationships with people within the business or organisation and within technology. Relationships with technology peers, seniors, and junior colleagues are invaluable; we need to not only look after a key stakeholder, but we need to have trusted relationships with people who know how things get delivered. Often, older senior developers and analysts have accumulated extensive knowledge about the business, as well as good contact and trust within that business. Testers can be a great source of functional knowledge. Engineering is key to having a successful lean and agile capability, so we need to be able to tap into their knowledge and support their capability. And don't forget the executive assistants, as they are great people with a tough job, so if you can help them, they can get you access, which is invaluable.

Within the business, the more you can build relationships with senior leaders, the better, but don't waste their time, as they are busy people. Focus on what they need, not what you need, and always be honest about the realities and limitations of technology; do not oversell, or you won't be trusted next time. That said you also must sometimes highlight blockers in their way and describe limitations. Find alternative options, as this is something they'll want to see.

But you also need to get to know people at the coalface of the business. What is the real-world reality of the day-to-day work? As they say in the Toyota management system, go to the Gemba, the real place of work, show respect, and ask questions. Sometimes managers have a good understanding of this real workplace, but sometimes they don't. In many industries, like insurance, digitalisation and automation are replacing many of the work hours closer to the coalface. There is much talk about what A.I. might be able to replace going forwards as well. In some industries, there are even concerns about where the next generation of subject matter experts and experienced leaders will come from if they don't get the chance to come into these entry level roles that might get replaced with technology.

Get fluent in the financials

If we are working on strategy or architecture, we need to be able to engage fluently on the financials and not just on technology and implementation estimates. Obviously, if you are dealing with a privately owned company, owners expect a return on their investment or are looking to grow the value of the company, often both. If it is a publicly listed company, then the shareholders certainly want their return depending on the nature of the risk involved (they might be more motivated by share price than dividends). Businesses such as technology companies with venture funding have a whole different cycle of financial pressures depending on where they are in the IPO cycle if going public is their objective.

For government agencies or government-owned entities they increasingly are under tight scrutiny on spending, particularly during certain times of the election cycle. Not for profits have other financial challenges with limited funding options.

We need to deeply understand the type of company and industry we are in and all the financial considerations well beyond simply the technology costs. We need to know how to frame our narrative in a way that is financially compelling, or at least informative, for the businesspeople making the decisions. We need to show that we understand their business pressures. If we do this well, then we can better serve our organizations and save ourselves a whole lot of frustration and pain.

Going back to insurance as an example, the entire concept of insurance is based on capital, understanding risk, and return on that capital, which really is at risk. A key measure to the shareholders is often RoRBC, which is Return on Risk Based Capital. This is probably the most important measure, though there are other measures used, but I like RoRBC as its name makes the value proposition clear.

I worked for a mutual insurance company in New Zealand in 2011 that was a leading personal insurance provider having been in business for over 100 years. It was so financially stable that a key challenge was how to release some capital best, as mutuals are not supposed to hold too much money. At 12:51 pm on February 22 of that year a vicious 6.3 earthquake directly hit our head office in Christchurch. The peak ground acceleration was over 2G of vertical shaking, meaning the 12-story building I was in was getting pulled back down at twice the rate of gravity. Surprised to find that the building didn't collapse and I was still alive, I quickly realized life in Christchurch would never be the same. A couple of days later, it was clear that the losses would be well over the $1bn reinsurance cap, and the company was insolvent. Over 90% of the Christchurch CBD had to be demolished. In only 45 seconds the 100-year-old leading personal general insurer was wiped out, with eventual losses over $2bn, which was about 4 times the maximum total losses actuarial modelling had predicted before the quake.

Every industry has its own brutal financial realities, which is why the subtleties of financial pressures really matter. Back with insurance, if I asked you to invest $100k in a company that absolutely can go bankrupt in 45 seconds, how much would you want as a return (on that risk-based capital)? Ok, many industries aren't that brutal, but things change, and you can lose money relatively quickly. Certainly, things can happen to collapse the share price rather quickly.

Beyond RoRBC in insurance, there are other high-level measures like Immunised Underwriting Results, Immunised Net Results, Written Premium, Net Earned Premium, Return on Equity, and many more. Companies, regulators, and markets tend to change their preferred measure

I've noticed, with companies often choosing the one with the best optics in their scenario.

In terms of the key insurance management financials, it seems like the Combined Ratio (CoR) is key to driving profitability. This really does tell you a whole lot about how the insurance margins are achieved and what narratives are going to work for our storytelling. The CoR can be across a financial year, quarter, or month. It can be for the whole company or for a distribution division (direct, broker, partner channel, or others like MGAs). Also, insurance is very informative at a portfolio or product level.

Again, this is used as an example, so you need to get this deep into whatever industry or sector you are working in. The Combined Ratio (CoR) has two key parts. The Expense Ratio, which is the proportion of the cost of running the business excluding claims, and the Loss Ratio which is the proportion of cost of paying out claims. If you have an Expense Ratio of 29% and a Loss Ratio of 69%, then you have a Combined Ratio of 98%; this means for every $1 of premium you get, you pay out 98c and make 2c profit. It is more complex than this, as you have other financial factors, but let's say you end up with a Return on Risk-Based Capital (RoRBC) of 2%. So, using the earlier example, if you invested 100k in an industry where you can lose it all in 45 seconds, would you be happy with a $2k return. I think not.

We know that our insurance leadership are, from the board down, going to be under a lot of pressure to improve the RoRBC, and the Combined Ratio might be used to guide and measure this improvement. To do that technology can help, but it is also a cost, so exactly how investments and benefits are realised is very important. Are we speaking this language? What I can tell you for sure is that they don't care about how loosely or tightly coupled our systems and services are. It might impact them, but we must be smart about how we tell the story, and more than anything, we must build trust. We also must be very careful about timeframes. The reality is leaders who won't have a job next year if they don't hit targets just aren't as highly motivated to worry about the long game; there is a bigger issue here for corporations and how they motivate their leaders, but we aren't going to solve that here.

Let's unpack the Combined Ratio and see what can be done. What makes up the Expense Ratio side, and how do we get this down from 29%. The Expense Ratio is made up of Administration Expenses plus Commission Expenses, divided by Net Earned Premium. One way of driving down the Administration Expenses is to find ways to reduce business costs such as staff, technology, buildings, licenses, etc; digitisation and automation can help, of course. But the technology total cost of ownership also comes into this, as well as paying back any capitalised investments in technology. Commissions in insurance tend to be paid to brokers and distribution partners, and improving efficiencies for partners can help commission negotiations. However, Net Earned Premium (NEP) can be increased, and if you can do this while holding the Administration Expenses steady, doing more for less, then that also improves the Expense Ratio (it turns out math did matter). You can increase NEP buy selling more policies or by increasing the price of your policies; both have implications, of course. For insurance, the accuracy of pricing is an arms race. The better you can use data and statistical modelling, the better you can price risks and win better business at a better price. To win more business digitally, a very smooth customer experience is needed, typically meaning you need to ask fewer questions while still pricing accurately; there is a tension between the digital experience people and the pricing people.

On the other side you have the Loss Ratio, and that is simply Claims Paid, plus Claim Handling Expense (CHE), although sometimes this is counted as an Administration Expense on the Expense Ratio side. This total is then divided by the Net Earned Premium to give the Loss Ratio. So here, reducing the cost of claims in terms of repairs, total losses, and of course, claims fraud, which impacts both. Technology is key here for process efficiency, fraud detection, and managing the supply chain. This is all highly audited and regulated, and reinsurers take a keen interest when reinsurance kicks in for catastrophe events. Processing claims quickly helps to reduce the cost of reserving as you need to reserve for the claim for a shorter time and, therefore, overall lower reserves, which frees up expensive capital. Paying claims quickly and fairly is the promise of insurance in the end, so doing this well has a big impact on reputation and, therefore, future premiums.

We can start to see where you need to aim your technology investment stories in this world. Yes, there is compliance and customer experience investment, but so much of it comes down to how it impacts the Combined Ratio in the end.

We need to understand the language of the decision-makers and of course, the people who ultimately entrust us with their money. They want a fair return on the capital they are putting at risk. We must get deep into how the financials work in the company, industry, or sector we are dealing with if we want to be relevant.

At a personal level, the better you understand this, the more rewarding and less frustrating your career life will be for you and your stakeholders. It is like suddenly waking up to the real world of strategy and architecture and clicking on what game you are actually playing, and you will wonder what the hell you were trying to do beforehand.

Understand the funding cycles

In each company and organisation, there is normally a certain pattern and rhythm of funding, both strategic and operational. We need to pay careful attention to these cycles as this is another key to being able to have a successful influence.

Often strategic funding rounds will be annual, but that might not be the case where you are, so you'll need to use those relationships you've established to determine how it works. There will normally be strategies that are funded over multiple years, so perhaps a major technology program to replace ageing technology, which might take 3 or more years to complete. But typically, there will be some new investments made each year, and depending on the situation it may take some time to get agreement on funding commitments. There often will be an investment slate that evolves several months before final decisions are made. Once the slate first comes together, it normally goes through rounds of refining it and culling items, not adding items, so you must ensure there is a line item in the early cut for any key initiatives you are advocating for.

The are only certain senior managers that can get potential strategic investments on the slate, and there is a lot of political credibility involved for them. So, how do we influence these? We can try to influence items that have momentum already, or we can try to get items on the slate that we think should be there. Either way, we need to be able to influence key players. Typically, I've seen people going directly into a logical pitch, often based on what makes technology sense. However, if you are asking for money, it must make *business* sense. Ultimately, it needs not only to make sense but it also needs to make more sense than most other items on the investment slate. Funding is a competition and normally a zero-sum game.

It is not uncommon for a company to have 2 or more times the number of good ideas with a positive return of value than they can afford to fund in any given year. So, having a good idea isn't enough; it needs to be a better idea than the other ideas or at least a better story.

The two things that, in my view, are the most important are: identifying and embedding a narrative and carefully choosing, or generating, the right timing. If you are in a situation where you can make the timing work in your favour rather than against you, then pay attention to when the conditions are right to make a play. You will need time to embed the right narrative so that the proposition seems to make sense to the senior managers who need to push for it. There are techniques for story telling which you can explore, such as the Minto pyramid for structuring your narrative.

The language of the business

As we've discussed above, learning and practising the language of your business or organization is key. Be it in the language of the purpose and strategy of the organisation, the dynamics of the industry, the financial language and nuances, or the language of the funding cycles.

We've all immersed ourselves in the language of technology; however, this is just not enough. We need to be able to listen to and speak with the various stakeholders of our business, organisation, and industry. In a lot of ways, it is a bit like speaking a foreign language; it can be scary, and you will get it wrong at times. But it is important you are brave enough to try, and that you persist. It will get easier. Most people will support you trying to speak to them in their own language and will cut you some leeway. Occasionally, you might find businesspeople who make you feel small but don't buy into it. People are complex, and there will be things going on for them. Trust your voice and use it.

Staying the course

Early in your career you can move around, and this can be valuable to gain knowledge and perspective. You'll meet a lot of great people along the journey. My first few jobs in technology were 2 years duration each. It gave me a view of a few different sectors, but you don't end up having time to really get deep into how the companies or industries work. There is no problem doing this throughout your career if you wish, as you add a lot of value as a generalist. A lot of people love contracting for this very reason.

But you can stick in an industry and even in a company and become an expert technologist in that sector. You will find things out about the business and the sector that just takes time to observe. You can also often stay at a large company or organisation and let it move around you. This is very achievable these days as companies restructure, merge, acquire, divest, and change focus. This is a way to use the impermanence that can be frustrating for us to enhance our careers.

If you do want to stay in one place and let things evolve around you, it is safer if you don't get too high in the management hierarchy. Certainly, you do see managers that stay around a long time, but it is a zone where you tend to get hit in many restructures; just something to think about. The good thing is that many companies now recognise that you can be a *leader* without being a people manager, and that can be very rewarding. In the end, leaders aren't appointed; they are leaders because they exhibit a vision and behaviour that people want to follow.

Ultimately, whatever approach you take, it still comes down to the business and the value technology brings to that. Remember that technology is defined by Britannica as "the *application* of scientific knowledge to the *practical aims of human life* or, as it is sometimes phrased, to the change and manipulation of the human environment". It is not about the technology.

CHAPTER 23

SPOTTING A NON-STRATEGIC STRATEGY

"The essence of strategy is choosing what not to do."
Michael E. Porter

What is strategy? This might be an odd sounding question, yet like other common concepts, it is something we all know the meaning of until we must give a clear explanation of it. Take a moment to define how you would explain what strategy is to someone who didn't just know. I have felt uncomfortable about what gets called strategy for many years now, not only in technology (including some of my own past strategy work) but also in corporate strategy overall. I have come to understand that a good technology strategy needs to be aligned tightly with a good corporate strategy. If the corporate strategy is poorly defined, then we are on the back foot to start with.

The entire strategic context has changed since the rise of the internet, mobile, GPS, platform business models, digital B2B models, data leverage, and A.I. or at least machine learning. Today, there are very few companies, governments, or other organisations where technology isn't simply a fundamental part of *good* business strategy. However, for it to be a good strategy, it must go beyond trendy soundbites and regurgitated industry cliches. It must be highly targeted, resource-constrained, action-based, and solve the most pressing challenges or take the most valuable opportunities where the company has an advantage that it can *leverage*.

A McKinsey email recommending must-read books gave me a breadcrumb to follow when it recommended *Good Strategy Bad Strategy* by Richard Rumelt. Richard, who was described in a 2007 McKinsey article as being "Strategy's strategist", is an uncompromising master at calling out bad strategy with some great quotable soundbites such as "many bad strategies are just statements of desire rather than plans for overcoming obstacles."

This chapter is not about describing how to *do* strategy, either business or technology, but rather it what even is strategy. I even think of it as differentiation, an actual strategy from something called a strategy that just isn't. This can include many technology strategies that simply give background information, perhaps with an ideal target or unconstrained roadmap, but don't address the hard problems of how to do it in the real business context. I can't cover *doing* strategy in just one chapter; there are some good resources for strategy available now via learning platforms like Udemy, EDX, LinkedIn Learning, and Coursera. For example, Udemy has Management Consulting Essential Training, MBA in a Box, and on EDX, Oxford Executive Strategy Programme, Digital Transformation Strategy (Yale) etc. In these courses, you will get an overview of leading methodologies and tools such as Porter's Five Forces, SWOT, PESTEL and others. Just be mindful that tools and methods help, but ultimately, there is no magic method to get a unique winning strategy. That is the point of competition. Imagine buying a guaranteed Football World Cup-winning strategy from a consultant; I hope they don't sell that to two aspiring teams!

In the end you can learn some concepts, but you'll learn a lot more when you just start doing it. If you can get to work with some fantastic strategic thinkers, as I have been lucky enough to, then you will learn much from them; pay attention and ask questions. Be respectful always.

Finally, be aware that, as with the business case game, strategy development operates at multiple levels. Getting acceptance of your strategy, or strategic advice, is one thing; being able to execute it is a separate issue, and then having the strategy actually work is another thing altogether. Also, recall the lesson from the *Bhagavad Gita*: you can only do the right actions, you cannot control all factors, so you cannot guarantee the outcome. Luckily, most companies tend to declare strategies successful or politely pivot and hope nobody asks about it.

Not a strategy

> "At the core, strategy is about focus, and most complex
> organizations don't focus their resources. Instead, they
> pursue multiple goals at once, not concentrating enough
> resources to achieve a breakthrough in any of them."
>
> *Richard P. Rumelt, Good Strategy Bad Strategy*

I do highly recommend reading Richard Rumelt's book Good Strategy Bad Strategy, and his follow-up The Crux, the former focusing *brutally*, and *amusingly*, on what is *bad* strategy along with defining good strategy. The later book has some good guidance on getting to the *crux* of the problem or opportunity to evolve the strategy. You can also find some good presentations from him on YouTube, and appearances on podcasts. Now for me, I tend to differentiate things into three categories: *good* strategy, *bad* strategy, and *non*-strategy being called strategy.

Richard identifies four hallmarks of a bad strategy, and if one or more are present, then be suspicious.

First is fluffy language. So, buzzwords or cliches would for us be an example, perhaps having phrases like *best-in-class* or one of my pet hates being the so-called *best practice*, along with any suggestion of an *out-of-the-box* implementation strategy, unless, of course, it is a coffee table from IKEA.

Next, Richard calls out failure to identify and face the real key problem. You must have a clear challenge to achieve or an obstacle to overcome. From my viewpoint, particularly with technology strategy, I'd say we are often identifying problems for us in technology but not very clearly showing why it is a top business problem, meaning in a way that the strategy would clearly solve a problem that the business cares about, and in a timeframe that matters to them. For example, the complexity of technology systems is often called out as a problem, challenge, or constraint. This might be true, but we need to be clear about exactly how this causes a real pressing problem for the business and why it is the most urgent problem for *them* to solve because resources are limited and there is much they need to do. We also need to be clear on specifically how and when our strategy will solve this problem.

Third, Richard identifies what is probably the most common hallmark of bad strategy, or non-strategy, we see in our businesses, which is defining goals and calling them a strategy. For us, an example might be an insurance company saying their strategy is to grow by 250 thousand customers and 500 thousand policies while reducing their expense ratio to 22% from 25%; these are goals and not strategy as they don't indicate how these outcomes will be achieved, and what the trade-offs are. It is just stating wishes. This would be like the coach of a Rugby team going into the World Cup Final saying his strategy is to win the game, which is a wish or hope. He might clarify this statement by saying that his strategy is to score more points than the opponent team, which is only restating to *win the game*.

Related to this we can include strategic objectives which are unclear, don't solve a real problem, or are just impractical. For example, a motorcycle manufacturer might have a strategy to become the leading truck manufacturer by the end of the decade by leveraging their motorcycle manufacturing expertise and supply chain economics. The expertise from designing and building trucks would seem very different than it would be for motorcycles, and even if they could figure it out, it seems unlikely customers would be keen on buying trucks from such a company. So, this doesn't really make logical sense.

In addition, the need to focus energy is key, so having too many goals and too many actions defined in a strategy is not going to work. Even if you pick good goals and sound actions to achieve them, if you just spread your focus too wide, you are unlikely to execute well. This is a common problem for governments who need to promise too much to all the various special interests they need support from to get elected.

A good strategy story

> "The most basic idea of strategy is the application of
> strength against weakness. Or, if you prefer, strength
> applied to the most promising opportunity."

> *Richard P. Rumelt, Good Strategy/Bad Strategy*

Good strategy is all about focus. Specific targeted actions, applying leverage where you have a potential advantage to achieve a defined strategic outcome, and giving up some things you would like to do or have because you understand you cannot do or have everything.

Strategy is often about choices, and I don't mean choosing between a new BMW or a Tesla but choosing between a new BMW or a second-hand Toyota, so you also have a deposit for a house; you are giving something up to achieve an important outcome. A nice clear example of this can be found in the sporting world.

On February 13, 2022, one of the greatest strategic gambles in sporting history paid off when the LA Rams won Super Bowl LVI. The Rams had moved from St Louis, Missouri, to the much warmer Los Angeles in 2016. The Rams had previously been based in LA for almost half a century (1946-94) until poor performance, an outdated stadium, and waning crowds motivated them to move to Missouri. Super Bowl LVI was played at the spectacular new 5-billion-dollar SoFi Stadium, which had tempted the Rams back to LA (along with tempting the Chargers there from San Diego). In the second season, the SoFi Stadium was open; it was the location for the season 2021 final, and the Rams desperately wanted to win it all; they wanted to win their division, the NFC West, their conference, the NFC, and the NFL title, the Superbowl. That was the objective, and they were prepared to go all in to achieve it.

The key to understanding the Ram's strategy is understanding the draft system and salary cap in the NFL, which is the top American Football competition and culminates in the Superbowl. As with everything in the NFL, it is complex and nuanced, but basically, there is a limit on how much each NFL team can spend on players, and this is to try to keep the game more competitive, meaning that as teams have more success, they have to pay their talent more, and therefore due to salary cap restrictions some of that top talent will go to teams that can pay higher because they have fewer top players already.

There are three main ways to acquire players with the main one being the NFL draft, where top talent from College Football can be drafted by teams. There are seven rounds, and teams normally get to pick one player per round. Importantly, the lowest ranking teams pick first to give them a chance to improve, and even more importantly, for this strategy, you can trade draft picks in future years and cash to acquire players from other teams, which is the second way to get new players. Finally, there are free agents, which are players that are off contract that teams can pick up.

The basic strategy for the LA Rams to win Super Bowl LVI was to go all-in for one big season. They targeted the 2021 NFL season with the Superbowl in their new stadium on 13 February 2022 and were prepared to accept the following years would be much tougher. They targeted proven veteran players and traded early-round draft picks to teams to get them. This included Mathew Stafford, Von Miller, and an important cameo by Odel Beckham Jr. There was some sound logic because picking stars from college football often doesn't pay off in the more intense NFL. They did have a good base of home-grown top talent like Cooper Kupp and Aaron Donald to blend the acquired veteran talent with, along with a few rookies. The Rams accepted they'd get good players, but they'd not get them for long. The strategy was to try and *peak* in *all phases* of the game at the same time: offence, defence, and special teams. Getting a top-running game and passing game at the same time is hard to do under the salary cap. They really had *one* shot.

The biggest bet was trading their star franchise quarterback, Jared Goff, who had taken them to the Super Bowl in the 2018 season but lost to some chap called Tom Brady. In the following years, the team didn't gel, and the Rams traded Goff for veteran Detroit Lions quarterback Matthew Stafford, for whom they had to throw in a valuable first-round pick in 2022 and 2023 to Detroit as well as a third-round pick in 2021. Goff has since had huge success at the Detroit Lions, largely motivated by a massive chip on his shoulder. Sometimes, you have great pieces, but they just don't quite fit, which needs a strategic change. Identifying that was a masterstroke for the LA Rams. Trading for the veteran Matthew Stafford, they knew he would be able to quickly build cohesion and lead the stitched-together collection of veterans, existing players, and rookies. It was a bit like The Expendables 2, with Stallone, Schwarzenegger, Van Damme, Willis, Lundgren, and Norris.

To be fair there are many teams that have tried a similar all-in strategy over the years, and it hasn't paid off. The LA Rams did this in a balanced way and executed it very well. In competitive areas like football, like in business it is a competition, and no strategy is a guarantee, but you can give yourself a good shot.

Beyond just winning the Superbowl and winning it in their brand-new home stadium, their longer-term strategy was to build a very loyal and committed fan base in LA that would be a foundation for decades. The loyal fans do indeed seem to be accepting a couple of lean years since then.

In Richard Rumelt's view, the kernel of a good strategy has 3 elements, which are: a diagnosis of the challenge (we can't afford to have top talent in all positions), a guiding policy, which I'd call a strategic approach for dealing with the challenge (go all in on one big season), and a set of coherent actions to carry out the policy (trading draft picks for proven talent). Importantly, the outcome was also very clear, being that they aimed at winning the Superbowl in their new stadium, so it was do or die; there was no option for partial success. I think the 2021 LA Rams got this right, and with some luck at times (e.g. few injuries, so not exposing depth weaknesses), the Rams did win it all. Don't underestimate chance; the lesson from the Bhagavad Gita.

Technology strategy

> "A hallmark of true expertise and insight is making
> a complex subject understandable. A hallmark of
> mediocrity and bad strategy is unnecessary complexity—a
> flurry of fluff masking an absence of substance."
>
> *Richard Rumelt, Good Strategy Bad Strategy*

All the above regarding good and bad strategy applies to technology strategy. That said, any technology strategy must be part of, complement, or execute actions of an overall business strategy. I cannot think of any reason you would *only* have a technology strategy; even if you are doing it for a technology company, it is still a company, and it does not exist in a financial vacuum.

I can imagine situations where you don't need a stand-alone technology strategy, which is not to say there are not strategically aligned technology actions; you just might not need to make it a big, separate thing. There is an interesting relationship between technology strategy and the definition of a technology target state or roadmap. I see a lot of target states and roadmaps created without clear and tight linkage to business strategy. I see a lot of target states and roadmaps created in an unconstrained manner, where it is a theoretical ideal but not aligned with investment appetite or overall financial reality for the company. It might be intellectually fun, but I don't see the point in doing these. More about this in a later chapter called *The Nature of Target State Architectures.*

An example of the type of business strategy-aligned technology problem that insurance companies have faced in recent decades is increasing their digital capability while managing risk and reducing the total cost of ownership of ageing legacy core insurance systems. It is a tough balancing act. There have been similar problems for banks.

Thinking about Richard Rumelt's kernel of a good strategy, it is often deemed clear what the diagnosis of the above challenge is. However, I'd caution against jumping too quickly to any conclusions. We need proper analysis of the technology and business challenges to ensure we clearly understand the real problem for the business. The problem is *not* that we need to replace core systems; that might or might not be the approach to solve the problem, but the shareholders, customers, and other stakeholders don't really care what the underlying core systems are.

The guiding approach for dealing with the challenge is crucial to get right. So, for our ageing legacy core systems, remember the earlier chapter with the story about the container full of frozen mackerel; sometimes, the most sensible approach really is to kick the can down the road. Also, there could be an approach that can allow you to bleed the asset for longer. Core systems are not like old Toyotas; you don't get to trade them in and get some value back, so bleed the assets for as long as it makes sense; just be careful about the total cost of keeping it, including risk and opportunity costs. Therefore, your approach might be to defer, with some uplift, or to replace the core system. If you are going to replace it, you might go for a full replacement or incremental replacement using something like a strangler pattern to shrink it incrementally over time. Replacing a system is sexy, but consider carefully how much capability you are uplifting verses just replacing and what the value of that uplift is to the business. I'd estimate that most insurance core system replacements involve replacing 80% or more of functionality that works well enough already, such as the policy lifecycle functions like renewal processing. Even with the 20% that doesn't work well the approach is often to implement like-for-like with uplift to happen later. Alternatively, an approach some banks use is to decouple their legacy core, if that core is stable, from their digital layer, sometimes with fully asynchronous data decoupling patterns. This is very complex, but if done well can greatly improve digital capabilities while not involving a risky core replacement. All these approaches can be appropriate in various situations. Make sure you understand the problem carefully, from a business perspective, and be honest about what approaches might work. Above all, don't believe your own propaganda as, in the end, your company will wear the impact.

And finally, a set of coherent actions to carry out the chosen strategic approach. This gets very nuanced, depending on the situation. I do often see a large gap between the problem definition, the overall policy or approach, and the specific actions that get defined. Care must be taken to ensure there is tight, logical cohesion between these. If the approach is to replace the core, then actions might be to select a package or compare that to a build-your-own approach. If you are going with a strangler pattern, then it might make sense to go with a more modular approach like microservices. The key is to ensure that all these choices are coherent. Don't forget to look beyond the technology and patterns and consider your expertise as well. You might need to re-train people and perhaps mix it with new hires; remember, the LA Rams brought in proven veterans. If you are doing a decoupled pattern, then you really need to try to blend in some old war horses that have some scars from previous implementations. If you are going with an event-driven architecture or event streaming, then start slowly with low-risk areas and not with the most important areas first. Be realistic.

Finally, my pet-hate: if you are providing strategic options for leadership do not put forward an option that they cannot realistically pick. If you look at an approach that is not viable, call it a discarded approach and explain why. In the last few years, I've started relying on MECE pyramids to frame up possible approaches and discard approaches based on feasibility, desirability, and viability. MECE is a great tool for the toolkit from the management consulting world and something you should explore yourself. It works very well for communicating to the executive level as it shows them your logical thinking and makes it easy for them to be confident you haven't missed anything, or importantly communicating to you something else you should consider. Call what you triage out discarded approaches rather than calling them options. Do not call them options until they can be selected. You know what it is like when you go to a restaurant and pick the baked cheesecake for dessert, only to be told they don't have it available. Why was it an option to pick?

CHAPTER 24

NOT FORCING

"Paradoxical as it may seem, the purposeful life has
no content, no point. It hurries on and on, and misses
everything. Not hurrying, the purposeless life misses
nothing, for it is only when there is no goal and no
rush that the human senses are fully open to receive the
world."

Alan Watts

How much energy do we spend as strategists and architects, getting
frustrated about our strategies and roadmaps not being approved, funded,
and implemented as we know they ought to be? If you find yourself
behaving more like a salesman than a trusted adviser, then perhaps a
famous ancient Chinese philosophical text called the *Tao Te Ching*, written
by Lao Tzu 2500 years ago and an approach called Wu Wei, can help.

Does forcing work?

"A good traveler has no fixed plans and is not intent on
arriving."
Lao Tzu

We are *conditioned* in most Western cultures to believe we ought to *force* the desired result. We should define the desired outcome and force things to align with that. Willpower! Brute force! How else do things get done?

As strategists and architects, we often look at the corporate strategy the current state technology, and then conclude what logically must be implemented to obtain the desired outcome; we then state factually what initiatives need to be funded and executed. It all seems very logical. But it seldom seems to get the required support, and we have always been prone to the charge that we are idealistic and unrealistic. We tend to blame the company for this, while the company views us as being out of touch with commercial reality. More than anything else this disconnect contributes to our ivory tower reputation.

Perhaps this is because many of the strategies are *populist* in nature! "Are those your new clubs? Nice! Hey, have you got the AI yet? We're doing the AI, have got to, can't afford to get left behind!". Often, these strategies are what the business thinks they should talk about, but not ultimately what the business has an appetite to really commit to when the cost and implications are made clear. Maybe our company wants to become customer-focused, as is the trend, and a good trend, and therefore, logically, we need to understand the customer, which could mean executing on CRM and even customer master data management; expensive, difficult, hard to comprehend, and therefore not something business leaders want to prioritize just now. This all makes sense.

So, what is Wu Wei? Who is Lao Tzu? And what has this to do with strategy and architecture? Well, you might not have heard the name Lao Tzu but you would have heard some of his insights.

> "The journey of a thousand miles begins with a single step."
>
> *Lao Tzu*

Lao Tzu and the Tao Te Ching

The *Tao Te Ching* – pronounced "Dao De Ching" – is believed to have been written by Lao Tzu in China around 600 BC (published 200 years later) and is one of the most popular texts in Eastern philosophy. It is the central text of Taoism, and heavily influences Confucianism and Zen Buddhism. Goodreads shows over 1400 editions of this very popular text.

The title translates very roughly as "the way of integrity". In its 81 verses, it provides a treatise on how to live in the world with goodness and integrity. Lao Tzu translates to something like "Old Master", and there is much debate about this figure being a real person or a personification created to explain the ideas of one or more other philosophers. There are similar debates about Socrates, and they both were supposed to exist around the same time. There are many quotes that originated with Lao Tzu, and many have been later reattributed.

> "Those who know do not speak. Those who speak do not know."
>
> *Lao Tzu, Tao Te Ching*

Wu Wei

Central to the concepts in the Tao Te Ching is something referred to as Wu Wei, which literally means *non-action* or *non-doing*. It is probably easiest to understand in terms of many martial arts where the central theme is to go with the energy and direct it as desired rather than going against the energy in a toe-to-toe slugfest. In the Tao Te Ching, this theme is connected to the natural world and how the world naturally works to get things done.

Wu Wei is related to flow, or effortless flow, which in sporting terms could be when we are *in the zone*, with full conviction and concentration. Some of the most successful companies do seem to be *in the zone*, with almost effortless action. All of this is of course, much easier in an authentic purpose led company, with that purpose providing the direction of flow. According to Lao Tzu we ought to seek to respond to the true demand of the situation, which can only be done if we are quiet enough to really listen.

The key example cited by Lao Tzu relates to waters ability to, over time, erode and shape solid rock. Water has properties beyond simply patience and persistence; it is also flexible, moving without concerns into lower places and small crevasses. It finds any position without judgment or preference.

> "Water is fluid, soft & yielding, but water will wear away
> rock, which is rigid and cannot yield … what is soft is
> strong."
>
> *Lao Tzu, Tao Te Ching*

Effortless action in strategy and architecture

As strategists and architects we must make decisions about what we will pursue for the benefit of the entity we are working for. We seek to determine the *best action*, which implies the *best action* that will *actually work* and achieve the *desired outcome*. Often, we will look at various professional resources or industry stories of successful implementations of a strategy or architecture. However, we are quite prone to underestimating sample size and context. Do we understand how often this has not worked? For whatever reason ("it was the right idea, but the stakeholders lacked vision")? Perhaps we don't fully appreciate the unique context which allowed success for others.

We could choose to allow quality space for thinking about strategies that ought to be pursued when the conditions are right so we are prepared to recognize and take opportunities that arise. Not locking in and getting caught up in these strategies or specific timelines for execution. The conditions will present themselves if we are prepared.

> "Writing is good, thinking is better. Being smart is good,
> being patient is better."
> *Hermann Hesse, Siddhartha*

We can take the time to listen deeply to the energy and flow of the company and consider what truly is the current condition, including what is just rhetoric and what there is really an appetite and commitment to follow through on. For example, recent high-profile data breaches get the attention of Boards and CEOs and provide good conditions for pursuing long-stalled data classification strategies; often, when a threat is perceived, people's bias to act comes into play, and if you have a well-prepared business case and plan on the shelf ready to refine and move forward then this can become the path of least resistance, allowing you to leverage the flow and energy of the company rather than fighting against it.

We can consider not only the existing conditions but also what might be able to be done to make it more likely for favourable conditions to arise. Now, to the prior paragraph, I'm not suggesting we out hacking other companies to panic our boards; seriously, though, don't act in an inappropriate way that causes harm to get any advantage. Quite an effective way to make favourable conditions more likely to arise is to create a repeatable narrative that aligns with the desired direction. Perhaps we connect businesspeople to stories that resonate with them and naturally lead to the desired path. At many companies, this is a powerful approach, and the feeling when you hear your narratives coming back to you from leadership is very special. You need to resist any claim of ownership of the narrative; it is not about your ego; it is about being effective and doing the right thing for your company.

We can also temper some of our expectations and use our skills to find other pathways. Some of our desired approaches, like core system replacements, will always be hard sells, and it may be more a matter of considering other less aggressive strategies, such as strangler patterns mixed with microservice implementations or whatever else might make sense.

We do, above all, need to always act with integrity and authenticity for the good of all stakeholders. Intentions matter. We ought not manipulate situations for personal advantage.

Think back to some of the most frustrating situations in your career as a strategist or architect where you went toe-to-toe pushing for what you thought was the right thing to do, but you could not gain the support for what you thought logically ought to be done. Do you think it might have been your approach in the situation that could have been unskilful? Could Lao Tzu's advice help you see things differently?

> "In the summer of 1998, I got an opportunity to talk with [Steve] Jobs again. I said, "Steve, this turnaround at Apple has been impressive. But everything we know about the PC business says that Apple cannot really push beyond a small niche position. The network effects are just too strong to upset the Wintel standard. So, what are you trying to do in the longer term? What is the strategy?" He did not attack my argument. He didn't agree with it, either. He just smiled and said, 'I am going to wait for the next big thing.'"

> *Richard P. Rumelt, Good Strategy Bad Strategy: The Difference and Why It Matters*

CHAPTER 25

THE NATURE OF TARGET STATE ARCHITECTURES

"Nature does not hurry, yet everything is accomplished."
Lao Tzu, Tao Te Ching

As strategists and architects, we talk a lot about the mythical *target state*, or even more elusive *strategic* target state, which is odd because a strategy is *action*-orientated and a state is, well, a *state*. Anyway, do we ever get to this *target state*, and would we want to be there if we did? Nature can teach us much about how we ought to think about the *target state*. We returned above to the ancient Chinese philosophical text called the *Tao Te Ching*, written by Lao Tzu 2500 years ago for one of its most profoundly deep quotes: "*Nature does not hurry, yet everything is accomplished.*"

I wrote about one reading of this quote in the previous chapter about not forcing. Wu Wei is related to flow or effortless flow. This reading of the quote is about not forcing and not hurrying, and for a long time, I thought that was the whole point of the quote. However, part of Lao Tzu's enduring genius is that he liked to focus on multiple layers of meaning in simple statements, and you could continue to unpack them carefully over long periods of time and lately, I've been thinking about the second half of the quote "… everything is accomplished". This part is doing a lot in the quote. What is this *everything*? Is *everything* the target, or in our terms, the *target state*? No. That is not the correct understanding.

Evolution to target

So, let's consider the *evolution* of the Giraffe. Was there an explicit or implicit *target state*? Just set assign the idea of a designer and consider if there was a *correct* way the Giraffe had to end up being. OK, we've all heard about the Giraffe evolving to reach the high leaves of trees in Africa, but there are a whole lot of trees around the world, and only the Giraffe is, well, *Giraffe-like*. If you think about it, the Giraffe is a strange-looking thing.

We are told, and it seems reasonable, that evolution is driven by environmental adaptation. Does this explain the Giraffe? Is the Giraffe now at *target state*, or does it, like all living things, continue to adapt and evolve? If so, what is it adapting and evolving to? Apparently, the Giraffe evolved about 7.5 million years ago, and like all living things, it is still in a *transitional state*, so that is a long roadmap, even by large corporation standards. I want to see the cost vs benefit analysis and assumptions made during the business case for the Giraffe.

> "Nature does not make mistakes. Right and wrong are
> human categories."
> *Frank Herbert Jr. (Author of Dune)*

The errors of nature

Does nature make mistakes? I'm inclined to align with Frank Herbert Jr's view that right and wrong are human constructions and that nature just does its thing without judgment. The same natural process that created the Giraffe created the Bat, the Shark, and Tick. What principles was its Architectural Review Board using when it endorsed all these designs?

However, we do understand that the basic principles of evolution and adaptive design are based on gene mutations that are carried forward due to adaptive advantage. Effectively, nature is running a series of experiments and selecting the most advantageous adaptations to carry forward and, therefore, build on for the next generation. The direction things end up going is somewhat random with regard to what adaptations can rise to the surface.

So, the concept of a *target state* in nature is not relevant because species don't stop evolving and, therefore, don't reach a target, and steps forward have their origin in randomness.

What if Lao Tzu was a technology architect

I'm not so sure that Lao Tzu would tackle technology architecture even if he walked the earth today, but I'm fairly sure he'd smile about our ideas around target architectures and roadmaps. What are your experiences and observations on target architectures and roadmaps in the real world? How often have you seen a strategic target state (not just a program one) come to fruition at a large complex organisation? How many roadmaps worked out the way they were envisioned? There are always a lot of things to blame for this, like funding, lack of understanding, inadequate support from above (or below), poor execution etc. But perhaps Lao Tzu would say that it is because roadmaps are self-deceptions, and the target state is a mirage.

Can evolutionary architecture help us?

Our architectures evolve due to both business drivers and technology drivers and typically well before we arrive at any target state. We are expected to know what is needed in 3-5 years' time, but we cannot possibly know this from an epistemological viewpoint i.e. a justified – true belief.

There are emerging concepts like *evolutionary architecture* that have got some attention in recent years. Let's face it, our enterprise architectures will evolve and in ways we cannot anticipate. So, leveraging the principles of evolutionary architecture might makes sense, but I think of the concept as a *countermeasure* to what will happen while we are drawing visionary diagrams. We don't *do* evolutionary architecture, as that will happen regardless, but we are using the concept called evolutionary architecture as a measure to response to or counter any adverse impacts.

An evolvable architecture supports guided incremental change across multiple dimensions. In *Building Evolutionary Architectures* by Rebecca Parsons, Neal Ford and Patrick Kua, who evolve out of the ThoughtWorks stable, they state that the first principle of evolutionary architecture is to enable incremental change in architecture over time. This makes a lot of sense, and it aligns with the whole concept of DNA and its ability to adapt. They define evolvability as an additional 'ility to all the usual nonfunctional abilities like scalability and maintainability. Evolvability is defined in Wikipedia as "the capacity of a system for [exhibiting] adaptive evolution".

The authors leverage something they call *fitness functions*, which is a term used in genetic programming and genetic algorithms to guide simulations towards optimal design solutions. These fitness functions are intended to evaluate how well the solution fits the various 'ilities; which is to say, the characteristics of the architecture. Preferably, these are automatically executed (e.g. coded in Java), but in some cases, they could be manual or semi-automated. A nice example they talk about is a legal department needing to know if open-source licences have changed, and the company is writing a fitness function that is hashing the licence files and comparing them to detect a change to the file. Another example might be checking that software versions are upgraded as necessary. These are intended to be implemented within a CI/CD pipeline, which is key to an evolvable architecture.

Fitness functions have a couple of effects on architects, firstly architects need to be specific about defining 'illities that can be deterministically tested, and secondly, architects have more time to focus on the issues where their skills are most valuable to the organisation, such as ensuring we preserve optionality, which if you think about it is the ability to evolve. So, there is work in defining these fitness functions, but unlike our mostly ignored standards, these functions, particularly if automated, are really used and benefit the organisation. These become new guardrails and inherently focus more on outcomes than implementations, giving teams more freedom to make decisions closer to the real place of work.

Under this concept, the target would become a combination of the fitness functions and platform/modular boundaries, using the most appropriate technologies at the time. This is particularly well suited to PaaS and FaaS based micro-service implementations while still being applicable to other styles. Often, people ask about COTS (commercial of the shelf) packages, and in this case, the focus is more on the integration points, fitness functions, and making the package work with CI/CD pipelines. From my personal observation we often see packages having certain key capabilities we want, then other functionality that is more there as a presales *filler*, and we need to take care about leveraging these. I tend to favour applying the strangler pattern to COTS packages from the first implementation or soon after by swapping out generic functionality to specific where it is important to the business.

Your architecture will evolve, and although it is far from certain that the concept of evolutionary architecture has solved it, you need to determine some practical way to managed it beyond just ignoring it or hoping. Hope is not a strategy.

Onward to target

So you will get to a target of a sort, but it likely won't be the one you expected it to be. Nevermind. Just make sure that whatever the target is it has evolved to a point that supports the business evolution. The best possible architecture under the conditions as they are, and anyway, it isn't really the target state; it is still evolving.

CHAPTER 26

LEARNING FROM ENGINEERING

DISASTERS

"Those who ignore the lesson of the past, will be
doomed to repeat it."
George Santayana (using the paraphrasing of a 1941
columnist in The Union-Banner)

Do you regularly fly on commercial aircraft? Is it for work, or for leisure, or perhaps to visit relatives. Does the safety of flying worry you?

There are a lot of people who do worry about flying, but most people know that driving to the airport is a higher risk than flying on a plane; that said knowing it and feeling it is not the same thing. However, this safety was hard won and was based on learning from many air disasters or significant incidents. The search for root causes and iterative improvements is relentless, with large investments made in investigations. To put this in context, there have been 52 hull loss accidents with the massively popular Boeing 747 since 1969 (over 1500 built), with the DC 10 having 33 hull losses since 1971 (over 440 built), and the modern Airbus A320 workhorse having 41 hull losses since 1987 (over 11,000 built). Each and every one of those were extensively, and often controversially, investigated. The current high level of safety with aircraft like the newer A320 is based on painful experience, extensive investigation, and careful implementation of improvements to people, processes, and technology.

If your executives are flying to a workshop to discuss the kick-off of a major strategic technology program, are they more worried about the plane crashing, or the program being a disaster and damaging the company or if they are sponsors, damaging their professional credibility? There are strategic risks around the program being the right thing to do in the way it is envisioned, delivery risks on the ability to deliver it on time and on budget, and operational risks on what will be delivered in the end.

When you jump on a plane, at least you have confidence that the pilots, ground staff, air traffic controllers, and even the other passengers are all trying to get to the same place and want the trip to be successful. Unlike on a project, when you and your wife or husband board a plane to go on holiday, your wife or husband isn't sitting next to you hoping the plane will crash on the way to Berlin, so you will have to admit that the two of you should have picked Hawaii for your holiday like they said.

Lessons from documentaries

There are several documentaries I regularly enjoy when I'm chilling out on the couch. *Abandoned Engineering* (History Channel) is compelling because it reminds us that constructions are new and innovative at one time and become old and irrelevant for a variety of reasons, and often over unforeseeable timelines; my absolute favourite episode was on the Cold War era Caspian Sea Monster (look it up on Youtube).

I also like *Air Crash Investigation* (called *Mayday* in some countries), along with *Seconds from Disaster*. All three shows are entertaining; I can relax without having to think too hard. However, I can still passively learn facts, which I can use to become even more annoying while getting some inspiration on how to analyse causation and risk.

Often, there is death and injury in these programs. So, am I some kind of sadist who likes seeing human misery? No. What I like is the exact opposite. These shows tend to follow a specific formula, particularly Air Crash Investigation and Seconds from Disaster. They start with the very basics of the story and the impact on humans, often bodily harm, but sometimes only financial loss. Then, they go through the timeline of what happened in detail. What was the factual flow of events? Next is the investigation into the root cause and contributing factors, which normally includes politics and drama to get to the truth. Finally, there are the learnings to avoid the situation occurring going forward. How engineering as a discipline gets better has always been a continuous improvement cycle.

If we think of building architecture and wider design and engineering, for example, with aircraft, then the disciplines have matured through a lot of accidents, disasters, and even just subpar outcomes e.g. an inefficient distribution centre design.

When we consider technology strategy and architecture, thankfully, we don't often see a large loss of life when things go wrong. There are exceptions to this, of course. There can be simple bugs like patients not getting system-generated appointments that have significant impacts on individuals, and there have been some high-profile cases. And there can, of course, be real harm done to companies, which can have some serious flow-on effects on people, but we don't tend to end up in the headlines in the way that direct human tragedy does. However, this is a double-edged sword. We don't tend to get the high-profile scrutiny and blame game, with potentially large direct or indirect penalties, but we also don't get the baked-in continuous improvement feedback loop. In some organisations, there is a *feedback loop*, but mostly, these tend to be perfunctory, if they happen at all. Either that or some type of political bloodbath. Either way, not a whole lot of learning going on.

There are many well-known engineering, procedural, or human-based disasters, like the Crash of the Concorde, Space Shuttle Columbia, TWA Flight 800, Titanic, and many others that we'd be familiar with. The nuclear meltdown in Chornobyl was a particularly interesting one, and the book *Midnight in Chernobyl* is well worth a read to understand systemic human failure on a global scale. However, as an example, I've picked a less-known disaster, particularly outside the US, which has many of the common factors explored in *Seconds from Disaster*.

The Hyatt Regency Skywalk Collapse

The 1981 Hyatt Regency collapse was the deadliest structural collapse in the United States at that time. Around 1,600 people gathered for a dance in the atrium of the Hyatt Regency in Kansas City on Friday, July 17, 1981. The recently opened hotel had innovative glass skywalks, which were unusual at the time. At about 7:05 p.m. guests heard popping noises, and moments later, the fourth-floor walkway fell onto the second-floor walkway, and 65 tons of steel and glass then fell onto the crowded lobby. Ultimately, 114 people died, and another 216 people were injured.

This disaster caused a media storm. During the multiple extensive investigations' significant changes to the original design of the walkways were identified. The final report cited structural overload resulting from design flaws where the walkways could barely hold their own weight, let alone the crowd of people that were on them. The walkways were suspended from steel hanger rods. At the root of the causes were both flawed initial designs and changes to the design of the walkway's steel hanger rods, which ultimately led to the failure. The original design specified three pairs of rods running from the second-floor walkway to the ceiling, passing through the beams of the fourth-floor walkway, with a nut at the middle of each tie rod tightened up to the bottom of the fourth-floor walkway, and a nut at the bottom of each tie rod tightened up to the bottom of the second-floor walkway.

A design change intended to reduce damage during construction proposed that two separate and offset sets of rods be used: the first set suspending the fourth-floor walkway from the ceiling, and the second set suspending the second-floor walkway from the fourth-floor walkway. This design change would be fatal. In the original design, the beams of the fourth-floor walkway had to support only the weight of the fourth-floor walkway, with the weight of the second-floor walkway supported completely by separate rods. In the revised design, however, the fourth-floor beams supported both the fourth- and second-floor walkways but were only strong enough for 30% of that load. There were other compounding factors.

Investigators concluded that the underlying problem was a lack of proper communication between the architects, engineers, and manufacturers; sound familiar? Manufacturers were working off early designs, not knowing they were not the final approved designs. Processes for changes and approvals were either inadequate or not followed. There was disagreement about who was responsible for doing the crucial calculations to ensure structural safety. Finally, some issues that had been noticed by construction workers had not been adequately followed up.

Lawsuits sought a total of $3 billion of damages, equivalent to $9.66 billion in 2022. However, in the end, only $140 million, equivalent to $451 million in 2022, was eventually awarded to victims and their families.

Paul Munger, chairman of the Missouri Architectural Board, stated that "[The design] is one of the worst examples of people trying to push off their responsibilities to other parts of the team ... Since the Hyatt, there has been a lot of activity in the engineering profession to address quality, the final product and how you attain quality". The American Society of Civil Engineers now has a policy that structural engineers are ultimately responsible for reviewing shop designs by fabricators.

Implications for Strategy and Architecture

Have you been to a post-implementation review of a significant project, a project that perhaps didn't go so well? If you have, did it seem to get the attention we see in civil engineering reviews after significant problems have occurred? There are several factors in the engineering reviews of the type discussed in the Hyatt Skywalk collapse that could be useful.

First, identifying something happened. In the case of engineering, it often becomes clear that something has happened because it is highly visible, particularly if there has been loss of life or major disruptions to public services.

With technology programs that go wrong it is often possible for people, motivated to change the optics, to find ways to obscure the real situation.

The people motivated to do this can include a very broad range of stakeholders, from business sponsors to technology leaders, delivery partners, architects, and even delivery teams on the ground. Often, programs just continue to completion with mediocre or poor outcomes declaring the project a success if timelines and budgets are achieved, regardless of the real business impact. Sometimes, this is achieved by descoping the of the original business case; phase two, anyone? However, these subpar outcomes do lead to a significant erosion of confidence in technology delivery.

This point can be well made by paraphrasing Ronald Regan's famous quote that the 9 scariest words that businesspeople can hear is: *I'm from corporate technology, and I'm here to help.* To start to turn this around, we need to begin by being open and honest about identifying when things have gone wrong or not as right as they should have.

Second is determining the root causes and contributing factors. Once we have something we want to investigate we need to methodically look for the root causes of problems, which often can start back at the business case, but can be anywhere through the process. Our delivery maturity as a relatively young industry is such that there will often be issues right the way through the process. We are particularly interested here in architectural design issues, but the pressures that lead to those issues may well be earlier in the process.

The issues might be post-architecture and more around the implementation of the design. It could be due to inappropriate or flawed external technology. It could even be a mismatch between the sophistication of the design and the ability to execute, such as trying to implement CQRS patterns for the first time in large complex programs with no real-world experience in the delivery teams with using the pattern.

It is normal for people at all levels to want to avoid being blamed for issues they caused and for things they didn't. We need to foster a culture where we want to learn from failure more than we want to avoid blame. To be fair it is unlikely that this is common in structural engineering or many other disciplines either, so it must be *baked into the system*.

Third we need to learn from mistakes and use them as an opportunity to continually improve processes, standards, principles, governance, patterns, education and more. If we cover off the first two steps, we can take a bit of a breather in step 3, where we take the learnings and try to make improvements. Although this is hopefully easier, it is unlikely to be pain-free. It takes time to define and implement improvements. Also, none of this is free, so the time must be paid for. It takes time to implement these and can seem to slow down future delivery, although if done well, the problems it avoids should compensate and ultimately lead to better and quicker outcomes. Using lean continuous improvement can be a way to uplift practices efficiently and ensure they don't atrophy or bloat over time (which they are inclined to do).

Holding people to account

> "Don't let us forget that the causes of human actions are usually immeasurably more complex and varied than our subsequent explanations of them."
>
> *Fyodor Dostoevsky*

There is no way around it. At times, you must hold people to account, and yes that might motivate people to avoid identifying problems. It will also encourage people to try to avoid being blamed. However, to really change future behaviour, there are situations where we must have consequences for people.

In many industries regulators have brought in regulation to ensure that boards of public companies have penalties in place for executives and other senior managers. Many also have mandatory anonymous whistle-blowing processes. These changes are intended to uplift the risk culture at companies. Often there are consequences for negligence, but worse consequences for hiding the negligence.

CHAPTER 27

THE 7 WASTES OF ARCHITECTURE

"There is nothing so useless as doing efficiently that
which should not be done at all."
Peter F. Drucker

The concept of the seven wastes comes from *lean thinking*. Lean is based on the Toyota Production System (TPS). Lean thinking has provided significant benefits to many people through its impact on manufacturing, service provisioning (including healthcare), and technology development, along with many other industries. Importantly, these people benefits have been to customers, shareholders, and employees; not only can lean thinking provides a win-win, but it is baked into the way it works.

I believe the principles of lean thinking can provide great benefits to architecture, including enterprise architecture, to the extent that it might even *save* enterprise architecture from itself.

There is a long history of how lean evolved, and I'm not trying to explain the history and all the key players here other than to say that a key moment in the lean journey was the release of the book Lean Thinking by James

P. Womack and Daniel T. Jones in 1996. The earlier book, The Machine That Changed the World, is another key moment, and was written by the same two authors, along with Daniel Roos, all of which were conducting research at MIT. Other influential players in the lean world include Jeffrey Liker and Mike Rother, but there are many others. Also, I always enjoy the real-world lean thinking CEO lessons from Art Byrne, as in the end, lean thinking is something you do, not just something you think.

The core idea of lean has been summarised as *maximising value to the customer while minimizing waste.* It is said that lean thinking changes the focus from optimizing separate technologies, assets, and vertical departments to optimizing the flow of products and services through entire value streams.

Lean does relate to the more widely known agile practices. However, I'd agree with people who say agile is a subset of lean. Exactly where lean demarcates with systems thinking, human-centred design, product thinking, and other contemporary approaches are topics outside the focus of this chapter and of this book, but it is true that many of these things tend to *hang-out* together.

The lean process and waste

The overall process described in the book Lean Thinking is 1) identify value, 2) map the value stream, 3) create flow, 4) establish pull, and 5) seek perfection. All the time you go through this process, there is a key focus on minimising waste. There is a whole lot involved in unpacking this process, and I'd encourage people to explore the many great books, videos, podcasts, and training sessions on lean thinking. The key callout I'd make is that lean is principles-based, not process-based. It is called lean thinking because lean is, more than anything, a way of thinking and acting. There is probably more than an accidental relationship between my love of the concepts in part 1 and my love of lean thinking; these ways of thinking do seem to overlap.

You don't have to do lean perfectly to get value, and if you are doing it perfectly then you just don't understand lean thinking. There is value in simply understanding the concepts, taking action, observing, and refining in cycles; you could argue that, in the end, that is all there is to do.

For this chapter the wastes are key for us. Lean came from manufacturing, where there are seven wastes of manufacturing defined, which are: over production, inventory, waiting, over-processing, transport, defects, and motion. These seem very logical, and it is a bit easier to measure when you are dealing with real physical items being *manufactured*. These wastes are somewhat generic outside manufacturing; however, tweaks tend to get made for different industry types.

There have been seven wastes of software development defined, but I'm not sure who originally defined these, and there are slight variations. One of the lists I've seen is: task switching, partially done work, motion, waiting, extra processing, extra features, and defects. These seem reasonable, though some might need to be carefully interpreted, particularly extra features, which is a concept that could be exploited by project managers to claim *gold-plating*.

The value of enterprise architecture and architecture waste

> "Time waste differs from material waste in that there can
> be no salvage. The easiest of all wastes and the hardest
> to correct is the waste of time, because wasted time does
> not litter the floor like wasted material."
>
> *Henry Ford*

Technology architecture, and particularly enterprise architecture (EA), has long been questioned about its real value to the business.

For me, the central charge, which I'd observe as being a fair question, is that we spend way too much time navel-gazing and thinking about EA, and not enough time actually adding value. I've long believed that lean thinking is a great countermeasure to help EA to become disciplined enough to realise its value. Focusing on the many rabbit holes we are tempted down, recognising them as forms of waste from the viewpoint of the business, and minimizing this waste would be very useful.

The (top) seven wastes of architecture

Below is an initial list of the top seven wastes of architecture. Are these irrefutably the top seven, well that can always be debated, but I think this is a good place to start.

Unclear purpose
Performing architectural thinking without having a clear business purpose for that thinking. Generally, architectural thinking, at least when it is on-

the-clock (paid for by the company), ought to be clearly aligned to business purposes and outcomes, which might be indirectly aligned, providing this is still reasonably justifiable as beneficial to the business.

At times, it might be appropriate to have some focus on professional development or architectural community uplift, for example, presenting at an architectural conference under the company's name, benefiting both the company reputation and the wider architectural community.

However, the vast majority of activity must clearly align with business purposes and outcomes.

Over production

As with manufacturing, overproduction is where something is produced, and there is no business-defined need. For architecture a common occurrence of this is the production of target state architectures, roadmaps and strategies where there is no business request or identified funding pathway.

We need to carefully consider when to enact the removal of this waste as we do want some premeditated high-level thinking in some areas, particularly where we see that there is strategic alignment and we want to get ahead of the business request, or where we want to try to build the narrative and desire for the roadmap as we strongly see a benefit to the company.

It is all about finding the right balance of being reactive versus being disconnected from the actual business appetite, and this will be different by company, industry, and factors like economic cycles.

Over-processing

As with manufacturing, performing more processing work on architectures than is needed to get to the next decision point or handover point.

As always, context matters, and the level of work needed for an enterprise architect, domain architect, solution architect, or other will be different depending on the business, the skill of individuals, their interest level, and other factors. Funding can have an impact. For example, I've worked in teams where enterprise architects didn't recharge, but solution architects had to, and therefore, project managers were greatly incentivised to try and get the enterprise architects to go into as much detail as possible. We need to be very careful about how we manage these situations.

I always advocate applying what I call a *dead-cat test*. We don't want to throw a *dead-cat* over the fence, hoping it magically pops back into life on the other side. We ought to do enough that it can reasonably be used to make the required decision and be taken forward with the next level of detailed solution or design work based on the full context of the initiative and the team's skills.

Reprocessing

Unnecessary reworking of architectures. This might be because appropriate patterns have not been defined or used; therefore we create another architecture which really could have just been pattern reuse. This could also be where there has been a handoff to the next architect and they cannot, or do not, pick up from where the architecture has evolved to, and there is no contextual change necessitating rework.

Architecture is not deterministic, so different architects can legitimately come up with different solutions, and this is not a problem. It can be very hard to pick up someone's work and continue from there. We just need to try to minimise the rework.

Task switching and partially done work

Combining two closely related wastes from software development, the amount of *task switching*, which often strongly correlates to *partially done work*.

Given the nature of architecture, and particularly enterprise and domain architecture, there is inherently a need to be across many programs, projects, and initiatives, as well as supporting business case development, root cause analysis, strategic planning, investment slates development and more. We must be available for many stakeholders, and so we will have many spinning plates.

But we do need to be mindful of how much work we have in progress. Managing the other wastes will help with this one. We need to focus on creating efficient flow in our work.

Waiting

As with manufacturing and software development. Waiting time is almost always a key waste and a key metric to measure to improve flow. The degree of wait time will often be related to interdependences.

Architects are often a bottleneck, either in reality or at least perception. Architects both cause others to wait and have to wait for others. Having an architecture principle to move decisions as close to the real place of work as practical will greatly help to reduce this bottleneck, and in both directions. Effectively, this is one of the key benefits of microservice architecture – technology operating model decoupling.

Re-litigation of decisions
Unnecessarily revisiting decisions where there has not been significant new information or a significant context change.

We need to ensure we have the right architectural governance, including responsibility and accountability, so we can make good decisions the first time and then commit to those decisions, acknowledging that we won't always get it right. We need to have lightweight documentation of when and where the decision was made, by whom, and the basic rationale. Generally, we should avoid a decision by committee and have a small number of responsible decision-makers, but they ought to consult wider.

Revisiting decisions if there is new information makes sense, but only if there is new information or a context change. If we must revisit the decision because we just got it wrong, then we need to use it as a learning opportunity and apply continuous improvement to get better.

How to start

The idea of lean is not necessarily to eliminate all wastes, as that just never happens, but we should continually look to bring in countermeasures to reduce these wastes. It needs to be a continual improvement because conditions change and new wastes creep in.

The top 7 architectural wastes for your specific situation may well be different depending on the type of company you are in, the architectural operating model (centralised, decentralised, federated), your maturity level, the mix of personalities you have, and many other factors. Lean thinking ought not to be prescriptive. There is no magic formula that just works.

It is a way of thinking and improving. The countermeasures you need depend on your specific situation at that specific time.

The key is to start where you are and reduce waste and friction in the architectural process. Be diligent about focusing on business value.

A chapter doesn't really do this topic justice. One day, I might expand this out to a book of its own, but for now, I'll stop here; just cracking the door open a little and giving you a tantalising peak. But be curious. Keep your beginner's mind.

> "We improve by 1% every day. In just 70 days, you're
> twice as good."
> *Alan Weiss*

CHAPTER 28

BAD KICK – GOOD CHASE

"[Sometimes in Rugby the difference between a good kick
and a bad kick, is a good chase]"
Unknown Rugby or Rugby League Commentator

In Rugby and Rugby League there are many times when a team will kick the ball back to the opposing team in general play. A good kick might go deep into the opposition territory or might go very high, so the kicking team can put pressure on the receiving team. Some kicks are good, and some are not so good. Sometimes the kick might be quite good, but the chasing players, who need to defend against the receiving team, might be slow or fragmented, and the receiving team can make a lot of progress; and then sometimes the kick might be poor, such as off the side of the boot, but the chase is fantastic, and the receiving team might even fumble the ball, turning it over.

Hence the quote opening this chapter: Sometimes in Rugby, the difference between a good kick and a bad kick is a good chase. I don't recall who said it. Technology implementations can be a lot like this. For example, core system replacements are very hard and tend to be wobbly old kicks at best.

What matters is what you follow it with and if you did the right things to enable a good chase.

Horizons and foundations

McKinsey's Three Horizons Model has become a mainstay of corporate strategy for some time, and for good reasons: it is simple, people get it, and it works. When I say it works, it *can* work if you get it right.

For example, organizations often define a strategy where Horizon 1 is something like process or technology simplification and standardisation, all delivered in a short timeframe of three to 12 months or perhaps 18 months; this first horizon is often called a foundational phase. Horizon 2 builds on the first, and might be business model extensions, product uplifts, or new capabilities that will be ready 24 to 36 months out; this is often where financial benefits are starting to be realised. Finally, Horizon 3 might be creating new disruptive products, or business models delivered 36 to 72 months out.

I've occasionally seen Horizon 1 declared done, though sometimes extended, and then a formal transition to Horizon 2. I cannot, however, recall a company declaring it has *done* Horizon 2 and is starting Horizon 3. This is ok. I think one of two things happen: either the company runs out of puff and hopes people politely don't ask about it again, or the three horizons are a rolling three horizons, so they redefine the next 3 phases, and it all moves right.

Technology foundation

Often, as part of a three-horizon model, there is a foundational technology phase in Horizon 1. Alternatively, there might not be a stated three-horizon model, but there might still be a foundational technology initiative, which, for our purpose, is a similar situation. Thinking about physical buildings, you don't build a foundation if you don't intend to build something on that foundation; by definition it wouldn't be a foundation. The big difference with a physical building is that you need to have a clear plan of what your end building will be, whereas with technology, and particularly with cloud, you might not have a clear picture; for example, you can build for horizontal scalability without knowing the final scale.

The technology foundation might be for one or more new business capabilities, in which case we need to carefully consider if the business realistically *knows* how to define the capabilities adequately or does the business needs to explore one or more of the capabilities, where using hypothesis testing and iteration is probably a smart play. For example, an insurance carrier that sells business insurance to micro-SME businesses (companies with 1-5 employees) via brokers might have decided to open a new direct sales channel via a direct-to-customer digital platform. This is an example of something that is very attractive in the insurance industry but which few carriers have got quite right, so implementing a fixed budget foundation and experimenting to test and learn would be smart.

Alternatively, the technology foundation might be an existing capability, for example replacing legacy core platforms at an insurance company. In this situation, there might not be an overarching need to experiment at a business level, but then you do have existing customers and policies to deal with; you need to change the foundation in a way that you don't harm the existing business. This is very hard. I heard one vendor during pre-sales, an old warhorse with many scars, describe this as being like changing the engines on a Boeing 747 (Airbus A380 these days) while the plane is flying and full of passengers. I'm not sure it is *that* hard, but it is very hard, and many careers have come unstuck on such projects. Understandably, these expensive programs tend to be very careful about managing their scope and almost always have a principle of *like-for-like* functional replacement, with uplift to be done after the foundational replacement, meaning after the program. Like-for-like for a home-grown legacy system always throws up a lot of surprises, and if you are going with a package, there are a lot of painful compromises for the business. Don't worry; we (you) can fix that after the foundation.

Watch your step

> "One thing I have learnt time and again over the years
> with technology programs and transitional states: do not
> step somewhere you cannot afford to live as a business,
> in terms of operational efficiencies, because you will
> probably be living there a lot longer than you think."

Michael D. Stark, advice to many business executives
and senior stakeholders over the years

If the technology foundation is a new business capability, then success can come down to how well-understood the requirements for the capability are and if the implementation is funded to implement those requirements fully. It might be that it is a new play like the earlier example of an insurance carrier that sells business insurance to micro-SME businesses (companies with 1-5 employees) via brokers who want to try to open a new direct sales channel via a direct to customer digital platform. What is the initial foundation? Is it a proof of concept or an experiment? What does success look like? What will you do if it is a poor outcome, such as pivot, cancel it, or keep going? What future investment envelope will you have?

Alternatively, the technology foundation might be an existing capability, and we had the example of replacing legacy core platforms at an insurance company. Typically, the estimate is underbaked to get the business case over the line, and either way, you quickly find complexities in the legacy you didn't know about. Scope comes under pressure, and you descope some things, saying they will be done later. Perhaps part of the legacy technology remains, or perhaps some suboptimal business processes are accepted *for a short time*, and that can hit operational expenses, customer experience, and colleague job satisfaction. And then there are the recriminations.

In either situation, you just must sometimes take some interim steps and set some type of foundation to get anywhere. But during this phase, you can give yourself a chance by being open and honest about ongoing funding and focus. What will it look like after the initiative? What is success for the business itself, not just the top players and *their* careers? How do you set your business up for a good chase?

Good chase

> "Such programs fail to recognize that turning innovation
> or change into an event rather than part of our daily work
> can never produce significant or lasting results."

*Jez Humble, Lean Enterprise: How High Performance
Organizations Innovate at Scale*

We opened with the rugby analogy that sometimes a *good chase* can turn a bad kick into a good kick, and even a good kick won't help you if you don't chase well. If you look at how a *good chase* is done, you'll see that some or all the players are prepared for the kick, get a running start, and time it carefully. They don't just say, "Oh, someone has kicked the ball; we better do something like run after it". That doesn't work. Neither does implementing a foundation and then wondering what to do. A wobbly foundation phase can work out if you are prepared to follow up with the right actions.

Putting aside the business case itself, as we have covered that, we do need to try to advocate for defining what the ongoing funding will be post-foundation. This is important as it will inform what technology options and architecture are appropriate. We need to be careful about strangler patterns and scaffolding if there is no ongoing funding. We should, even if ongoing funding is indicated, ensure that the solution is good enough to last if things change and funding that was reasonably expected just cannot be provided. For example, another pandemic and severe fiscal pressures for the company.

We need to determine if funding will be perpetual, such as product funding, or case by case. We also need to advocate for thinking about the post-foundation delivery operating model. If we are going with an operating model based on a product ethos, then a microservice approach is a good candidate, and this product operating model should be embedded during the foundation to ensure there is no vacuum once the program ends.

We also need to advocate for the foundation program to be responsible and sponsors accountable, for ensuring that an appropriate capability for ongoing agility is delivered during the foundation phase. A good way of doing this is by defining technology functional requirements around delivery capability, and appropriate non-functional requirements. Also, deliver the foundation incrementally, therefore operating in a way that will work post-foundation; even mocking live deliveries but not really going live as you go.

We need to ensure that continuous improvement is supported by technology and that this is seen as a key strategic enabler for the company or organization. All the good things in DevOps: are continuous integration, continuous delivery and deployment, source and version control, infrastructure as code, provisioning, containerisation, logging, and automation. Test automation is vital, including unit, integration, and user acceptance to the extent possible. Process automation can be important, but it must be used and funded appropriately. Enabling AB testing and toggle switches is often important, particularly for digital. Investing in good API portals for internal developers and external developers is normally important.

Unless we have been living in a time-warp, we know all the good things in the previous paragraph, but what we need to realise as strategists and architects is that these *are* key concerns for us; they *are not* someone else's problems. We must enable and support engineering excellence. These are key strategic concerns for most businesses and organisations today, even if they often don't know it.

We need to ensure we champion funding and executive focus on these capabilities, get these concerns baked into foundation implementations as success criteria, and we need to build trusted relationships with engineering and DevOp teams. If we look at some of the darlings of modern platform businesses, like Amazon and Google, then it does seem some of their difference is that they are engineering-based companies, so they get the strategic importance of engineering excellence, often right up to the board level.

Engineering excellence is the foundation of a good chase in business transformation, innovation, and major program delivery. There are other factors, but this is the one we, as strategists and architects, can help ensure.

Those of us from non-engineering backgrounds can get it, but we need to put in the hard yards, get some base knowledge, and build relationships. Having engineering at architecture governance forums is helpful if you can get them to attend. Above all don't go running into engineering domains throwing your weight around. You know nothing, and you are there to learn, provide support, and remove obstacles at a strategic level. Remember the advice of Fujio Cho, which is worth repeating.

"Go see, ask why, show respect."
Fujio Cho, honorary chairman of Toyota Motor Cor-
poration, referring to going to the Gemba (real place of
work)

CHAPTER 29

A COLLECTION OF RATS AND MICE

(SMALL TOPICS)

"The older I get, the more I'm conscious of ways very
small things can make a change in the world. Tiny little
things, but the world is made up of tiny matters, isn't it?"

Sandra Cisneros

Before we finish this book with the final chapter on diversity of thought, there are a few smaller topics that have been bundled into this chapter. The chapter is named after the rats and mice idiom, which is generally considered to mean *remaining small and insignificant details*. Well, they might be smaller concepts, but maybe not all that insignificant. You decide.

Strategy and architecture needs uncertainty

> "Uncertainty is an uncomfortable position. But certainty
> is an absurd one."
> *Voltaire*

Strategy and architecture need uncertainty and ambiguity because this is the oil that keeps our trade viable. This is where we ought to shine; we just need to embrace it.

Of the techniques commonly used to alleviate the anxiety caused by uncertainty in strategy and architecture, the most common is the trusty *assumption*. Often the *assumption* is used like the ultimate Teflon disclaimer. However, the overuse of assumptions can be lazy and sloppy, and they are quickly discarded by stakeholders who just take the dates and dollars as commitments. Often, assumptions are just preferences that people want to articulate early, for example assuming we will use SQL Server, where the database choice might not matter. We can be prone to using assumptions to remove uncertainty intellectually, but this can be deluding ourselves, and we often would be better off leaning in, recognising, and dealing with the uncertainty.

The most dangerous is the *critical success assumption*, which is an assumption that *must* hold true for the strategy, business case, design, or concept to be feasible and viable. You will often find that the *critical success* assumption is a premise of a logical argument (see appendix for more on logical arguments). For example, making an assumption that you can get governance approval from a regulator to store the personal data of customers in an offshore cloud service; this could have a large impact if it doesn't hold true, and even if it does, it could be a long process.

The best antidote to the errant assumption is honesty and logic; this is easier said than done. Ask yourself if the assumption is necessary; again, imagine it is a premise. Do you need it for the argument to stand; if you don't need the assumption, don't have it there. Is the assumption reasonable in terms of being probable, so no reliance on magic tricks, please. For real uncertainty with critical success assumptions, it can be good to use the *hypothesis-driven experiment*, providing it focuses on the actual key unknowns with objectivity and not on proving what is already known.

People are *hard coded* to look for or, where necessary, manufacture certainty. As strategists and architects, we know our stakeholders crave certainty and so we end up trying to give them it. We pride ourselves on being devoid of bias. However, providing certainty without biases is hard to do at the best of times, let alone in a high-pressure meeting with senior stakeholders or when formulating the business case with all the associated pressures and expectations.

We've talked a few times about Daniel Kahneman and his book Thinking Fast and Slow, in which he also identified the strong drive of cognitive ease, which in our case is nicely supported by a few comforting assumptions. Providing our stakeholders with a comfortable and cohesive story is very effective but can also be very dangerous for our companies.

"Our comforting conviction that the world makes sense
rests on a secure foundation: our almost unlimited ability
to ignore our ignorance."

Daniel Kahneman, Thinking, Fast and Slow

There are countermeasures to uncertainty aversion. Use assumptions sparingly and ensure that any critical success assumptions are clearly identified, along with implications, and accompanied by a specific approach to prove or disprove these assumptions as early as possible. Also, "Do your job!" – the famous mantra of New England Patriot's five-time Superbowl-winning head coach Bill Belichick. It generally should not be our job to *sell* the business case. You need to be a trusted and objective advisor to the business. You can practice saying "don't know" – these two words (Zen saying) are very hard to say, but these words will help liberate us from bias while gaining the respect of our peers. And finally, if you have to make a call, then make it, but take care with your bias.

So, uncertainty is essential to strategy and architecture, that is, if we can live with it and embrace it. Although, I'm not entirely sure about that. Are you?

"As one judge said to another: 'Be just, and if you can't be
just, be arbitrary.'"
*William S. Burroughs, Naked Lunch (notorious Beat
Generation author, and grandson of the founder of the
Burroughs Corporation, which after the 1986 merger
with Sperry UNIVAC was renamed Unisys)*

Architecture arguments are not a bug; they are a feature

An exchange in the movie Argo:

> C.I.A Operative Tony Mendez: "There are only bad
> options. It's about finding the best one."

> C.I.A Director Stansfield Turner: "You don't have a better
> bad idea than this?"

> C.I.A Deputy Director Jack O'Donnell: "This is the best
> bad idea we have, sir... by far."

It is said that the collective term for technology architects is an *argument* of architects. It is probably a fair term to use for us, as we do seem to debate quite a bit, and with great passion.

Architecture in the technology domain is not easy. We always get to see problems with the options we do choose, and not the problems that would have happened with options that we don't choose. Often, there are no good options, so agreeing on the best-bad or least-worse option is a point of debate.

Another feature of architectural decision-making is that there is an element of chance. One of the key jobs of an architect is to preserve optionality. We want to enable the business to change its mind about its business model, operating model, or requirements. Maybe none of those changes, but the business feature is far more successful than imagined, like a platform business model, and must scale beyond the originally anticipated scale; that is a good thing for the business but tough for architecture. I always like the example of a sprinkler system in a building. We want the option to use it, but we might spend all that money and never actually use it. That is still a good investment, as the option to use it was worth it.

So, given the uncertainty and variation of options, it is a good thing that there are debates in architecture. It is important to be kind and be respectful. But in the end, someone must make the call. An EGM I worked for would often say, "committees don't make decisions, people do".

It is important to be clear about who is the responsible decision maker, which literally means able-to-respond, along with who is ultimately accountable, which literally means held-to-account, and is often someone much more senior like an executive. I think these days, many companies are going for a Chief Architect which would be a level that could be accountable, potentially also responsible. This makes sense because it is hard for most executives, even CIOs, CDOs, and CTOs, to really know enough about architecture to understand what they are taking accountability for fully.

As architects involved in the process, we should state our viewpoint clearly and concisely and then accept that the decision maker, be it another architect or senior leader, needs to make a decision. We need to be able to support the decision maker in the end once any counter-opinion is stated. If necessary, get your view documented, and then let it go. Don't get too tightly attached to your viewpoint; you might just be wrong.

You can't get an ought from an is

> "You can't get an ought from an is."
> *David Hume*

This famous concept from the great Scottish philosopher David Hume (1711–76) has interesting implications for us. Hume observed that people seem to derive what ought to be done by citing facts about what is, yet logically, there seems to be a gap, and there must be some other point of reference. As strategists and architects, we often fill this void with principles, but we need to take care of how we use these. But first, the ought-is gap.

Just the facts

To clarify this ought-is problem, consider the issue of pro-life verses pro-choice while trying not to take a moral or ethical position. Often, each side will look to medical *facts* to validate their position, however, these facts typically need some other guiding ought. For example, one theory is that up until the time of brain activity, which can be determined by science, there is no person, therefore, no right to life. But the fact about brain activity still requires some other rule to say that no brain activity means no person yet. There is a theory that we intuitively determine what feels right and then determine the ought statements to fill the logical gap that makes this correct.

Why use such a hotly debated example? The pro-life versus pro-choice debate is one of the most polarizing debates in recent human history and also one where most people can feel their intuition in the driver seat. This is also an area where ambiguity cannot be accommodated, as the lawmakers must pick a position. As stated by a giant in this field, Baroness Warnock, the law [in the West, at least] requires precision more than it requires accuracy.

Back to safer ground

The key here is that in many situations, we *intuitively* determine what is right, then reverse engineer the ought statements to fill the logical gap that makes this correct. We are also remarkably efficient at finding evidence that our intuition is correct. Relying on intuition is not necessarily a bad thing; it has largely been responsible for our success as a species, along with opposable thumbs, of course (try operating your iPhone without using your thumbs). However, it does expose us to bias, again not always a bad thing, but it can be.

A principled solution, or not

> "I am a man of fixed and unbending principles, the first
> of which is to be flexible at all times"
> *Everett Dirksen*

As strategists and architects, we need some other reference to get us from the fact (is) to the guidance (ought). We normally fill this logic gap by defining architectural principles. These principles are themselves ought statements (thou ought to loosely couple thy systems). We can be prone to determining principles out of context so they 'feel' safe in their abstraction. We then kind of forget we did this when we applied them.

However, sometimes accuracy does matter more than precision if architects want to be trusted advisers rather than pedantic lawyers, assuming here that being pedantic is a useful trait for a lawyer, just not for an architect.

Architectural principles have their place, but we need to use them carefully as guides and not positions to defend at all costs. A better approach might be to consider the desirability of certain architectural characteristics within the context of the solution being provided. For example, you may have a buy before build principle and a loose coupling principle, but many COTS packages can put these two at odds. It might be more useful to have guidance that we need to determine if the characteristics of interchangeable components are more important than the characteristics of prefabrication within the specific context.

Hume was right; we cannot get an ought from an is, but we do need to make the best decisions we can in context.

Do nothing is always an option

> "Never put off till tomorrow [that which] you can avoid
> all together."
> *Preston's Axiom (one of many variants)*

I recall a wise old, dog-eared project manager explaining to me that *doing nothing* is always an option for executives and sponsors and that we should always include *do nothing* as an option. From where we sit, it might seem that something must be done, but for executives and sponsors, they are often presented with more *must-do* scenarios than they *can do*. Therefore, some of those things cannot be done. Our job is to give them the information they need to decide.

The Bhagavad Gita points out that doing nothing is an action in itself. This is true. For example, neglecting children can be punished in court in extreme cases, even though it is all about not doing an action. If someone slaps you at a party, it certainly feels like an action, or at least quite an effort, to restrain yourself from responding. So, you can take the action of no action.

Often, for a business case or proposal it makes sense to frame a do-nothing option genuinely. It can mean we should frame the costs or risk associated with this option and potentially even recommend against inaction, but then we need to accept that someone must choose between many more *must do* actions than can be done. Typically, this is not our decision, and we are not the ones held *accountable* for picking which actions are not done. We need to respect the decision-makers and the tough calls they must make.

Knowing less makes it easier to understand and be comfortable

> "It is the consistency of the information that matters for
> a good story, not its completeness. Indeed, you will often
> find that knowing little makes it easier to fit everything
> you know into a coherent pattern."
>
> *Daniel Kahneman, Thinking, Fast and Slow*

We were introduced to Daniel Kahneman, the Nobel prize-winning psychologist, in Chapter 6 when we looked at the intellect. Kahneman had developed the System 1 verses System 2 concept from his groundbreaking book *Thinking Fast and Slow*. His broader focus was on judgment and decision-making. His empirical findings challenge the assumption of human rationality prevailing in economic theory at that time and had significant implications for all areas of judgement and decision-making, from economics to wider business. I would argue his findings certainly have implications for strategy and architecture.

Beyond the understanding I got of cognitive bias and heuristics, and his System 1 and System 2 concepts, was the a-ha moment around his emphasis on cohesive storytelling. He builds his case on the prior foundation, backed by empirical evidence, of how ensuring everything fits together nicely is very powerful because we really aren't wired to spot missing information easily; if we can fit the pieces that we have neatly together, then we feel comfortable. I could suddenly see why putting together extensive presentations that completely cover all details of a proposal or analysis often wouldn't land well with executives and senior leaders, while someone with shiny shoes and a flash logo would take that information and tell a very basic story with it and get the tick. Covering every detail just made it hard for most busy people with limited time and attention to *feel* comfortable that they understood.

It is well worth buying this book; I'd recommend it as audio and unpacking the lessons in detail. Alternatively, studying the various management consulting story telling methods probably gets you to the same place with this aspect if you don't want to understand the psychology. But I do, as the psychology of it is fascinating.

> "The most coherent stories are not necessarily the most probable, but they are plausible, and the notions of coherence, plausibility, and probability are easily confused by the unwary."

> *Daniel Kahneman, Thinking, Fast and Slow*

There is a closely related concept that, as people, it is good to be aware of. Kahneman's work has shown something that many marketers and dictators have known for a long time. Our brains are not good a distinguishing familiarity from truth. Novelty, for much of evolution, was a risk, and familiarity was safe. This is not in itself good or bad; it depends on the context and how it is used. Just keep it in mind.

> "A reliable way to make people believe in falsehoods
> is frequent repetition because familiarity is not easily
> distinguished from truth."
>
> *Daniel Kahneman, Thinking, Fast and Slow*

Saying No when No is the right answer

> "I canna' change the laws of physics."
> *Montgomery "Scotty" Scott, Chief Engineer, Star Trek*
> *(original)*

We can sometimes struggle to say no, but we are seen as the experts in our domain, and we must say no when no is the right answer. This story from Sadhguru reminds me of many architectural conversations:

A patient goes to their doctor with terrible pain in the middle of their torso. The doctor does blood tests and X-rays. The doctor shows the x-rays to the patient, pointing at a blockage and says, "this is the problem here, and you need to have surgery and spend two weeks in the hospital and another ten weeks off work". The treatment will be twenty-five thousand dollars.

The patient says no. They do not want surgery, do not want two weeks in hospital; and they cannot take ten weeks off work; and certainly, they are not paying twenty-five thousand dollars for all this. No way! There is silence while they look at each other; the doctor says nothing. The patient says, "Ok, I'll make you a deal; look what can you do right here and now for two hundred dollars, no more, that is it, what can you do?" The doctor thinks about it, looking at the X-Ray, rubs his chin, grabs an ink marker, and says "well … okay … for two-hundred dollars I can touch up your X-Ray right now for you."

There are times we are asked to add a feature, make a change, or resolve a problem with technology where it is just not possible or not possible within the cost or time constraints required. And by this, I mean not possible at all, and not just something that we don't like or don't think is a good idea. We can be under a lot of pressure. But it only gets worse if we agree to something that is not possible. We shouldn't game this to get our way. We do, however need to say no if no is the correct answer, and then stand by it.

Micro-Management

> "Even though you try to put people under control, it is
> impossible. You cannot do it. The best way to control
> people is to encourage them to be mischievous. Then they
> will be in control in a wider sense. To give your sheep or
> cow a large spacious meadow is the way to control [it].
> So it is with people: first let them do what they want and
> watch them. This is the best policy. To ignore them is not
> good. That is the worst policy. The second worst is trying
> to control them. The best one is to watch them, just to
> watch them, without trying to control them."

Shunryu Suzuki

The Zen monk Shunryu Suzuki eloquently describes above what is wrong with micro-management and how leadership ought to be done. Notice I say leadership and not management. I'm not entirely certain that if leadership and organisation are done right, we even need management, or at least, we might need a lot less of it.

There is not much to say about micro-management. It happens and is frustrating. If you are the micro-manager, then just stop doing it. You are making your people miserable, and worse, you might be making them dependent. You are harming your company. You are also making your own life harder as it all goes through you.

If you are the one being micro-managed, then I recommend using one of two juxtapositioned countermeasures. Either tell the manager very little or tell the manager everything. The right choice depends on you, your manager, and the situation.

Telling the manager very little can work if you are confident in what you are doing. Respect the managers role and responsibilities, but keep turning the conversations around to outcomes and away from methods. Focus on *what* needs to be done, not *how*. Still, ensure you communicate on progress and update them on issues, particularly if they might get blindsided. I would often send an email so it is documented and start the title with "No action required:", and then say I'm just giving them a heads-up but have it under control and will reach out if I need help. Often, if you gain their confidence around this, they will ease up. I'm a bit of a fan of verbally the saying, "this is not my first rodeo", and often this makes the point firmly but with kindness and humour.

The other approach if you can't make the first one work, or perhaps if you are less experienced, is to tell them every small detail and keep asking questions. This floods them and overwhelms them to the point where they must start trying to give you more autonomy. Then, you can switch to the first approach.

Be careful with both approaches, as they can backfire depending on what else is going on with the manager. Some managers are unfortunately prone to throwing their teams under the bus, but the good news is they tend to flame out, so just bide your time in this case. Remember impermanence from Part 1 of this book; you don't always have to force things to change; they just will.

Of course, beyond manager and subordinate, we are all people, so if you feel comfortable it can be best just to have an open and honest conversation, and that will quite often do the trick. You will often find that the manager says something like they know they do it and try not to. Then you can use the "not my first rodeo" with a wink to remind them if they do it, and you can both have a laugh at yourselves.

Remonstration of leaders

> "In serving his parents, a son may remonstrate with them,
> but gently; when he sees that they do not incline to follow
> his advice, he shows an increased degree of reverence,
> but does not abandon his purpose; and should they
> punish him, he does not allow himself to murmur."
>
> *Kongzi (Confucius), master Kong*

Kongzi, meaning master Kong, in the West inaccurately called Confucious, had a focus on how we ought to behave in the family, government, and society. He was firm on the need to respect parents and other authority figures. However, he also promoted an acceptance, or even duty, to remonstrate these authority figures when necessary. The advice of Kongzi, captured in something called The Analects, has underpinned society in China for millennia.

The Merriam-Webster Dictionary defines remonstrate as "to present and urge reasons in opposition". The Colins Dictionary defines it as "If you remonstrate with someone, you protest to them about something you do not approve of or agree with, and you try to get it changed or stopped."

In the paper *Remonstrance: The Moral Imperative of the Chinese Scholar-Official*, by Anita Andrew and Robert André LaFleur they say, "[…] the remonstrance ideal in a Chinese context called upon an underling — an official of government or a child within a family — to provide guidance and even criticism for a superior, when necessary, regardless of the risks encountered." Just to emphasise how strong this guidance was they also say "[…] and especially in troubled times — this included the very real possibility of death."

We can take some learning from this in our corporate world. It is alright to provide such feedback to leaders, and in most companies and organisations, we could consider that we have a duty to provide such feedback, even to the extent of remonstrating leaders. We probably aren't going to be risking death, but we can do ourselves harm and might find we don't have a seat in the next reshuffle. However, we have greater obligations. This does depend on your personal circumstances as well. We can have conflicting duties and obligations. If you have a young family and a large mortgage and think you would not easily find another job, then you *must* put your family first, of course.

You will often find if you are brave, and provide the feedback clearly, concisely, and respectfully, it is normally well received and might well help your career. Be mindful of where you provide the feedback; for example, if you remonstrate an executive in front of other executives, then that won't go well for you. Be smart.

Show don't tell

> "Don't tell me the moon is shining; show me the glint of
> light on the broken glass."
> *Anton Chekhov,*
> *a nineteenth-century Russian playwright.*

This is a simple one. Show don't tell. This rule is often attributed to Anton Chekhov, a nineteenth-century Russian playwright.

As of the writing of this book, Wikipedia has what I think is a good description stating that: Show, don't tell is a narrative technique used in various kinds of texts to allow the reader to experience the story through actions, words, subtext, thoughts, senses, and feelings rather than through the author's exposition, summarization, and description. It avoids adjectives describing the author's analysis and instead describes the scene in such a way that readers can draw their own conclusions. The technique applies equally to nonfiction and all forms of fiction, literature including haiku and Imagist poetry in particular, speech, movie making, and playwriting.

That is a good way to describe it, and in particular where it says that the readers can draw their own conclusions. That is what we want for our storytelling.

As an example, I've seen many enthusiastic enterprise or business architects presenting capability maps to business leaders, explaining what they are, how they work, and why they are important. Typically, the business leader's eyes glaze over, and they quickly loose interest. What is wrong with these people? Who doesn't love business capabilities? They are fascinating.

Hard to believe if you have got this far into this book, but some people really don't love abstract concepts. And business capability maps are highly abstracted. What to do? Show don't tell.

Where I've had success with business capability maps is to use a concise high-level diagram when discussing business or operating models, for example, helping to shape an underwriting agency engagement at an insurance company. The business capabilities must be carefully matured to a point where business leaders can see their business in them without explanation. So, you have got to have the right diagram. Then, I've started heat mapping it with them. Who will do the pricing capability, the insurance carrier (us) or the underwriting agency? Who owns the customer? Who does the claims handling? What about the claims supply chain? Who is responsible for the reserving and reinsurance? If it is shared, then does this work, or do we need to click down lower so we can clearly define responsibility? These conversations were very engaging, and the business leaders were able to focus on the issues that mattered to them and for the success of the initiative. Gaps were spotted in the business thinking, and key decisions were able to be framed up early. The model facilitated it but wasn't the focus. That is a good model. That is a useful tool.

You end up showing them what a business capability diagram does by just using it in a situation that matters. At the very end, I've often said, "Oh, by the way, this type of diagram is a business capability map; did you find it useful?". Job done!

A good analogy goes a long way

"One good analogy is worth three hours discussion."
Dudley Field Malone,
politician and advocate of women's suffrage

It is normally hard to succinctly explain complex or highly abstract concepts to people. Often, when you try to, you find the discussion drags you into all sorts of pedantic details that are not so important for the point you are trying to make. You end up debating nuances that don't matter at that stage. Or worse still, you get the blank stare.

Nowhere is this more noticeable than when you are explaining complex nuances to executives and other senior leaders where you normally have very little time, and perhaps even less attention, to work with. A good analogy can go a long way to helping. This could be an analogist story or perhaps a simpler analogist concept. I'll use an analogy as an analogy for this.

The situation
We needed to integrate two systems together in an effectively headless pattern. One system was the core system, being the 'body' in this 'headless' pattern, and it was to remain the master of the information, including a lot of financial data that was needed for regulatory compliance and general financials. There were many integrations from this core system to other internal and external systems, so the data needed to be up to date. The system to be the 'head' in this pattern was basically a case management system, and this would be the user interface. We were going to need to push a large load of data to the 'head' case management system to start the case, with most updates happening in the case system, but there were a lot

of entities and attributes that needed to be pushed back to the core system. Sometimes, this was in large payloads, but sometimes in small payloads.

Obviously, in this situation there was quite a lot of integration work involved. A lot of entities and attributes to map and values to align between systems. Performance and scalability were factors, so a lot of work on balancing synchronous and asynchronous patterns. It was going to be a large effort, so relatively expensive and time-consuming. At some stage it was communicated that there were going to be dozens of APIs required. Quickly, the conversation at the executive table turned to a number of APIs driving the complexity, cost, and timeline, therefore, the need to reduce the number of APIs. I'm not going to get into what is an API versus and endpoint on this one.

So, the challenge for me was to explain that the number and size of APIs was certainly something for some people to think about and probably argue about at some point, but this ought not to be a consideration for the executive level, and trying to reduce this number artificially wouldn't lead anywhere good for anyone. But this is a nuanced topic, even for architects and engineers.

The analogy
So, a good way to understand this is to think about a time you've moved house. Let's say you have a four-bedroom house you've been in with your young family for a few years, and you've got a lot of stuff to move. How hard is that move? What determines the amount of effort required? Is the biggest deciding factor the number of moving boxes you use? No.

So, obviously, the number of boxes is analogous to the number of APIs. It's not perfect, but it is good enough to talk to executives. Not only boxes but all the storage needed, so perhaps also car boots, trailers, small trucks, large trucks, or shipping containers. These can all be analogous to APIs. What you put in is the payload. Now there are good and bad size boxes, cars, trailers etc. At some stage, it does matter which ones you pick. But first, let's understand the things that can impact the size of the job.

If you are just moving to the house next door, you can probably carry boxes and couches. If you are moving within the neighbourhood, you might go with cars and boots. Across town or between towns, then trucks and trailers. But if you are moving overseas, you are probably looking at a shipping container. But you might be moving across town to a house still being built, so you might still want a shipping container.

The complexity of the move is largely driven by the distance and timeframe of the move, but also other factors. How organised is the house? How messy? Are you moving from a large house to a much smaller house? Are you moving to a house with poor access, where you have to walk up small pathways and stairs. And, of course, the weakness in the analogy is when moving house, you don't have to be anywhere near as particular about what goes in each box, or what the definition of kitchen utensils actually is at both ends. There are many factors that you should consider to be able to select the right size and number of boxes and other storage for moving. Starting with a rule that the fewer boxes you have, the simpler is not a good rubric.

What can change the equation of complexity would be changing the number of things you need to move. If you sell the house with the refrigerator, freezer, spa pool, trampoline, outside furniture, and pony, all included, then that will change the equation.

<u>Bringing it home</u>

It is important not to overplay the analogy as it is rare that it is a perfect fit. You need to be clear this is conceptual.

In the above case the key message is that the number of APIs, like the number of boxes, is not the important factor. People close to the work will care about how many, and it matters a lot at some level, but the executives don't need to get caught up in that. Look at what is driving the complexity. The amount of information being moved and the mapping and decision-making involved.

Another example of a useful analogy was talking to an executive about the potential adoption of a specific type of emerging AI for a very important business function. The type of AI was in the early stages of the classic hype cycle; though it certainly had potential, but it needed time to mature. In this case, the executive was a motoring enthusiast, so the analogy was going all in on electric trucks for a national truck fleet. Will it be a good idea in the future? Possibly, or even probably. Is now the right time for the company? It might be a first-mover masterstroke, but it could be a very expensive misstep as there would be a lot of challenges to solve. An electric truck fleet for inner city or last leg delivery is one thing, but long haul is not a mature option yet, regardless of how enthusiastically visionaries talk it up. It is a strategic decision that needs to be weighed carefully in line with the broader corporate strategy. The executive got the point on strategic timing and understood the nature of the decision to be made.

A good analogy can do a lot of heavy lifting if used wisely.

Guarding a tree-stump waiting for rabbits

Cherish those who seek the truth but beware of those who find it.
Voltaire

As strategists and architects, we are acutely aware of the big success stories in technology or in the industry we are in. Companies that change the paradigm or achieve an outstanding first-mover advantage. What is less common, though, is to hear about the role chance plays in these successes, and certainly, we hear less about the non-successful stories beyond those we are involved in directly or some high-level statements around failure rates.

We have stories about startups that achieve unicorn status, being valued at one billion dollars or more, while pre-IPO, owned privately or funded via venture capital. Well-known examples are OpenAI, Databricks, Canva, Figma, DataRobot, and Webflow. But depending on what statistics you look at, only 10% to 20% of tech startups survive in the long run. We like a good story about why some succeed and give a lot of credit to the founders, which can be true, but we can miss the role chance plays in these successes, which includes the timing.

Another storyline the resonates loudly are the platform companies that get the chicken-and-egg problem solved correctly and achieve massive growth. We all know about Uber, Airbnb, Amazon, Netflix, Alibaba, PayPal, and many others. And we hear the *disruptor* word used a lot. There are cases of course, where there has been huge disruption to industries, for example, Uber disrupting traditional taxi companies and Amazon with books, but sometimes they are more of a change agent than a full disruptor, such as Airbnb. And there are industries where much hype disruption hasn't happened at least yet, for example insurance, where there is a lot of regulatory friction. Insurance is interesting as the real disruption seems to be coming from a hardening capital market impacting reserving, reinsurance and share market demands, combined with increasing perils, particularly around weather and fires. Again, chance plays a big part in the success of some platforms, particularly around timing. Sometimes, you just cannot replicate that or create those conditions.

> "In every business I tried, I can see now, it wasn't me that failed. Something was missing. Even if I'd known what it was, there's nothing I could have done about it because you can't create this thing. And it makes all the difference in the world between success and failure ... War"

> *Oskar Schindler's character in the movie Schindler's list.*

The rabbit and the tree stump

When we are looking at the successes of others with technology and business innovations, it is good for us to take note and leverage where we can, but also consider where chance or conditions out of our control might lead to different outcomes. We have to work at what is right for our situation ourselves. Otherwise, we'll be *guarding a tree-stump waiting for rabbits*; it is a fantastic idiom from China.

The story typically goes something like this. One day, a long time ago, a farmer was working hard in his field, preparing for next year's crop so he could feed himself and his family. He was taking a break from the hot sun under a small tree when he saw a rabbit carelessly run at speed into an old tree stump, breaking its neck. Bad luck for the rabbit but great for the farmer, who took the rabbit back to the farmhouse and cooked it, having a great meal for himself and his family. It occurred to him that it was pointless doing all this back-breaking work when he could simply wait by the tree stump for more rabbits. He stopped farming and merely sat at the stump, waiting for rabbits to come and run into it. Although there were a few rabbits running around, by some weird turn of bad luck, none of them ever ran into the tree stump again. It didn't end well for the farmer.

We need to consider the part played by chance and timing when we consider ours, and others, successes.

Guarding a tree-stump waiting for rabbits; it is a fantastic idiom.

CHAPTER 30

DIVERSITY OF THOUGHT

"You have your way. I have my way. As for the right way,
the correct way, and the only way, it does not exist."

Friedrich Nietzsche

Diversity is an important value for many modern companies and organisations. This is a good thing, given the richness of experiences and variation of thinking that having a diverse mix of employees can bring. It is also, importantly, the fair and the right thing to do. It can be challenging, in a good way, and leads to win-win outcomes. By diversity, we are talking about diversity of gender, ethnicity, race, age, religion, disability, sexual orientation, geography, social economics, temperament, neurodiversity and more.

There are some hot debates regarding diversity topics, such as DEI programs covering Diversity, Equity, and Inclusion. I'm not getting into debates around DEI, but I think in principle, *most* people believe that diversity is a good thing, even if the implementation and growing pains can be hard to navigate at times.

There are many reasons why this diversity is good, but I think I'll summarise it with two main lenses. One is the lens of fairness for individuals and overall benefit for society, and the other is the benefit to organizations and companies.

In this chapter, I'm focusing on the later organizations and companies, which does also relate to individuals and the wider society, as all of these are not separate in the end. The real benefit of diversity to an organisation or company, beyond widening the employee pool numerically and aligning with a wider range of customers, is to introduce new ways of thinking and new approaches to solving problems and taking opportunities. I do worry that many companies and organisations are stifling or not leveraging these new ways of thinking. They are perhaps ticking the diversity box and might be relying too much on some kind of trickle-down impact on thinking rather than really embracing *diversity of thought*.

This must be much broader than just moving diversity metrics.

It is important that we can bring all aspects of ourselves to our roles, including our cultural, emotional, and spiritual selves. But not just that. We need to bring our storytelling approach, our narrative style, and bring our logical or scientific ways of thinking, or perhaps it is our non-dualistic or holistic approaches; bring it all. My advice: be yourself, be authentic, and be brave. Living this, you will go beyond corporate platitudes and will meaningfully encourage and support diversity in others.

In this chapter, I mainly try to ground things in terms of philosophy, but there is overlap with psychology, culture, and religion; most non-Western areas do not fit well with explanations using these terms. These are Western concepts and are ways Western intellects divide things. For example, if you consider Hinduism, Islam, and Judaism, we might think of them as religions, yet they all have significant aspects of philosophy, psychology, culture, and health (don't eat the pig, which I haven't for 30 years). I have no idea how Buddhism can be classified as a religion any more than psychotherapy can; the language is different, but to me, the objectives, and in a way methods, are very similar. I use terms like philosophy and psychology as the best language I can to express my thoughts to most of you, but please be aware I'm not making value judgements or truth claims with these terms. The whole world is indeed beautiful and diverse.

Beyond Inclusion

> "All things are subject to interpretation. Whichever interpretation prevails at a given time is a function of power and not truth."
>
> *Friedrich Nietzsche*

Inclusion is important. Including a range of people is the right thing to do. I'm no *expert* on it, but in my way of thinking, inclusion means having a range of people *participate* in the game. Literally, inclusion means to include. Your gender, ethnicity, age, religion, disability, sexual orientation, geography, social economics, temperament, and neurodiversity do not limit your involvement or position in the game. This is good; it is necessary, but is it sufficient? Is it enough? I don't think it is.

We see people being included in the *old* corporate game and let us be frank here, we mean the straight white, able-bodied, male-dominated game, with extra credit for being a good, bubbly extrovert.

So, we have a diverse range of people being included, but they soon learn they need to adhere to the old unwritten rules of the game. New, new-looking players, but the same old game. What we need is to change the game or just start a new game. An example I've seen of changing the game was a Chief Digital Officer I worked with a few years back. She was a forty-year-old woman who didn't play the normal male-dominated executive game, which was common at that time with executive teams. She didn't join the old boys club. She didn't try to be boisterous and loud or make deals outside the office at bars and golf courses. She brought her own way of using soft power (mostly but could fire up when needed), willow tree strength, and building deep, genuine connections with all areas of the business. I think she didn't want just to tick the gender diversity box in the executive team but wanted to bring her own strengths and style. I'm sure it wasn't easy for her, but perhaps she made it easier for others to follow. Things are changing.

I am not ascribing characteristics like being quieter, gentler, and using soft power and building genuine connections as female traits here. That is not the point. The point was that she didn't perform to an executive stereotype, which I'm sure doesn't suit all male executives either, and would suit many female executives.

We often talk about diversity in our corporations, yet we seem to be slow to embrace what I feel is the most important diversity, which is diversity of knowledge and wisdom. Diversity of thinking, and not just *what* to think, but *how* to think. It is common for people to be told something like, "you can bring new ideas as long as they are logically sound and backed up with data and evidence". This isn't the only way of thinking and reasoning. This isn't real diversity of thought. And this is very challenging to hear if you have been brought up in the post-enlightenment Western-influenced world.

I'd encourage people to bring their full selves and be authentic, and to encourage and support others to do this also. Perhaps it is a colleague that comes from a culture, perhaps an indigenous culture, that has a more holistic way of thinking. This is a very good fit for strategy and architecture, and we should encourage this way of looking at things. It aligns very well with systems thinking and is a good antidote to the Westerners intellectual default of slicing and dividing things and not optimising the whole. We can all learn and grow. There are times when slicing and optimising components is good. It is about balance. That is the power of true diversity.

Eastern thinking

"When you listen to someone, you should give up all your preconceived ideas and your subjective opinions; you should just listen to [them], just observe what [their] way is. We put very little emphasis on right and wrong or good and bad. We just see things as they are with [them] and accept them. This is how we communicate with each other. Usually when you listen to some statement, you hear it as a kind of echo of yourself. You are actually listening to your own opinion. If it agrees with your opinion, you may accept it, but if it does not, you will reject it, or you may not even really hear it."

Shunryu Suzuki

We covered some Eastern philosophical concepts in part 1 on getting out of your own way, including our relationship with our ego, our understanding of impermanence, the Yogic view of the intellect, non-dualism, time and causation, and a lesson from the Bhagavad Gita. These were very basic discussions based on my limited understanding and viewpoint. The Eastern philosophies I discussed from India do have many more topics than those I lightly touched on, and these are all very big topics, with many varying and sometimes conflicting opinions and viewpoints.

In a similar way, I covered some Eastern philosophical concepts from China and Japan, such as keeping your beginners mind from Shunryu Suzuki (Zen), remonstration of leaders from Kongzi (Confucianism), Wu Wei from Lao Tzu and Zhuangzi (Taoism), along with the useful lesson about guarding a tree stump waiting for rabbits. Again, these are just basic discussions based on my viewpoint, and these are also all big topics with lots of angles and opinions. That said, these are very useful concepts, in my experience, even if you only take a basic initial understanding. One of the nice things about many of these concepts is that they are intentionally vague, so you have to think about them and interpret them for yourself. You bring as much to the concept as the author, and your understanding of these ideas will change over time as your context changes. They are the gift that keeps giving.

There are so many other areas of Eastern philosophy that I have not tried to talk about, largely because I either don't yet know about them, they didn't link to the purpose of this book, or I could not fit them into the narrative. All the areas of North, West, East, South, and Southeast Asia have rich histories and philosophical knowledge, sometimes adapting to those of other areas of the globe. For example, Buddhism has travelled throughout Asia and now further around the world, and it has changed and adapted in each place, sometimes blending with other local beliefs; this is a feature, not a bug. If you look at how Zen Buddhism landed in the USA in the 50s and 60s, you can see how it blended with the beat generation and hippy culture, respectively.

One thing that has become clear to me over the years, beyond just that this wisdom has much to offer us all, is that there is often a disconnect between these philosophies and people who have come from Eastern countries. Sometimes, people understand the concepts very well, and sometimes, the concepts have infiltrated the culture even if the explicit terminology and origins haven't.

This happened with many philosophies from India, where during colonial times, the British Empire cynically tried very hard to devalue and undermine the extensive historic wisdom of India, which, in my view, was much more advanced than anything in Europe at that time, and arguably even now. For example, with regards to Buddhism and psychology; India was two thousand years ahead in almost all regards. Freud would, in my view, be the first Westerner to really take a step towards where India had been with psychology more than 2000 years earlier, though some Western philosophers did get glimpses of psychological wisdom along the way.

In the case of China, the wisdom of Kongzi, known (or mis-known) as Confucius, was dominant in political and administrative areas up until the time of Mao, who systematically tried to eradicate the Confusion influence. It has made somewhat of a comeback in the last few decades. However, even then, the underlying philosophies of the greats, such as Kongzi, Lao Tzu, Zhuangzi, Mencius, Mozi, Sun Tzu and many others, have had a profound influence on culture and belief systems the entire time China has existed (since the waring states period). Another area of historic influence is with holistic approaches from China, which can be traced back to Lao Tzu or even earlier thinkers.

Anyone with an Eastern heritage should be proud of what their cultures has given the world, and I would encourage them to learn more about it, celebrate it, and bring it into their working life. The enlightenment moved Western thinkers towards logic and reason, and that was good, but we need to realise that this was largely an antidote to the prior religious and superstitious dogma and that we ought not to turn logic and reason into a dogma of its own. Datapoints are great, but as nicely said by William Bruce Cameron in 1963: "not everything that counts can be counted". The quote is so good I'll expand it out in full.

> "It would be nice if all of the data which sociologists require could be enumerated because then we could run them through IBM machines and draw charts as the economists do. However, not everything that can be counted counts, and not everything that counts can be counted."

> *William Bruce Cameron in the 1963 text Informal Sociology: A Casual Introduction to Sociological Thinking (often misattributed to Einstein)*

For those of us who come from cultures based on Western thinking, we can *respectfully* learn and benefit from the rich ways of thinking from the East, while still being proud of the sources of knowledge from our own culture. We are building our futures here, not only for ourselves but for those to come, and we want that future to be as rich and diverse as possible.

Indigenous thinking

"We all come from the same root, but the leaves are all
different."
*John Fire Lame Deer (1903 - 1976), Lakota holy man,
a Mineconju-Lakota Sioux born on the Rosebud Indian
Reservation*

I have had limited exposure to indigenous thinking, not due to a lack of
interest or it having any less importance or relevance, but I just cannot
cover everything, and I haven't been able to focus on these areas yet. I
have some limited understanding of Māori ways of thinking about the
world, mātauranga, because I've grown up in Aotearoa, New Zealand.
I have some understanding of Polynesian thinking giving how close
the South Pacific countries are nowadays. I understand almost nothing
of Australian Aboriginal thinking, but I do know it is the world's oldest
continuous culture and is very rich. I've done some reading on Native
American thinking, mainly through reading John Fire Lame Deer (a Lakota
holy man), and found this has some similarities to Eastern philosophy but
with rich nuances.

There are many indigenous philosophies around the world, and they all
differ, so grouping them is not valid. My understanding, which could be
wrong, of course, is that there is a tendency toward holistic and non-
dualistic thinking and that there is a much better understanding of systems,
balance, interdependencies, and flow on impacts. Also, most indigenous
cultures that I'm aware of are master storytellers, being able to speak
powerfully and convincingly with great integrity; in Māori culture, this is
called *mana*, meaning prestige, authority, control, power, influence, status,

spiritual power, or charisma. This all sounds like it would be useful in strategy and architecture, and again, I can only see bringing these ways of thinking into our worlds as being a win-win for the modern corporation and people from these cultural backgrounds.

There is a much broader post-colonial lens that I'd love to apply, but that isn't an area I can cover here. Colonialism has had a very large impact on the world, and much of what was done must be seen as problematic. We cannot turn back the clock. We must move forward, but we must recognise the historic wrongs. These are among humanities toughest challenges. I have no idea how we resolve them but resolving them appropriately is in all our best interests in the end.

> "Until the lions have their own historians, the history of
> the hunt will always glorify the hunter."
> *Chinua Achebe, Nigerian novelist, poet, and critic*

I'm not entirely sure how to accurately categorise the different ways of thinking around the world that would build out full diversity. I've gone with Eastern, Western, and Indigenous, but then these aren't discrete, and there is overlap. There are many other important philosophical traditions such as African, Arabic or Middle Eastern, and many others.

The same advice holds true for all the various ways of thinking around the world. It is all valuable, and we all benefit from the diversity. Bring it all to your work. Celebrate it all. Don't participate in someone else's game, but try to make the game better for everyone.

Leveraging Western philosophy

"It is hard enough to remember my opinions, without
also remembering my reasons for them!"
Friedrich Nietzsche

Western philosophy has had a significant impact on the thinking in Western societies. And Western thinking has had a profound impact on many other societies for a variety of reasons. There have been some very cynical techniques used, particularly during colonial times, to elevate Western thinking while suppressing non-Western thinking.

Although I advocate for diversity of thought and have gained much from non-Western philosophies, even preferring to focus more on them, this is not to undervalue the huge contribution of Western philosophy, and that is where my love of all philosophy started for me. In many ways, these Western philosophical concepts are familiar to us. However, we often don't understand that many beliefs that seem self-evident and irrefutable in the West are, in truth, products of a couple of thousand years of philosophical debates, many of which continue today. Our entire democratic system and our concepts of human rights have come out of Western philosophy for just two examples. But many of these concepts are so ubiquitous we just don't see them; similar to the way a fish doesn't detect the water it swims in. We can't be sure that fish don't know they live in water, but we assume they don't, at least until they are removed from it, which is a bit like the culture shock we might find travelling to other parts of the world. We never see our culture, including our underline philosophies, so clearly as we do when we are not in it.

We tend to assume that we have a much better grasp of logic and reason than many of us do (and that includes me). A wider exploration of Western philosophy didn't quite fit with the broader theme of this book. However, in the appendix of this book, you will find an exploration of how I think Western philosophy could help strategy and architecture mature as disciplines. You will also find a very brief introduction to the four main branches of Western philosophy: Epistemology, what we know; Logic, how we reason; Ethics, what ought we do; and Ontology, what is and is not. There are also some initial thoughts on how these could be applied to our work.

Emotional diversity

> "And those who were seen dancing were thought to be
> insane by those who could not hear the music."
> *Friedrich Nietzsche*

If you swim in a modern corporation or organisation, you would have heard of Emotional Intelligence, known as EQ, with a good chance that you have been formally or informally evaluated for your EQ score. Perhaps you were assessed when applying for a role or as part of some type of team *self-reflection* session; if not, then your boss probably has had some training sessions, and they've thought about where you might score.

We mostly come across the model introduced by Daniel Goleman, who is described as a science journalist. EQ gained popularity after his 1995 bestselling book *Emotional Intelligence*. EQ is described as the ability to identify and manage one's own and other people's emotions. His model identifies the following five key competencies: self-awareness, self-regulation, social skills, empathy, and motivation.

There is nothing wrong with these competencies or with trying to improve them. In this book, I cover most of these areas in one way or another. However, we need to avoid getting carried away with these as the key to corporate or personal success. I would also advise that we need to be cautious with empathy as it doesn't scale and can impact you to the degree that you become ineffective (e.g. if you work with victims of violence and take on their pain every day); it can be better to favour compassion over empathy, as compassion is boundless and can scale to include all sentient beings. You feel for the person or being and want to take action to help them, but you don't feel their emotional pain. It is subtle but powerful. I've been exposed to this through Buddhist methods, but if you do your research, you'll find it has wider support as well. It provided great benefit to me recently when my elderly mother was dying; I think it was of comfort to her also.

Although an understanding of the EQ competencies has utility in practice, I'm not sure about the usefulness of *measuring* these EQ competencies. Modern corporations and businesses love to try to maximise anything that is deemed *good*, but that means we dualistically tend to define the opposite as being *bad*. Measuring these competencies in people sets up a duality and judgement. First off, measuring anything psychological is problematic, and if you doubt this, Google the *replication crisis in psychology*. Second, applying these measures to individuals is even more problematic. I suspect that having a balance in any population is useful and natural, but these traits will be distributed on a bell-curve.

Think of all the impactful people in history who probably have not had high EQ. I can't know for sure, but I'm thinking of Winston Churchill, Malcolm X, Friedrich Nietzsche, and Fyodor Dostoevsky. I'm sure we can put Elon Musk on that list on both the impactful and low EQ measures. According to a 2017 Forbes article by Tomas Chamorro-Premuzic, leaders such as Walt Disney, Steve Jobs, Mark Zuckerberg, and Jeff Bezos appeared to have had low EQ. But it is not just about famous people; think about all the wonderfully interesting people in your own world who might have low EQ but add that magic richness that makes life surprising and exciting. Many of these people also add significant business value by coming up with ideas that other high EQ people might not have, as well as often being able to turn a flat, boring workplace into a high-energy, creative, and fun place to work.

> "[...]the only people for me are the mad ones, the ones
> who are mad to live, mad to talk, mad to be saved,
> desirous of everything at the same time, the ones who
> never yawn or say a commonplace thing, but burn, burn,
> burn like fabulous yellow roman candles exploding like
> spiders across the stars and in the middle, you see the
> blue centre-light pop, and everybody goes "Awww!"
>
> *Jack Kerouac, On the Road*

The 2017 Forbes article by Tomas Chamorro-Premuzic says that "most of the academic research — thousands of independent studies and several meta-analysis studies - suggest that EQ is just a sexy name for personality." Effectively this would equate to the big five personality traits, each of which exists on a continuum. The big five are neuroticism, extraversion, agreeableness, openness, and conscientiousness. A few people, of which I am one, think that this whole EQ fad is just clever marketing which taps into the desire businesses always have to find a magic answer and a way to turn human diversity into cold hard data that can then be measured and therefore *optimised* (targets anyone). Nature does not make mistakes. Diversity of any type is *not* a mistake. As we've discussed, if you discount low EQ humans, you don't get many of the great people who add a rich flavour to life.

We've talked about low extroversion, i.e. introversion, previously; we have described how there is nothing at all wrong with being introverted. It is similar to neuroticism. In the early days of psychology, thought leaders like Freud and Jung had the view that neuroticism was a problem to be cured rather than just a normal variation. It can be a good thing; some neurotic people use their worries to fuel creativity. It depends to a degree on how we process these neurotic feelings and if we can manage our negative conversations with ourselves and use them in a positive way. The worries we have might come from an active imagination. But by thinking more about problems in an imaginative way many people can find much more creative solutions.

Interestingly, a 2019 World Economic Forum article highlighted that when it comes to EQ, there is a bit of a bell-curve in terms of average score, with regards to individual contributors at one end and executives and CEOs at the other end. The highest EQ was in the middle, with supervisors and managers, with CEOs, on average, having the lowest EQ scores.

The same World Economic Forum article has some good practical advice: acknowledge the feelings of others, reflect on your emotions, let go of grudges, get plenty of rest and look after yourself, avoid getting caught up in negative self-talk, and show appreciation. It is all based on self-reflection but without judgment and blame. It is good to take each person as an individual with strengths and weaknesses, and the key is to find out how they best contribute in a way that gives everyone a positive outcome.

"Always remember that you are absolutely unique. Just like everyone else."
Margaret Mead
(original source is unclear)

Relax, create a little space, and just be

I have made a lot of mistakes in my interactions with people over the years. As do we all. All I can try to do is reflect without self-indulgent blaming and do what I can to learn and improve going forward. I think I've come a long way, but the road is long. Any improvement is better than no improvement.

But I try to be authentic. I don't want to live as someone I'm not. I don't want to be some type of caricature of myself worrying about trying to tick the EQ or Myers-Briggs boxes. For example, I don't want to act extroverted in a performative manner; I think I am perfectly *normal* and valuable as an introvert.

We are all *supposed* to be different from each other, whatever that difference might be. Differences in gender, ethnicity, race, age, religion, disability, sexual orientation, geography, social economics, temperament, neurodiversity and more. We are not built to fit neatly into boxes for counting and sorting.

Alan Watts has said in well many times: did you ever see a cloud that was misshapen, or one that questioned itself about how it was? No. All clouds are cloud-shaped.

"If we are intent upon answering our most serious questions, from climate change to poverty, and curing diseases to designing new products, we need to work with people who think differently, not just accurately."

Matthew Syed,
Rebel Ideas: The Power of Diverse Thinking

CONCLUSION

We made it to the end, or at least to the point where I am going to stop writing. As my first book, this has been a marathon effort and a massive learning experience for me. Thank you for trusting me with both your illusionary time and your most precious resource, which is, of course, your attention.

If you didn't make it through Part 1 of this book, *"Getting out of your own way"*, then now might be a great time to give it another try. It really is the foundation, as it might disrupt your familiar ways of thinking or at least give you a glimpse of something very rich. Recognising and letting go of attachments, including your ego, will provide the space and freedom for you to just be. Recognising the impermanence of existence is truly liberating. Understanding how beautiful and powerful your full intelligence is beyond your intellect will open a new world of possibility. Having an appreciation of how we create our universe ourselves, how this relates to non-dualism, and the true interconnectedness of all is the ultimate systems thinking. Understanding how time and events exist in a complex web of causation gives us a much better understanding of what happens around and to us. We also saw the value of keeping an open mind, a beginner's mind, and met one wonderfully rich part of the famous *Bhagavad Gita* that advises against getting caught up in outcomes.

It takes some work for Eastern philosophy to *click* for most of us, but the rewards are boundless. You will find your own path, which for me, started with the warm, rich recordings of Alan Watts. These ideas *blew my mind* in a really good way.

Some of the most important lessons were covered in Part 2, "*Understanding the game*", which helps us to see that we shouldn't take the game, or ourselves, too seriously. The game is important, but leave just a little space, a gap. This is true for business cases, where all sorts of subtle games are played. We found we could leverage the subtleties of language to help our work. Knowing how our roles interact with various levels of abstraction makes us more effective, but there are pitfalls of abstraction, which we see with the very clever storytelling in the movie *The Big Short*. Some of the other useful concepts were the tragedy of the commons and understanding complexity. This included a useful story about rotten frozen mackerel, which allowed us to understand better some behaviour that seems unhelpful logically but would make sense to the people directly involved, given their situation. Introversion was also an important part of the game that many of us get caught up in, and we learn some ways to help understand, accept, and value this trait.

Finally, we got to look beyond the standard skills we learned in our roles in Part 3, *"The other strategy and architecture skills"*, including ensuring that we deeply know the business, from the corporate purpose and strategy to the nuances of the industry, and getting deep into the financials. We saw what makes a good strategy and what doesn't. We had a couple of lessons from the East about not forcing and choosing our timing, along with understanding from nature what evolutionary architecture could add to our work. We considered how building and mechanical engineering disciplines learned from mistakes and asked ourselves if we could better learn from these. We also questioned what we do in our work that could be considered waste. We learned about the power of a good follow-up in technology delivery, and how we set ourselves up for this, including what role architecture can play. There were a number of rats and mice topics including how to leverage analogies in our work, understanding the part luck plays in success, and much more. One of the most important areas of the book for me was covered in the final chapter on diversity of thought, where we found that we need to bring our true diversity to our roles and not get caught up in modern-day dogma.

I'm hoping that you now understand the reason for the name of this book and have some new insights on how you might be able not only to *survive* but truly *thrive* in the highly rewarding world of technology strategy and architecture and how you can be your authentic self. How you can approach things differently from the norm, and how you can leverage wisdom from any place and time in the universe.

As I said in the introduction, I hope that by reading this book, you will be a more successful strategist and architect; however, I am even more motivated by wanting to help you to become a happier one with more satisfaction, understanding, and contentment in your career and your life. But in the end, it's your life. It's up to you.

It feels like we should finish with a story. Perhaps my take on a classic from Sadhguru.

A middle-aged man finishes a long week's work and heads home at the end of another 13-hour day. It was 7:30 pm, and his wife's rule was that he had to be home for dinner at 8 pm. Still, time for one quick drink at the club. Had a drink, and a drink, and a drink; he looked at the watch - it was 2 am. Trouble. Must get home for dinner. Trying to walk down the street; it is so unfair a man has to walk on a round planet, a ball, and if that is not hard enough, the thing is spinning. You only really know this when you are drunk.

He stumbles home at last. Falls into a rose bush Scratches face. Crawls slowly up the stairs. Makes it into the bathroom. Looks into the bathroom mirror. Oh no, my face is a mess. Pulls the rose thorns out of his nose. Bleeding. Cuts covered with plasters from cabinet; slips quietly into bed. Must not wake the wife.

Six am. He wakes up suddenly when his wife throws a bucket of cold water over him. He hates that. Every Saturday. She yells, "You fool", and drags him into the bathroom, "Look!". The mirror in the bathroom is covered in all the plasters he put on his face.

We often stumble through life as if we were drunk. We see problems with us but try to *fix* the world. The world is the world, and mostly, we cannot control that, but we do get to control how we feel about it and our own actions. Just because everyone else seems to blame the world, it doesn't mean we have to play that game. We can find our own path.

Don't be a fool; it is never a bad day in the Universe.

> "The individual has always had to struggle to keep from being overwhelmed by the tribe. If you try it, you will be lonely often, and sometimes frightened. But no price is too high to pay for the privilege of owning yourself."

Friedrich Nietzsche

Enjoyed the book?

Please review it on Amazon (or where you purchased it) and Goodreads

Kind regards
Mike

APPENDIX

WESTERN PHILOSOPHY FOR STRATEGY AND ARCHITECTURE

"We are doing philosophy when we engage in a dialogue about problems that are important to [us], but we don't agree about the method for solving them."

Bryan W. Van Norden
Taking Back Philosophy – A Multicultural Manifesto

Leveraging Western Wisdom

Note: For brevity, in this appendix, I refer to Western philosophy without qualifying it as Western philosophy. However this is what is referred to unless specifically stated as Eastern philosophy. As I hope you can tell by now, that is not because I think philosophy is, by definition Western.

Socrates, arguably the most famous Western philosopher, was put to death in ancient Athens for asking too many *inconvenient* philosophical questions. Death by drinking hemlock. Most strategists and architects feel like this might happen to them at times.

At this stage of strategy and architecture's evolution, I believe it is *useful* to consider it a *philosophical* activity. We can make the point by asking a simple question: do we have a *universally agreed* method for solving strategy and architecture problems?

We ask this question because among the wide variety of definitions of philosophy is the one below, which is the best I've seen and the one that really resonates with strategy and architecture.

> "We are doing philosophy when we engage in a dialogue about problems that are important to [us], but we don't agree about the method for solving them."
>
> *Bryan W. Van Norden*
> *Taking Back Philosophy – A Multicultural Manifesto*

Unpacking this quote, we can safely agree that when we are *doing* strategy and architecture, we are certainly engaged in dialogue; we've all heard the collective term '*an argument of architects*'. The problems are important in our context, centred around our corporate and technology objectives. But the key is that we do not *agree*, as a discipline, about the *method* for solving the problems. This is important – it is not that we just don't agree about the answer to the problems, but we don't universally agree on how we ought to go about getting the answer or how we can know for sure when we have the right answer. To be honest, we all know the answers, but they are different answers, and we just don't all agree, hence the *arguments*.

Many disciplines, for example, physics, started and matured for centuries within philosophy before evolving into their own disciplines; we can consider if philosophy can offer strategy and architecture paths towards becoming disciplines with universally agreed methods. If you look at the history of philosophy, there is a case to be made.

Don't we have frameworks and methods?
What about the architecture frameworks? Most of us have TOGAF training (or some other framework), but most people I meet instantly disclaim that they know it, but it isn't something anyone would actually *do*. Sometimes, people say they do TOGAF *lite* as a way of trying to tick the TOGAF box but not to get caught up in the key criticism that it is too heavy and impractical. It is good to know one or more frameworks, but would anyone say that, in general, we *agree about the method* for solving architecture problems? That would be going too far.

This is certainly true for enterprise architecture, and even going closer to implementation, in the solution architecture zone, we have more agreement on what is good and bad, but we still can't really claim that we universally *agree about the method* of solving solution architecture problems.

Maturing as a discipline

We can compare enterprise and solution architecture to more mature disciplines like medicine, physics, chemistry, biology, and mathematics, where there are plenty of disagreements, but in general, the method to solve problems and knowing you have an acceptable answer is agreed upon. Interestingly all those disciplines were once considered philosophy, but as they matured and the method for solving problems became (largely) agreed, they moved out of philosophy and into separate disciplines. Even engineering was arguably part of or influenced by philosophy, for example, with the influence of Archimedes in ancient Greece. Still today, fields like physics do occasionally hit areas that *shift the paradigm*, such as quantum physics, and at such times, they do find themselves going back and doing philosophy for a time until they get to agreed methods of solving problems in the new paradigm.

The suggestion here is not that we formally make strategy and architecture part of philosophy, which wouldn't help the ivory tower perception, but that we learn from philosophy; its main branches do correlate somewhat to our challenges, and there are approaches in philosophy to working through methodological challenges. At a minimum, we can detect some of the traps in logic and reasoning, and we can be more kind and more generous to ourselves and each other about what can and cannot be known.

Loose coupling - the villain of the story

The current definition on Wikipedia is that "a loosely coupled system is one in which components are weakly associated with each other, and thus changes in one component least affect existence or performance of another component". That is a good definition. This loose coupling concept sounds useful, so what is wrong with loose coupling? Nothing!

I pick on loose coupling as a concept because it is something that we tend to think is *always* a good thing, so it is exactly the type of concept we need to be willing to question. Loose coupling is normally a good thing, but there are times when it might not be a good approach, or at least not the best approach. It is easy for us to take loose coupling as a mantra. It can almost become a law of the universe. It is not.

The key point here is that loose coupling in technology is exactly the type of *common-sense* universal belief that philosophy is very good at challenging.

What is in the Western philosophy box?

There is a lot in the Western philosophy box, and in this appendix, we will touch lightly on the main branches of Western philosophy and how these branches have ways of thinking that might help strategy and architecture.

The main branches of Western philosophy are:

•   Epistemology - what we know

•   Logic - how we reason

•   Ethics - what ought we do

•   Ontology - what is and is not

For each branch, we look at a brief description and example and how it might be applicable to strategy and architecture thinking. We'll weave in how this might help you in your strategy or architecture role.

Philosophy – Epistemology Branch

Epistemology focuses on how we know what we *think* we know. It is the theory of knowledge. The famous reference here is that we have *knowledge* of something if we have a *justified, true, belief.* Not only must we be right, but we must be right for the right reason. It is not just having an opinion that ends up being true; we have an unbroken chain of reasoning in our belief that it is true.

Let's make up an example of when we might be right for the wrong reason. We might believe that a specific model of BMW is faster, from 0 to 100km, than a specific model of Porsche; it might be true that it is faster in this regard, but if we held that belief because uncle Bob said BMW's are faster than Porches, then we don't have *knowledge* of that. Some Porsche models might be faster than some BMW models, which is why you don't have a justified belief, even though you happen to be right in the specific situation; we do not have knowledge of this fact.

For strategy, there are many situations where we can get caught up in industry knowledge that is just accepted, but often, we find that strategy is just harder than that. If it was as easy as listening to industry experts, then every company would be number 1, and of course, that can't happen. For a long time in the insurance industry, there was common knowledge that the broker model wouldn't persist, or at least not with the penetration it had, yet business customers continue to want to get advice from brokers. Further to this, direct SME insurance was going to take over from broker

SME insurance; everyone knew it. Yet outside some good growth in commercial motor this has largely not been significant.

As the numerously ascribed quote goes, predictions are difficult, especially if they are about the future. We certainly shouldn't elevate these predictions to the level of knowledge.

For architecture, there are many areas where we need to check if we have a belief that raises to the standard of knowledge. For example, we might believe we know that loose coupling of a particular technology service is the best approach for a specific company in a specific scenario because it will lower the total cost of ownership over time. It makes logical sense to us that we should spend the extra on implementation costs to do this, but do we know this is true? Can we *prove* these things to sceptical businesspeople who have heard this for years, yet every time the cost of tech seems to increase, and any time they want a change made, they are told how difficult it is? It might be that loose coupling can be part of achieving optionality, but is it the irrefutably best answer in this situation. As we noted earlier, loose coupling comes at a cost, and that cost is complexity. If you have control over both endpoints, you might not want to pay the cost of the additional complexity of loose coupling.

Epistemology can help us question what we know and how we can know it. Epistemology tends to give us a bit of humility in our area of expertise, and that isn't a bad thing.

The centrepiece of epistemology is the proposition; this is basically a truth claim. There are several ways we might acquire knowledge that we make truth claims about: perception, introspection, memory, testimony, and reason. The philosopher Imanual Kant split knowledge into the following two categories: *a priori*, being knowledge prior to any experience using only reason, and *a posteriori*, being knowledge following, or after, sense experience, in addition to reason. There are people that believe all knowledge is *a posteriori*, or empirical (ultimately based on experience), and others that believe all knowledge is based on reason. We see an interesting slant on this with Eastern Philosophy, where largely knowledge is empirical but mostly looking inward, with many of the traditions being cautious about what outside ourselves can be known.

We also find, in the West, something similar called epistemological scepticism, which calls into question what it is possible to know at all.

Now, this epistemology is a big topic, and there is still a lot of debate within philosophy. For example, in the mid-20th century, Edmond Gettier found some rather important outlier cases, but for our purpose we are better to stay out of those; it is not only architects that argue.

Largely here, we have focused on propositional knowledge, which is to say, truth statements about the world. Another area of epistemology, which tends to get less focus, is practical knowledge. That is knowledge about how to do things. Think of playing tennis, riding a bike, or knitting. Let's get simpler and think of walking or talking. These are all types of knowledge, but not truth claims. That knowledge goes beyond just intellectual knowledge and into body knowledge, such as neuromuscular memory, that might allow you to perfect your golf swing.

It is said we are in a post-truth world. This is well understood at a geopolitical level and within societies, but perhaps this has bled out into our corporate narratives as well. Maybe it was always there. Perhaps rehydrating epistemology practices might be a good countermeasure.

How we reason

We've discussed the Enlightenment (1685 - 1815) and how, in the West, this epoch allowed us to move from the age of religious *belief and faith* to the age of *reason*. We suddenly have our reasoning to save us from having to just believe every word written in a book, regardless of which book it was. The 15th-century invention of the printing press helped spread knowledge, and in the 19th century, the steam powered printing press allowed knowledge to be spread on an industrial scale. The combination of the Enlightenment and the printing press was profound.

However, it feels like something has turned. Many of us wonder if our relentless advancement in knowledge and reasoning at a social level is continuing to make progress. Increasingly, we see situations where reason seems to be abandoned by people, and the huge explosion of information doesn't seem to be resulting, as we would have expected, with useful knowledge on the ground.

Our education system does not help this situation. Right through our school system and into higher learning, we often seem to confuse memory with intelligence; memory is part of the mix, but it is not by itself *intelligence*. Aided by the trusty Google search, Siri, or Alexa, it is becoming easy to appear intelligent or to have an intelligent viewpoint when, in reality, we are just regurgitating something we've read or heard. We want to read and listen, but we need to use it to foster our own thinking and reasoning and not to replace them.

Socrates foretold this

> "You offer your pupils the appearance of wisdom, not
> true wisdom, for they will read many things without
> instruction and will therefore seem to know many things
> when they are for the most part ignorant and hard to get
> along with since they are not wise, but only appear wise".

Socrates in Phaedrus by Plato

In Phaedrus, Plato records a conversation between Phaedrus and Socrates (the founder of - and generally considered the greatest - Western philosopher of all time). We see Socrates observations of writing in the quote above.

Socrates never had the chance to see the impact of writing through history and the impact of the printing press, let alone the internet and ChatGPT. Had he have seen this, we can only guess at what he'd have thought, but I'm sure he'd have softened this position or at least marvelled at it all. However, his point is well made, and worth reflection.

We need to take care about simply regurgitating information we've been spoon-fed. There are lessons from both Eastern and Western reasoning that can help us avoid this.

Philosophy – Logic branch

Logic is about valid approaches to how we reason. The philosophy of logic is defined by Brittanica as "the study, from a philosophical perspective, of the nature and types of logic, including problems in the field and the relation of logic to mathematics and other disciplines". This is one of the most applicable branches of philosophy to strategy and architecture, and ironically an area many of us probably have gaps in our thinking or have just got into bad habits.

Although we all assume we have a good grasp of logic and logical reasoning, it is harder than we think to get it right, particularly when we believe we already know the answer. I've found personally that I need to slow down and force myself to use a structured approach to logical reasoning. This can be a large topic, and we are not exploring it in detail here. Also, as noted, we are not writing an academic book, simply a guide to areas you might want to explore further if you think there may be benefit for you and your work.

In our work, we find that reasoning logically to get to the *right* answer is one thing, but convincing others of that logic is something else. That is where we find the logical argument.

Arguments

An argument in logic has a different meaning than the everyday usage of the term *argument*, which is typically the type of argument you might have with an errant uncle or aunty about politics at a family wedding dinner. According to the Monty Python Argument Clinic, "an argument is a connected series of statements intended to establish a definite proposition". Let's also consider the Collins Dictionary definition that "An argument is a statement or set of statements that you use in order to try to convince people that your opinion about something is correct".

Anatomy of an Argument

In both definitions we are talking about a series of statements, so what specifically are these statements? Statements, as opposed to other sentences, are either true or false in the real world; that applies regardless of whether us being able to determine the truth or not. For example, I could state that at the moment of the death of Queen Elizabeth the 2nd, there were 9,227 planes in the air; now, that is a statement as it will be either true or false, but we might not be able to determine its truth. In the simple case, the statements we are talking about with an argument are premises, which are reasons or justifications, and conclusions, which are truth claims. We can say that an argument is a way of taking our logical reasoning and making some type of communication so we can have other people understand that logical reasoning, and typically, we want them to accept the validity of that reasoning.

Example: Adam had two apples and gave one to Eve; therefore, Adam has one apple.

In this simple argument, we have two premises, which are information or evidence, and one conclusion, which is what we logically conclude from the evidence. We can document this in a structured manner as:

Premise 1: Adam had two apples.

Premise 2: Adam gave one apple to Eve.

Conclusion: Adam now has one apple.

This will typically be written in a sentence, paragraph, or several paragraphs. The conclusion is often signalled in a sentence with a word like *therefore*.

However, the structure of the sentence might go the other way with a word like *because*.

Example: Adam has one apple because Adam had two apples and gave one to Eve.

What must happen, though, is that the conclusion logically follows from the premise that has been provided, something called the inference. Were we to argue that Adam had a bag of apples and gave some away? Therefore, Adam has one apple, which would be a loose inference and, therefore, a weak argument. He might only have one apple, but this would not be logically known from this argument. You could say that Adam had a bag of apples and gave some away; therefore, Adam has fewer apples than he had. That would be a valid argument, just not very profound. If you said he had less apples, then that is just bad grammar, though I'm not sure English grammar and logic really go together.

Deductive and Inductive reasoning

The two types of reasoning you will most likely hear of are *deductive arguments* and *inductive arguments*. With *deductive arguments*, we have certainty as the conclusion must logically be true if the premises are true, and with *inductive arguments*, the conclusion is probably true if the premises are true.

There are other types of arguments, including *abductive*, covering the most likely outcome with limited available information. There is a type called *analogical arguments* or *arguments by analogy*, where you argue based on another more accepted argument (which could be deductive or inductive). And even one called *reductio ad absurdum*, which is a counter argument showing that its logical consequence is absurd or contradictory.

As much as we might say to ourselves, "Well, I'll just stick to the deductive arguments", in the real world of strategy and architecture, and most of life, we are likely to be dealing with inductive reasoning, at best. However, we do need to be able to spot a deductive argument.

Deductive Argument – if the premises are true, the conclusion must be true. Often, these arguments are either mathematical or true by *definition*, as in the below example.

Example: all men are mortal, Socrates is a man, therefore Socrates is mortal.

This can be more formally structured as:

Premise 1: all men are mortal

Premise 2: Socrates is a man

Conclusion: Socrates is mortal.

The above would be considered a *valid* argument as the conclusion logically follows from the premises. If the conclusion was *Socrates is a philosopher*, then the argument would be invalid because, even though it was true, the conclusion wouldn't logically follow the premises stated in the argument. So, we need to consider that validity is different from truth. You can assess the arguments separately from any truth evaluation.

Another good example of a deductive argument would be that people who have more birthdays live longer than those who have fewer. It is valid and true, just not very informative. The definition of the word *more*, as well as *birthday* and *live longer* are doing the work here; it is true by definition.

Inductive Reasoning – where the conclusion is based on probability but is not certain. Much of science is based on inductive reasoning, but also most of real-world business problems are only open to inductive reasoning.

Example: thousands of Swans have been seen, all Swans ever seen have been white; if there were non-white Swans, we would have expected to have seen them by now; therefore, all Swans are white.

This can be more formally structured as:

Premise 1: thousands of Swans have been seen

Premise 2: all Swans ever seen have been white

Premise 3: if there were non-white Swans, we would have seen them by now

Conclusion: all Swans are white

<u>Limits of Induction – Black Swans</u>
There are many examples of where inductive reasoning has gone wrong, with one of the best-known examples being the Black Swan. In 17th century England, the phrase *Black Swan* was equated with an impossibility. Nobody had seen a non-white swan, so the idea of a Black Swan was ridiculous. That belief was blown apart in 1697 when Willem de Vlamingh, a Dutch sea captain for the Dutch East India Company, discovered the Black Swan while exploring the coastlines of western Australia.

A century and a half later, the English philosopher John Stuart Mill used the bird to demonstrate what is known as the problem of induction. "No amount of observations of white swans," he said, "can allow the inference that all swans are white, but the observation of a single black swan is sufficient to refute that conclusion". Of course, the definition of a Swan could have been defined that it had to be white, in which case the argument that all Swans are white would have been true by definition and therefore deductive, though again, that wouldn't be much of an argument. Many deductive arguments are not very profound.

The Logic of Strategy and Architecture

In strategy and architecture, we mostly use weaker inductive reasoning, based on a whole lot of assumptions and a subjective probability assessment often supported by industry wisdom (e.g. Gartner, Forrester, Celent, McKinsey, Thoughtworks etc); we then tend to forget we've done it and believe (or pretend) we are using the stronger deductive reasoning. An example here is that we've all seen times when tight coupling caused problems, and from that form, beliefs that loose coupling is always better, even though it might not be in some specific cases. Generally, it is better to use loose coupling for sure, but just keep an open mind in specific cases.

We tend to want to avoid exceptions to widely held beliefs as we worry about the slippery slope argument, which is that making one exception will lead to everything being an exception. The slippery slope argument is regarded as a cognitive fallacy in logical reasoning, but that said, we've all seen this slope and may well have slid down it ourselves. The countermeasure is to look at each case on its own merit. For example, if a project manager argues that "you agreed over there, so you must agree over here", then know that it is a clever trick, so just wink and say, "nice try".

An important part of inductive reasoning is determining what cannot be true, which links to the scientific method and more recently, relates to the trend in technology and in business to do hypothesis testing. Of course, that only works if you are trying to find out something to use as a premise, which can mean finding out that something doesn't work is a good thing. We often seem to get that a bit wrong.

Evaluating probability is another important part of inductive reasoning, along with being able to quantify or qualify probability assessments. This might be most important for risk assessments, which are a key concern of strategy and architecture. We need to unpack the overall risk and ensure we consider the probability and severity of the risk. If we have a customer master that is a synchronous dependency for our online customer application, and it is a single point of failure, then our severity for an outage is we take down the application. Now, that might cost us money in sales or services, but if we are a bank, it might be a reportable event that might have a wider impact on the company or executives. So, the severity is very high, and that means even a probability of once in 3 years might be intolerable. We might, therefore, put up a strong inductive argument that we need to spend that extra money to move to an asynchronous pattern, perhaps distributed, to mitigate it.

Philosophy – Metaphysics branch

Ontology, or General Metaphysics, is all about the study of being; therefore, it is about what exists in terms of the kinds and structures of objects. In simple terms, ontology seeks the classification and explanation of entities. Ontology is about the object of inquiry, what you want to examine.

Ontology is concerned about what really exists and what are the causes, natures, and properties of what exists. Ontology addresses questions like how entities are grouped into categories and which of these entities exist on the most fundamental level. Commonly proposed categories include substances, properties, relations, states of affairs, and events. These categories are characterized by fundamental ontological concepts, including particularity and universality, abstractness and concreteness, or possibility and necessity.

Much of ontology comes down to language and definition challenges. A common example is analyzing the sentence "Santa does not exist". So, we can quickly agree that this is true: there is not a Santa, but then how do we refer to Santa in a way that people know what specifically we are saying does not exist. What is this Santa that does not exist? A concept? This all gets very deep, and we won't go too far down this rabbit hole here.

There is a lot that can apply to enterprise architecture, with ontological hierarchies, dependencies, causation and properties. Perhaps the most important area for us is abstraction, which is probably the core concept that differentiates enterprise architecture from solution architecture, which is also all about abstractions that are just less abstracted. Even the technology coalface, coding, is an abstraction. For those of us who learnt about 2nd, 3rd, and 4th generation languages, we know about these levels of abstraction; even if you talk directly to the CPU by coding in assembler language, it is still an abstraction of electrical charges. However, if we consider how much of what we deal with in enterprise architecture actually exists, we have a real challenge. It is a huge house of cards.

Software applications don't really exist in a concrete sense; they are a bit like Santa; they are concepts. You can run the application, but in what sense does it really exist?

Is it helpful to question the existence of an application? I think it is when we consider the boundaries and dependencies. Let's consider a legacy banking application. If it is old enough, it might have even started life as punch cards. If not the actual code that is running today, perhaps the logic represented in the code. Today, it is perhaps source code stored on a spinning disk or solid-state drive in a cloud service. But is that all the legacy banking application is? What about the documentation about the system, the legacy programmers without which the systems don't remain stable, or even the knowledge in the heads of those programmers? What about the business knowledge to make use of the application? Anyone who has looked at systems thinking will quickly see that ontology seems to be related. Having a more holistic appreciation of systems can help us better see how they fit within our businesses. As useful as loose coupling is, it doesn't get you out of the broader *system* impacts when making changes.

Ontology is also useful in more specific areas, such as modelling entities, hierarchies, properties, and characteristics. You also quickly get into the language games that are a large part of philosophy and certainly impact us in enterprise architecture.

Philosophy – Ethics branch

Ethics is a big area of philosophy concerned with determining what is good and bad behaviour in certain situations. There is some broader value for us in the area of applied ethics, specifically in the growing area of business ethics, which tends to help guide our overall business behaviour and is becoming key with evolving questions such as the application of AI and its impact on employees and customers. Business ethics is also useful in looking at existing questions such as automation, digitization, and offshoring. Other areas that broadly align with business ethics would include diversity, climate change, and shareholder vs stakeholder value.

However, in this appendix, we are mostly concerned with the more general domain of normative ethical theories, which relate to determining the moral, or 'right', course of action, what we ought to do in a particular situation. A normative ethical theory aims to produce a code that tells you how to be ethical in any given situation you find yourself in. Normative ethics also helps to inform applied ethics, such as business ethics, as discussed above. There are many normative ethical approaches, but two key ones can help us understand how ethics can help enterprise architecture.

Deontology – an ethical theory that uses rules to distinguish right from wrong. Importantly, this approach advocates that we ought not to consider the outcomes but focus more on the specific moral rules. This tends to talk about the duties that ought to guide peoples' actions in given situations.

Example: Immanuel Kant has the most well-known example; imagine your friend runs into your house saying they need to hide from an axe-murderer, and then that murderer arrives at your door asking if your friend is there. Kant is clear that you must tell the truth regardless of the outcome for your friend, given the moral rule that one should not lie. There are simply no white lies, so you must say, "Yes, they are hiding in the wardrobe".

Consequentialism – an ethical theory that judges whether or not something is right by what its consequences are. For instance, most people would agree that lying is wrong. But if telling a lie would help save a person's life, consequentialism says it's the right thing to do. Utilitarianism is often considered a type of consequentialism, but some would see it as subtly different, mostly with regard to how you evaluate the outcomes. This is a very complex and nuanced topic, so we'll leave it there.

Example: Often people use the trolley problem to introduce people to their consequentialist intuitions, where you have to decide if you will redirect a trolley or tram to save the many at the cost of the few. In public policy a consequentialist may support harsh punishments for contravening laws because the consequence of the punishment acts as a deterrent. Some people will be punished perhaps unfairly, but in total, less people will break the law, so the harshness of the punishment is justified. Of course, in the earlier axe-murderer example, you should lie to save your friend and avoid murder.

For enterprise architecture, the leverage is around making rule-based decisions (Deontology), or making a more nuanced outcome-based decision (Consequentialism). It is very tempting to leap at the outcome-based approach, but deontologists would caution that it is much harder to really know the final outcome or consequence, than you might think. Also, you might find yourself in an analytical paralysis trying to figure it all out. In enterprise architecture, we try to balance these two approaches by using principles that basically say what you ought to do but leave room for specific variation based on the specific circumstances.

So, let's consider a situation where a company might want to add functionality to a legacy application to allow for better risk modelling for automotive lending due to the number of people defaulting during a post-pandemic recession. The architects correctly determine that this functionality forms a useful business capability across many value streams and design it as a loosely coupled micro-service with a nice restful API interface. The cost will be 2-3 million, including legacy system changes and the new micro-service. The business talks to the legacy team to see if there is a cheaper way to do it quickly (in this circumstance), and the old heads come up with a way to fudge it for 250k. Architecture pushes back, and after some heated discussions between executives, technology holds the line on the correct design. *This is the right decision, and the business will thank us one day.* The initiative can't be funded due to cost-cutting to meet shareholder commitments, delinquency rates climb, impacting many customers lives, leading to regulator intervention and fines, and 12 months later, technology is largely being outsourced after the technology executive was rolled for being out of touch with business reality. No good came out of this situation in the end.

We've all been in these types of decisions, though hopefully with less dramatic outcomes. We've also seen times when the tightly coupled work around was the start of a slippery slope of bad architectural decisions that ultimately led to a lack of flexibility and climbing run and maintenance costs. The point here is enterprise architecture has been wrestling with this for a few decades while philosophy has been trying to navigate it for millennia. These questions have been considered since at least the time of Aristotle in the West and Kongzi (Confucius) in the East. There is no quick and easy lift and shift answer, but there are ways to navigate these decisions.

Where to next

The above is a very light look at each of the core branches of Western philosophy and how they might be useful to strategists and architects. My advice here is to get curious, get humble, and explore some of these topics, being mindful of not going too far down each rabbit hole unless you want to and looking carefully for what might help your architectural skill set.

Now, there are many fantastic overview books on Western philosophy, such as the widely acclaimed *History of Western Philosophy* by Bertrand Russell (respect to Russel for correctly referring to it as *Western* philosophy, therefore making space for other types of philosophy). There are many great original works by Plato, Aristotle, Hume, Kant, Locke, Nietzsche,

Wittgenstein and many others in the West, and as many in the East and other parts of the world.

If you are like me, you will like listening to your philosophy, and there are many great resources for *dipping your toe* into philosophy, including:

- Philosophy Bites which is a fantastic introduction podcast to a broad range of philosophical topics done as interviews.

- Philosophize This which is another great podcast that goes a bit deeper on specific topics.

- Then and Now – Philosophy has many key concepts covered as videocasts.

- The Philosophy Academy is a more formally structured collection of videocasts.

There are thousands of resources freely available, including many university lectures, if that is your thing. Also, many of the original philosophy works are now in the public domain and available on YouTube or apps such as LibriVox.

ACKNOWLEDGMENTS

- Bernard Seeto, who gave me confidence, built on that confidence, and trusted me.
- Peter Chandler, who valued all my eccentricities and encouraged me to be myself, while highlighting the need for technical curiosity.
- Keng Yeo, a deep-thinking and wonderful human, who supported me and was always generous with illuminating the magic of management consulting techniques.
- Tony Craddock, who was normally the smartest guy in the room, and led by example with soft but highly effective governance, and taught us to start with the answer, then explain how we got there.
- Corrie Schoonbee for his trust and confidence, allowing me to use what I've learned.
- Steve Schaffer, who talking to is like drinking from a firehose of knowledge, and also the person that pointed me at Alan Watts, which started my Eastern exploration.
- Nick Draper, my longest work colleague, for his friendship, support, and for helping me understand internal politics.
- Barry Vorster and Steve Askey for their support, guidance, and friendship.
- All the many wonderful architects, strategists, and other technologists that I have grown with and learned from; I can't list you all, but you have been a huge part of my growth.
- All the very generous businesspeople that have shared their time and knowledge.
- Georgia and Sam for their editing contributions, along with Abusina Salah Uddin on Fiverr.
- My family for their support and tolerance: Sherryl, Samantha, Georgia, Gizmo, Luna, (Oxford comma) and Monty.

END

FACTORY F

Let's keep in touch

www.michaeldstark.com
www.thinkingea.com
www.linkedin.com/in/michael-stark-thinkingea

www.ingramcontent.com/pod-product-compliance
Lightning Source LLC
Chambersburg PA
CBHW071540210326
41597CB00019B/3061

* 9 7 8 0 4 7 3 7 3 3 4 9 0 *